PROGRAMMING ON PURPOSE
II
Essays on Software
People

P.J. Plauger

PTR Prentice Hall
Englewood Cliffs, New Jersey 07632

Acquisitions editor: Paul Becker
Editorial assistant: Noreen Regina
Cover design director: Eloise Starkweather
Cover designer: Lundgren Graphics
Manufacturing buyer: Mary E. McCartney

 Published by PTR Prentice-Hall, Inc.
A Simon & Schuster Company
Englewood Cliffs, New Jersey 07632

The publisher offers discounts on this book when ordered in
bulk quantities. For more information, contact Corporate Sales Department,
PTR Prentice Hall, 113 Sylvan Avenue, Englewood Cliffs, NJ 07632.
Phone: 201-592-2863; FAX: 201-592-2249.

Printed in the United States of America
10   9   8   7   6   5   4   3   2   1

ISBN 0-13-328105-1

Prentice-Hall International (UK) Limited, *London*
Prentice-Hall of Australia, Pty. Limited, *Sydney*
Prentice-Hall Canada Inc., *Toronto*
Prentice-Hall Hispanoamericana, S.A., *Mexico*
Prentice-Hall of India Private Limited, *New Delhi*
Prentice-Hall of Japan, Inc., *Tokyo*
Simon & Schuster Asia Pte. Ltd., *Singapore*
Editora Prentice-Hall do Brazil, Ltda., *Rio de Janeiro*

In memory of Joan Hall,
who taught us
that both adults and children
need steady supplies
of kindness and ice cream

PERMISSIONS

TRADEMARKS

TYPOGRAPHY

This book was typeset in Palatino, Avant Garde,
Bitstream Cloister, and Courier bold by the author
using a Compaq SLT/386s-20 computer running
Ventura Publisher 4.0.1 and Corel Draw 2.01L
under Microsoft Windows 3.1.

Table of Contents

Preface

𝕴 began a journey in July, 1986, that continues to this day. That month marks the first installment of my column "Programming on Purpose" in the magazine *Computer Language*. Many years and many issues later, I find myself still writing those monthly columns. And, *mirabile dictu,* I have yet to miss an issue.

Do something every month for six or more years and material accumulates. I have been asked repeatedly by readers to make some of that accumulated material more widely available. For many years my excuse was that I was too busy to do so. I was president of my own software company, Whitesmiths, Ltd. Then I sold the company to become a full-time writer. Packaging these essays has at last risen to the top of the queue.

This particular collection concerns itself with the people who write software. I began by poking gentle fun at them (and myself). But before I knew it, I was poking into all sorts of people-related matters — from business ethics to pragmatics, from our search for artificial intelligence to our desire to be loved. Writing and selling computer programs is a most human activity. It has brought out the best, and the worst, in many of us these past few decades.

You will find some technical content here. I can hardly resist, being a techie at heart. You will find more than a little humor. You will also find *lots* of useful advice for surviving in the business world. I speak as someone who has worked for the largest corporation in the known universe (AT&T before divestiture), and the smallest enterprise (myself). In between, I spent several years at a rapidly growing seminar company (Yourdon inc.) and started my own company (Whitesmiths, Ltd.). I sold the latter a few years ago, content that ten years as an entrepeneur was enough for me.

Frankly, I believe this collection represents my best writing in many ways. Much as I love a good computer program, people are my principal interest in life.

Thus, you will find this collection suitable for supplemental reading in an intermediate or advanced course in software engineering or engineering management. For "remedial software engineering," it can be quite useful. The independent reader can read for pleasure or for a unique perspective on the people side of making computer software. That can help you as an entrepeneur, a manager, or one of these creatures in waiting.

I follow each essay with a brief Afterword. That gives me the opportunity to fill in historical context where necessary. It also lets me excuse away the worst naivetes. I chose to present these notes as Afterwords rather than Forewords so as not to bias the reader up front. Mostly, the essays speak for themselves.

Other collections from "Programming on Purpose" deal with other themes. Besides people issues, I have written essays on (among other things): software design, programming technology, and software standards development. Some essays are humorous, some are deadly serious. A few are gems, but I like to think that all are worth reading. If you enjoy what you find here, please consider the other collections as well.

The magazine business sees considerable turnover of editorial staff. Miller Freeman, the publisher of *Computer Language,* is no exception. I have thus enjoyed the services of many editors over the years. All have worked hard to rescue my prose from its more florid excursions. They have nevertheless permitted me to retain a certain colloquial illiteracy that I find comfortable. I thank all the people at Miller Freeman who, over the years, have helped make these essays more readable. You should too.

Two people in particular deserve oak-leaf clusters. Regina Starr Ridley, now a publisher at Miller Freeman, was one of my earliest editors. And Nicole Freeman, now a managing editor there, has cheerfully haunted my career in many editorial guises. I am happy to acknowledge their continuing assistance in making "Programming on Purpose" better. I am also happy to count both as good friends.

Having given credit where it is due, I must issue a warning. I re-edited these essays from the original machine readable. I certainly strove to recapture the spirit of *Computer Language* edits, but I make no pretense at following them to the letter. If any have lost ground as a result, you can blame me.

P.J. Plauger
Concord, Massachusetts

1 Honestly, Now

$\mathbb{L}$et's talk about ethics. Some of you may find this a boring topic. If so, then I suspect you are probably masking discomfort with boredom. Some of you may be more open about your discomfort. If so, then it's about time you took a close look at your own ethical position. Some of you may simply wonder what ethics has to do with computer programming. If so, then you're very much at risk. Ignorance is not bliss, in this arena.

I was pleased to discover, in the early 1960s, that I could work my way through college as a computer programmer. To me, this was much less of an effort than delivering pizzas or shelving library books. I was bemused to discover, upon earning a Ph.D., that I could command twice as much salary as a purported computer scientist as I could with full-blown credentials in nuclear physics. I was astonished to discover, as a budding entrepreneur, that I could parlay a few tens of thousands of dollars into a business with an annual turnover in the millions, in just a few short years.

Understand, if I had chosen to open a restaurant or a dry-cleaning shop in Manhattan, it would have been next to impossible to do so on the same amount of money. And there isn't a banker alive who would have loaned me the stake necessary to get off to a proper start. I had no experience in running a business, much less in starting one. I didn't even have any courses on business or accounting in school. It turned out, however, that there were any number of people prepared to educate me, in trade for varying size chunks of the cash I found myself administering.

You'd be surprised how dishonest some people can be for a mere hundred thousand dollars. Well, maybe you wouldn't, but I certainly was. And you might be surprised at how numerous and varied are the temptations put your way in the course of everyday business. Even if your programming career has been confined to working salaried jobs, I'm sure you've faced situations where just a little dishonesty could earn (or save) you a significant sum of money. As the old joke goes, we've established what you are, now we're arguing about the price.

In summary, computer software is a high-paying business. Technically trained people tend to be naive about business matters. It is not uncommon now for techies to end up tending a cash engine much larger than the real world would ordinarily entrust them with. There are people who prefer to divert an existing flow of money their way, by whatever means, rather than generate wealth directly themselves. This is an explosive situation.

𝔚riting computer software is all the more perilous because it is so easy to steal the final product. Software is an intellectual creation only loosely tied to concrete representation — much like recorded music, or lithographs. It is even easier to steal than those art forms, because it doesn't degrade when copied. And its per-copy value is substantially higher than its per-copy cost. (The makers of digital sound recordings are just coming to grips with these selfsame problems. Witness the maneuverings surrounding the introduction of digital tape recorders.)

On top of everything else, producing software is a new industry. We are all learning, a day at a time, what works and what doesn't. How do you balance licensing protection against the need to expedite a sale? There's been a different answer every year for the last decade. How much should you charge for the use of a computer program? Beats me — the only formula I've seen that I believe involves the relative humidity and the Dow Jones Industrial Average. When does a program infringe on someone else's design, and when can you build on technology that has gone before? That's a hot topic of debate today, particularly with Lotus suing and being sued for copying the "look and feel" of successful software.

The software industry is too important to wait for scholars and judges to puzzle out a coherent set of laws. We need pragmatic answers now, even if they form a patchwork of guidelines that sometimes conflict. Needless to say, there are those who cheerfully exploit the current inconsistencies, as an excuse to be morally lax in a profitable field.

Ethics touches computer programming in many different places. This essay is a not-quite-random walk past some of those places where I have found myself face to face with ethical lapses. I begin with lapses that are most peculiar to larger companies. It is easier to distance ourselves from those nameless people who try to screw us in the name of United Whatever, even though the actual decisions are made by people just like you and me. I end painfully close to home, discussing the sins that you and I struggle with every day. Are you ready?

𝕺ne of my first shocks as a fledgling business person came just a few months into the mission. My company, Whitesmiths, Ltd., offered a compiler that attracted the eye of several techies working in different branches of a major computer hardware manufacturer. (The company shall remain nameless. Let's just call it the MCHM.) Plagued with a fear of outside software, that company throttled all such purchases, even when the per-copy price was a mere $550. Eventually, however, the central purchasing department felt moved to act upon this repetition of requests, and they sent us a purchase agreement.

It was not the agreement we sent to each of the techies. It did not contain our standard software license. It made no attempt to replace the license with any similar protections. Instead, it offered to purchase a single compiler from us at the full price of $550 — with the understanding that this MCHM could purchase two additional compilers from us each at half price. Further, once we had been paid the princely sum of $1,100, the MCHM would subsequently have unlimited internal use of our compiler.

I sent back a letter stating that I would be happy to sell our software on the terms they outlined — with the understanding that they would sell us their most popular superminicomputers on exactly the same terms. I sent a copy of the letter to the president of the MCHM. I got back a letter from the public-relations department. It explained politely that these were the terms initially offered to all software vendors who wanted to sell to the MCHM. We had to understand (it said) that some vendors accepted those terms.

I drafted a letter pointing out that merchant shipping did not truly flourish in the Caribbean until rampant piracy was suppressed. It is true that some merchants permitted pirates to board their ships and make off with their gold, valuable cargo, and assorted female passengers. That did not mean that the merchants necessarily approved of this practice. That certainly did not make the practice right. I reread this letter with relish three times, then I threw it away.

It was just as well, because several years later we had occasion to explore a joint marketing agreement with this MCHM. One of the first things I had to deal with was the file that the MCHM had accumulated on dealings with our tiny company. A prominent entry in the file was the letter I sent to their president back in the previous decade. Even though the representative of the MCHM with which I was dealing was in full sympathy with our earlier stance, he still had the task of justifying why the MCHM should do business with us! We were, after all, known troublemakers.

This is a clear application of the well known principle, "Might makes right." Being part of a large enterprise can be a heady experience, and it is easy for employees to become enamored of wielding that sort of clout. There are, of course, companies in the business of going out of business, like some famous shops on Times Square. But the good ones treat each deal they strike as if it were the first of many with that party.

You face an ethical dilemma when a large company offers you piratical terms and you really need the business. Your duty, to yourself and to the ownership of your enterprise, is to say no. Don't be a victim, don't blame it all on the big guys. It does you no good to strike a deal that is not profitable. As the old saying goes, you can't lose money on every sale and make it up on volume. So the principle to keep in mind is:

Just because they can get away with it, that doesn't make it right.

We at Whitesmiths were fortunate at that time that we did not need a potential $1,100 bad enough to sell our birthright for a mess of pottage. (Eventually, the MCHM came back and bought compilers on our standard terms anyway.) Still, it was a sobering experience.

It's nice to know that there are laws to protect your person and your property. Gone are the days when pirates roamed the high seas with impunity and robber barons distorted markets to their personal advantage. If you believe that, then eat your cookies, drink your milk, and go to bed.

I read in the Wall Street Journal every week about modern-day robber barons who still stay one step ahead of the SEC. I read in the Boston Globe almost as frequently about modern-day pirates who prey on merchant ships, despite the protection offered by dozens of well equipped navies. And we all see daily how ineffective the courts are as civil referees.

You'd think that if people owe you money, they have to pay it. Try collecting from someone who either hasn't got the money or who is willing to fight you for it. It can cost you so much time, additional money, and aggravation that the game is simply not worth the candle. Prudent people have learned the wisdom of safeguards. You run credit checks, you insist on down payments, you ship the software COD. Even then, you still must set aside some fraction of revenues as a provision for bad debt. Some folks are just masters at stiffing us more honest folk.

It's bad enough to have to sue someone and know the suit is not cost effective. It's far worse to be sued and know that you can't afford to defend yourself. Yes, the courts are supposed to throw out nuisance suits, but most judges bend over backwards to entertain any suit that has the least whisper of merit. (Would you want it any other way, if you were the wronged party?)

Again, the software business is at a disadvantage here, because the product is both complex and intangible. You've read those horrible disclaimers that come with the software you buy. Would you buy a car on similar terms? Probably not. I anguished for weeks, when Whitesmiths first got started, over how to write a software license that promised something other than delivery media that was more or less free of defects. But what can you promise, in simple terms, about a product as complex as a compiler or an operating system? You can say that its quality is high, and that you will fix bugs as quick as you can, but you can't quantify either of those statements. In the end, prudence and a litigious society led me to adopt the same arrogant boiler plate that everyone else uses.

But even that doesn't keep you from being sued. There are all sorts of laws about implied warranties of merchantability and fitness of a product for its advertised purpose. If a customer decides, even after months of using your product, that it's no good, there's a fair chance you will be asked to refund the purchase price. (And how do you know when a customer has destroyed all copies of your product and has stopped using it?)

Whitesmiths was once sued by a customer who had been using a product for two years! And he admitted that he was still making good use of part of what he'd bought. Yet he sued for a complete refund, plus unspecified damages, mostly because he no longer had any use for the rest. And we had to spend time and money preparing a defense. In the end, at the strong urging of the judge, we settled the matter by making a partial refund. That was far cheaper than proving that we were right in the courts.

The simple fact is that the civil courts can be used as a blunt instrument by anybody who wants to give you a hard time. It's a form of legal blackmail that is widely practiced. It can also be used, by someone who doesn't want your money, to consume your precious time and psychic energy. But if you need to use the courts to redress your own grievances, you will find them to be an equally blunt instrument. You can bludgeon but you can't easily compel. So the principle to keep in mind is:

𝕵𝖚𝖘𝖙 𝖇𝖊𝖈𝖆𝖚𝖘𝖊 𝖞𝖔𝖚'𝖗𝖊 𝖗𝖎𝖌𝖍𝖙, 𝖙𝖍𝖆𝖙 𝖉𝖔𝖊𝖘𝖓'𝖙 𝖒𝖊𝖆𝖓 𝖙𝖍𝖊𝖞 𝖈𝖆𝖓'𝖙 𝖌𝖊𝖙 𝖆𝖜𝖆𝖞 𝖜𝖎𝖙𝖍 𝖎𝖙.

Does this mean you're hopelessly at risk when you sell software? Not at all. First, you have an ethical responsibility to produce the best product you can. You are responsible for obeying the law. You are responsible for striking fair agreements and keeping your end of the bargain. If you simply do these things, you greatly reduce your need to sue and your risk of being sued.

Beyond that, I have found two principal ingredients in every lawsuit with which I have become entangled:

- There was an ambiguous understanding, so both sides could argue that they were right before a court of law.
- Someone had a stake in being right at all costs, either because there was a lot of money involved or because his or her feelings got hurt.

And when you come right down to it, the ambiguity and the money are mere excuses. I believe all lawsuits stem from hurt feelings. If you contrive, in any way, to say to someone, "Look, I don't respect you and I don't have to respect you," then that person will find some way to respond, "Oh, yeah?" It's as simple as that.

So far, I've focused on other people who might do you wrong. Now let's get more personal. When was the last time you copied some commercial software rather than pay for a legal copy? Maybe you just made an extra diskette for a friend to try out, or to use on your PC at home. Maybe you bought one copy for the office and put the software on all the machines. We all know that software is overpriced, and they pad the price even more to cover this sort of thing. Right?

Hogwash.

If you write software for a living and you steal other people's software, then you're fouling your own nest. It costs money to make this stuff, and it costs more to keep it alive and evolving. Some of that money pays your salary, or your rent. Some is invested in making better software for tomorrow. The shadowy fat cat raking in the dough is shadowy because he doesn't really exist. The money comes back to you, and the person at the next desk, and your great aunt Amelia who invests in high-tech stocks. Or it doesn't come back at all.

The cynics among you are already muttering that I'm probably not a saint in this area either. You're right. I played fast and loose with licensed software in the past. Then I wised up and went back and paid for it. I still am pretty casual about putting PC software on one machine before I delete it from another. But if I find myself using multiple copies, I pay for them. It's worth it for the extra manual set, not to mention the clear conscience. And I flatly refuse to let my company violate software licenses. Otherwise, how can we expect others to respect ours?

Another delicate area — when you left your last job, what did you take with you? Did you take listings of source code? Internal memos? Diskettes? Dump tapes? Many programmers feel that all the software they have ever written (or worked on) is their personal property. Their employers simply exploit it for their own nefarious purposes. Even if they sign a confidentiality agreement that clearly spells out who owns what, there are programmers who feel ill used when asked to leave behind their toys.

I reviewed a manuscript, a few years ago, about how to get started in your own software business. The author chose as a unifying theme three typical examples of software startups. One was a guy who wrote a useful program for his employer, but his employer was not in a position to exploit it. So he quietly reworked it to run on a PC, then left his job to start selling the program. Another was a person who moonlighted for a year or so while building up cash flow in his new enterprise. A third was someone who bootstrapped his operation by luring away a customer or three from his previous employer.

It was a well written book. And it did indeed show three typical ways to start a company. But every one of those examples involved a clear violation of ethics, if not a clear violation of law. Even if you have a wash-and-wear conscience, you'd better not emulate any of these examples. As soon as you're at all successful, your previous employer has a golden opportunity to sue you blind. (See previous discussion.)

I was pleased that the author heeded my advice and replaced his examples with three that were morally more defensible. He even added a brief essay on the need for ethics in business, for what that is worth.

The principle that applies here is:

Just because you can get away with it, that doesn't make it right.

The last topic is the touchiest of all. Under what circumstances are you at liberty, or even obliged, to defy the law? The victors in World War II made it very clear, at Nuremberg, that we each have an obligation to be ethical, even if the current powers that be have perverted the law of the land. If you know that your company is intentionally selling defective software, then you have a moral obligation to stop it, even if that means violating the confidentiality requirements of your work agreement. It's no fun being a whistle blower, and martyrdom is rewarding only to those who can take the very long view.

But to do nothing is ethically untenable.

You may feel that the society you live in is supporting some unethical behavior. Richard Stallman, of Project GNU fame, has stated loudly and repeatedly that he feels software should be "free." I use quotes because his definition of free is a rather precise one that is easily misinterpreted. Read his writings to see just what he means (**Gar90**).

Now, I personally disagree with him. I think he is a person who delights in stirring up a roomful of responsible adults by calling them names. But I also respect the fact that he has a consistent belief, that he works hard to make it a reality, and that he causes no bodily harm in working toward it.

If you want to defy law and society for a living, then I strongly urge you to do your homework. Reread the Declaration of Independence. Read Henry David Thoreau's essay "On Civil Disobedience." Read a book on the life of Gandhi. Above all, be so in touch with the rightness of your position that you are willing to endure ostracism and financial discomfort to prevail. If you feel, however, that it is okay to damage property or hurt people to get your reform, then you're off base. That makes you an anarchist. Anarchists are unhappy people, boring at parties, and seldom effective in achieving their goals.

Finally, what do you do when the bad guys have you cornered? (Remember, of course, that this is a relative term. To them, *you* are probably the bad guys.) More than one naive techie has signed away rights that later proved to be worth serious money. More than one naive entrepreneur has been driven out of his or her own enterprise by a barrage of legalese. No matter how legal the machinery, you know that the inevitable end result just ain't right.

You can either be a victim or take responsibility for obtaining an acceptable outcome. To do the latter, you have to be willing to exploit the clumsiness of law enforcement as much as the other guys (if not more).

At one low point in my checkered career I called a board meeting with just enough notice to satisfy the articles of incorporation, but not enough to inform everyone in time. (The meeting took place, aptly enough, right next door to Disneyland.) Needless to say, I got just the mix of attendees I needed to pass some very unfriendly resolutions. Were the resolutions valid? Well, sort of. I can say that they achieved the desired effect.

I also asked several loyal employees, relatives, and friends to pay an evening visit to a company office. They were accompanied by a locksmith and several moving vans. They nearly ended up in jail. Were they entitled to make that visit? Well, mostly. I can say that they achieved the desired effect.

I also was very slow to respond to a judge's order. I was sufficiently slow that my attorney advised me not to set foot in the state of New Jersey until we had talked the matter through from a safer distance. (Okay, New Yorkers, you can go ahead and say that that was no hardship.) Was I obeying the law? Well ... You get the drift.

The operative ethical principle is:

𝕵𝖚𝖘𝖙 𝖇𝖊𝖈𝖆𝖚𝖘𝖊 𝖙𝖍𝖊𝖞'𝖗𝖊 𝖗𝖎𝖌𝖍𝖙, 𝖙𝖍𝖆𝖙 𝖉𝖔𝖊𝖘𝖓'𝖙 𝖒𝖊𝖆𝖓 𝖞𝖔𝖚 𝖈𝖆𝖓'𝖙 𝖌𝖊𝖙 𝖆𝖜𝖆𝖞 𝖜𝖎𝖙𝖍 𝖎𝖙.

It was not until I realized that the law is a two-edged sword, with both edges dull, that I began to take responsibility for cleaning up the mess I put myself in. And that's what ethics is really all about, being responsible for the consequences of your actions.

I have give you four ethical principles in this essay. I'm convinced they're correct and complete, because they appear to contradict each other. If you can figure out which one to apply each time you face an ethical dilemma, you can't go wrong. □

𝕬fterword: This was my first foray into writing about the people side of the software business. It was a difficult essay to write. Several of the incidents I allude to here occurred during a fight for control of Whitesmiths, Ltd., the company I founded. It would be easy to say that I was naive and got took, but that is not entirely accurate. More to the point, I was driven by several emotional needs that mixed not at all well with business. Thus, I often failed to take responsibility for my actions.

I paid a high price for that fight, both in money and in emotional battering. It was arguably worth it, however. I grew up in some important ways and I eliminated some serious stresses from my life. (I even ended up in control of Whitesmiths, Ltd.) Writing this essay helped me realize how much I had learned about myself and about people in general.

2 You Can't Do That

$\mathfrak{G}$enius makes its own rules. When presented with a seemingly intractable problem, most people flounder about for a spell, then despair. They divert their energies to justifying why the problem cannot be solved. The truly ingenious apply their energies in a different direction, however. They focus on the rules instead of the problem. They challenge all of the assumptions, both explicit and implicit, until they find a weak spot to attack.

When presented with an ingenious solution to a seemingly intractable problem, most people simply respond, "But you can't do that!" To some, it is more important that the apparent rules be obeyed than it is to discover the meta-rules that set you free.

Alexander the Great is the prototype of all ingenious problem solvers. In the city of Gordium, he was shown the chariot of king Gordius. The chariot was lashed to a pole with a rope containing an intricate knot. You couldn't even see the end of the rope within the knot. Legend held that only the conqueror of Asia could undo this knot. Alexander had already demonstrated an obvious zeal for conquest which was not about to be deterred by a mere legend.

What did Alexander do? He certainly did not waste time, as so many others had done, trying to puzzle out the intricate way the rope was tied. Instead, he drew his sword and cut the Gordian knot.

You can be sure there were many in the crowd of onlookers who came to scoff at this upstart, but ended up bleating with wounded civic pride, "That's cheating. You can't do that!" You can be equally sure that Alexander was unimpressed by such objections. He was solving the general problem of advancing his cause — the conquest of the civilized world. With characteristic directness, he eliminated one small difficulty that lay in his path.

$\mathfrak{I}$n the more aethereal sphere of mathematics, ingenious solutions are often more abstract than the stroke of a sword. Hence they are harder to share with a general audience, even when the author of the solution is just as audacious (in his or her own way) as Alexander the Great. Once upon a time, however, I saw a friend solve a math problem with an annoying directness that is not too hard to convey. The problem is one you may have seen. It crops up regularly on calculus and solid-geometry tests to this day.

Consider a sphere with a hole bored right through its center. I will tell you the diameter of neither the sphere nor the hole. All I will tell you is that the height of the cylindrical hole left inside the sphere is 6 cm. Your job is to compute the volume remaining in the sphere.

The approach I took was to draw several pretty pictures involving triangles and arcs of circles, then dust off my high-school calculus. After several false starts, I set up the integrals properly. After several more false starts, I solved the integrals correctly. To my surprise, the result was independent of the diameter of the sphere (or of the hole, naturally). In fact, the residual volume is just the volume of a sphere whose diameter is 6 cm.

Flushed with success after only three hours of labor, and pleased at the result, I began to explain the problem to a friend. Before I could even begin reproducing my (correct and final) drawing, he told me the solution.

He reasoned that, since I was pleased with the elegance of the problem, and since the diameter of the sphere was not specified, the result must be independent of the diameter. For a sphere whose diameter is less than 6 cm, you can't possibly drill a hole with the required properties. For a sphere whose diameter is exactly 6 cm, however, you can drill a hole of zero diameter through the center of the sphere. The height of the (nonexistent) hole is 6 cm, as required. The volume of the hole is zero. Therefore the residual volume is the entire volume of a sphere whose diameter is 6 cm.

My first reaction was to say, "You can't do that." My second, I am happy to say, was to appreciate the elegance of his short cut to the proper solution. I have since seen others use the same approach to solving this problem, but nothing can diminish the pleasure of being present when that one warrior took a sword to this particular knot.

My favorite example of ingenious problem solving involves neither legends, nor mathematics, nor great names from the past. Credit, instead, goes to a young man who was a graduate student at Fordham University, in the Bronx, back in the 1960s. He was faced with the well known problem of meeting girls. (Pardon me if I don't give explicit citations from the literature for this problem. See, for example, the entire fiction section of your local library or book store.)

For reasons that I will not go into here, this young man was not content to meet just any girls. Far from it. He imposed additional criteria, which I believe are shared by a few hundred million other young men:

- He wanted to meet girls who were sexually active. You can probably guess why.

- Notwithstanding the above, he wanted to meet girls who were likely to be free of sexually transmitted diseases. Even in that simpler time (after penicillin and the birth control pill, and before herpes and AIDS) this was an important consideration.

- He was constrained to meeting girls who would tolerate a cheap date. Graduate students have never been overpaid.

So while his friends were joining the choir and the outing club, or hanging around smoky bars, this enterprising fellow did something completely different. He frequented the waiting room of the public VD clinic. (I have no knowledge that he ever told his mother about this practice, but you can guess what she would have said.)

Just in case the glorious elegance of this tactic is lost on you, let me explain. Among the patrons of such a clinic will be a certain number of attractive young girls. Only a few of those girls will be "those kind" that your mother warned you about. Many will be very nice people who made an unfortunate choice of boyfriends.

Our ambitious young graduate student learned that a few words of compassion, plus large doses of commiseration, broke the ice quickly. Having established a rapport with a girl who was demonstrably active sexually (the first and most important criterion), he could trace the progress of her treatment with occasional sympathetic questions. By the time the girl met the second criterion, their friendship was usually well advanced. Oh yes, and since it was a public VD clinic, the clientele were generally in the same economic straits as our hero. That satisfied the third criterion. *Quod erat demonstrandum.*

Ingenious, no?

This essay is nominally about computer programming and not world conquest, solid geometry, or (uh) socializing. My aim therefore is to show you a few solutions to problems in data processing that demonstrate varying degrees of ingenuity. These are all cases where your first reaction is to say, "You can't do that." But once you admit that you can, indeed, do that, then you have a clever addition to your kit of tools.

The exclusive-OR operator lies at the heart of more than one ingenious trick. (The British, who talk funny, also call this the *not-equivalence* operator, for fairly good reasons. Circuit designers, who think funny, call this the *half-add* operator, also for good reasons.) In C, you write **A^B** to form the bitwise exclusive-OR of the operands **A** and **B**. Each bit of the result is 1 only if the corresponding operand bits differ, otherwise the result bit is 0. Thus (in binary, octal, or hexadecimal) **0011^0101** has the value **0110**.

The exclusive-OR operator preserves information. No matter how curdled the result of **A^B** may appear to the human eye, you can recover the value of **A** simply by evaluating **(A^B) ^B**. Equally, you can recover the value of **B** by evaluating **(A^B) ^A**. This property forms the basis for the various tricks. Many methods for encrypting data, for instance, involve an exclusive-OR operation that is later undone by another exclusive-OR using the same value. The intermediate result is satisfyingly obscure.

Perhaps the simplest trick is also one of the oldest. I have no idea who originated it. It provides a clever way to exchange the data in two arbitrarily

large regions of storage. Now, it is well known that the way you exchange
the values in two data regions is to make use of a temporary region that can
hold data of the same type as in either of the two regions to be exchanged.
You permute the values among the three data regions, taking care to first
copy one value to the temporary. The common idiom for swapping two
values in C is:

```
t = a, a = b, b = t;
```

But if you can perform an exclusive-OR directly into storage, you can eliminate the temporary. In C, you can do this with integers **a** and **b** of any type:

```
a ^= b, b ^= a, a ^= b;
```

Since integers are relatively small, this is cute but not very useful.
System/370, however, has a nice instruction that lets you exclusive-OR one
region of storage directly into another. You can operate on 1 to 256 bytes of
contiguous storage with a single instruction. So for large enough regions,
it can make sense to swap them by performing three exclusive-OR operations instead of allocating a temporary of the same size:

```
xc  dest(len),src
xc  src(len),dest
xc  dest(len),src
```

It's a small trick, but an ingenious one nevertheless.

A much more clever use of the exclusive-OR is storing two pointers in a
storage cell large enough to hold only one. I believe this is one of the
exercises in Knuth's *The Art of Computer Programming* (**Knu68**). You say you
can't do that? Watch.

Let's say you have a list of data elements that can be very long, and that
you need to scan either backwards or forwards. The usual technique is to
declare each data element as a structure that contains both backward and
forward pointers. So if **p** points to the current element (again speaking C),
p->left designates the element to the left, and **p->right** designates the
element to the right.

If you feel you can't afford to set aside space for two pointers within the
structure, what you do instead is set aside a single integer large enough to
hold all the bits of a pointer. (Yes, I know there are implementations of C
that may require two or more long integers to represent a pointer. And I
know that converting between integer and pointer representations can
cause a change of representation. If you want maximum portability, you
should write all this stuff with macros so you can localize the machine-de-
pendent parts.) What you store in the integer is the exclusive-OR of the
pointers to the left and right elements. Let's call that integer cell **link**, and
assume it has some defined integer type **INT** that can represent all values
of the type **PTR**, which is a pointer to a list element.

Instead of a pointer to a single list element (such as **p** above), you must now maintain pointers to two adjacent list elements. Let's say **pleft** points to the left element and **pright** points to its neighbor to the right. Then you can move your two-element window on the list to the left by writing:

```
ptemp = (PTR)(pleft->link ^ (INT)pright);
pright = pleft;
pleft = ptemp;
```

And you can move your two-element window to the right by writing:

```
ptemp = (PTR)(pright->link ^ (INT)pleft);
pleft = pright;
pright = ptemp;
```

It is a fun exercise to write full blown versions of these functions. You need to make them safe for lists with zero and one elements. You need to ensure that stepping left or right will not take you off the end of the list. And you need to add functions for adding and deleting elements. Try it.

You can extend this ingenious trick to two dimensions. Say you have to represent the grid points within an arbitrarily large contiguous blob on a plane. Again, the usual solution requires that each element have four pointers, for the neighbors you reach by going up, down, left, and right from the current element. You can replace these four pointers in each element by two integers, one for each axis. To walk the list, you must maintain four pointers, to adjacent elements that form a square. You advance in any direction by sliding the square about the plane.

To span three dimensions, you need to store only three integers within each data element, instead of six pointers. But you must maintain *eight* pointers to walk the list in any direction. As you go to higher dimensions, you can see the classic tradeoff between storing information and recomputing it as needed. The exclusive-OR trick lets you squeeze considerable redundancy out of your stored data, but at a cost in computation.

Another technique that I dearly love lets you count up to a million in one 8-bit byte. I learned it years ago from Bob Morris, at Bell Labs, Murray Hill. Morris is an endless source of algorithms that take you from, "You can't do that," to "I wish I'd thought of that," in a matter of milliseconds.

Now, it is well known that you can represent only 256 distinct states in an 8-bit byte. To count to a million, you usually allocate a 20-bit counter, and increment its stored value by 1 for each count. It's kind of hard to imagine where you steal those extra 12 bits.

Let's say that you need to maintain a fairly large histogram, as an array of integers that we will call **hist**. It is so large that you can afford to allocate only one 8-bit byte for each element. From time to time an event occurs that results in an index **i**. For all **i** that are valid subscripts of **hist**, you want to increment the value stored in **hist[i]**.

You can obtain an execution-time profile of a program that you run, for example, if you can convince your operating environment to interrupt the execution of your program at regular intervals. The index i is (a possibly scaled version of) the program counter that was stored when your program was interrupted. Assuming that there are no nasty correlations between the timer interrupts and the execution of your program, you can obtain a good representative profile of where your program spends its time. Unlike profiles that count the number of times each function is called, an execution-time profile is automatically weighted by the amount of time your program spends in each function. Separately and together, both profiles are invaluable in measuring, debugging, and tuning your programs.

The pseudo code for a typical profiler reads something like:

```
IF (<i in range>)
    hist[i] := hist[i] + 1
```

This works fine if none of the counters overflow. It's even tolerable if counters overflow once or twice, provided that the peaks in the histogram spread over enough adjacent counters that the wraparound is obvious to the eye. You can also add logic to make the counts saturate, as in:

```
IF (<i in range> AND hist[i] < MAX_VAL)
    hist[i] := hist[i] + 1
```

That way, you don't miss sharp peaks, or mistake a broad peak for two smaller adjacent ones. All peaks get flat tops if they grow big enough.

But what if you need to distinguish between peaks that have 10 counts and those that have 1,000 and those that have 100,000? If you have to trade off counting range against the range of program counters that you can profile, you can end up running a lot of tests that are messy to correlate. Over such a broad range, you would cheerfully trade off an exact representation of any one count (or of certain counts, at least) to be able to capture the entire dynamic range in a single run.

What you would clearly like to do is capture in each element of the histogram not the total count, but a function of the total count. If that function is monotone increasing, and if it increases much more slowly than the total count itself, you can represent a broader dynamic range in each element. An obvious function that suggests itself is the logarithm. Let's say that you store in each cell the value of the function f(N), defined as:

```
f(N) = A * ln(N + 1)
```

You need to add 1 to N because ln(0) has annoying properties, and you do want to represent a count of zero. The coefficient A you adjust to obtain the desired dynamic range. For a count of one million to give f(N) the value 255, for example, A should be about 18.45.

Now your range problem is solved, because you can store in each element function values that correspond to counts between zero and one million. Granted, there are only 256 distinct values, but that is often plenty of magnitude resolution. It is almost as if you are representing the values in floating point, by keeping only the exponent and a few magnitude bits.

There is one small remaining problem. How do you increment the stored value? Adding one to a count is easy. Knowing when to change the state of **f(N)** takes a bit more thought. Consider, for example, when **hist[i]** contains the value 100. That corresponds to a total count of 224.89. If you change the stored value to 101, the corresponding count is 237.47. Clearly, you only want to increment the stored value after 12.58 events have occurred for the index **i**.

Here is the trick. You need to call a function that generates a random number. If the numbers returned by the function are uniformly distributed between 0 and **RAND_MAX**, inclusive, you simply test whether the random number is less than **RAND_MAX/12.58**. On average, the test will be true once every 12.58 times. When it is true, you increment the value stored in **hist[i]**.

So in principle, all you need is a table of 256 threshold values, one for each possible stored value of **f(N)**. And the increment code becomes:

```
IF (<i in range> AND rand() < thres[hist[i]])
    hist[i] := hist[i] + 1
```

Note that you can set **thres[255]** to zero if you want to prevent wraparound on overflow, as above. You don't need a special test to ensure that peaks get flat tops.

In practice, the logarithm is not the ideal functional form for **f(N)**. Until **N** exceeds about 80 counts, this form wastes a number of codes on fractional values that you don't need to represent. Worse, it requires you to muck up the simple code shown above, to deal with cases where you may have to add more than one to **hist[i]**. But remember, the only real requirement on **f(N)** is that it be monotone increasing. You can define each value of **hist[i]** to represent any count your heart desires.

A good definition for **f(N)** is:

f(N)	represents
0-15	0-15
16-31	17-47
32-48	51-111
49-64	119-239

And so on. In other words, the first 16 states represent exact counts. If you set **thres[j]** to **RAND_MAX+1**, then an event always causes a count. There is no statistical uncertainty. For the next 16 states, you count by two. You do this by setting each of the **thres[j]** to **RAND_MAX/2**. Then you count by four, then by eight, and so on. If I have done my arithmetic correctly, this scheme lets you count up to just shy of one million with an 8-bit counter. If you don't care about flat tops, you need to maintain only 16 distinct thresholds:

```
IF (<i in range> AND rand() < thres[hist[i]/16])
   hist[i] := hist[i] + 1
```

And there you have it. You can vary this scheme in many ways. You may want, for example, to maintain exact counts up to 200, then progressively coarser approximations for code values up to 255. If **rand()** is an expensive function, you can call it only when **thres[j]** doesn't have a degenerate value. All of that is icing on the cake, once you learn how to count with bits that you don't own.

There is yet another area that has seen a lot of ingenuity these past few years that I think more people should know about. It lets you prove to someone else that you know a secret, without revealing what that secret is. It lets you receive secret messages from your friends over public channels, even when your enemies know as much as your friends do about how you want your messages made secret.

You say it can't be done? Then you don't know about the exciting world of public key cryptography. It is a topic that is worth far more than just part of an essay on assorted clever tricks. It is, in fact, the subject of another essay or two. (See my essays, "Programming on Purpose: Locking the Barn Door," *Computer Language*, October 1988, and "Programming on Purpose: Half a Secret," *Computer Language*, November 1988.) □

Afterword: I think this essay is interesting for the tricks is presents. More important to me, however, is the examples it gives of how people can be ingenious. Too many people decide early on that they're not creative. So they stop trying to solve problems that appear intractable. The rewards of persistence should not be so quickly sacrificed.

3 Protecting Intellectual Property

The information that you traffic in has a value that you must protect. Typically, you protect the value of your information by limiting access to it. Some of the information you own may be extremely difficult to hide, however. I am referring to intellectual property, the kind embodied in the hardware or software you may be selling for a living.

The single largest problem in our volatile and cash-rich business is the out-and-out rip-off. Computer software shares the same weakness as videotapes and music. All are very cheap to copy, if the copier feels no obligation to pay a royalty to the creators of the recorded information. Software is particularly bad because you can copy bits exactly. There is no degradation of signal you get when copying analog signals. (Digital recording techniques now pose a similar threat to the entertainment industry.)

Even hardware can be knocked off, of course. Avoid the costs of development, use cheaper components, piggyback on someone else's advertising budget and a pirate can turn a tidy profit at just a fraction of the price that the legitimate vendor must charge. Everything from Apple computers to Yves St. Laurent fashions are vulnerable to cheap imitation.

Most fast-buck artists have no interest in obscuring what they do. They are not going to reimplement your algorithms from disassembled binaries, or alter your screens in subtle but significant ways. Nosiree, they're going to knock off exact copies, sell them, and move on when the heat arrives. This is a classic industry in 2 1/2th world countries that are scrabbling to raise the standard of living of their citizens (or at least a select few of those citizens). You can get all the big sellers for a fraction of the fair market cost, because the copiers keep their R&D overheads low. The same service is available in the U.S. through various unscrupulous bulletin boards, computer clubs, and enterprising individuals.

The good news here is that you've got lots of law on your side. Once you detect someone ripping you off, your major concern is to document as clearly as possible that someone is making money selling products without proper authorization. You want to work your way up the chain until you're sure you can implicate the principals. You don't want to nail a few underlings and leave the instigators free to start over in the next county.

You must suppress the urge to make angry phone calls, or tip off the pirates in any way, until you have an iron-clad case. Get a lawyer to help you, and be sure to work through the appropriate law-enforcement agencies. When you strike, you want the case to be open and shut. Despite what you see on TV, lawyers seldom rush to defend people who are caught red handed. It is the gray areas, the equivocal evidence, that encourages people to fight it out in court.

I have never produced a product so wildly popular as to attract the attention of mass-production pirates. (At least nobody tipped me off if that ever happened, and someone almost invariably does.) On occasion, however, I have been alerted to someone shipping the odd compiler without bothering to secure permission. Or pay a royalty. Usually, such fair-weather pirates are just trying to move some hardware. Free software makes a good lubricant. Faced with the choice of paying up or getting sued, they usually blush, stammer, and pay.

Copy protection seems to be going the way of the buggy whip. It interferes too much with the usability of your product by your legitimate customers. You can't afford to deter a few thieves at the cost of your customer base. You must tolerate a few losses, but keep a weather eye out for the mass producers. There's where the real hemorrhaging must be stanched.

𝔄 more pernicious problem, in the long run, is not the verbatim copiers but the idea thieves. If you make hardware that is enjoying good sales, you can be sure that one or more agents will eventually reverse engineer it to find out what you did so well. They will then endeavor to profit from your discovery and subsequent hard work by bringing a competing product to market. Since they have to invest less hard work, they can often undersell you.

If you write software that sells well, you have more to fear than just reverse engineering. Rare is the software package that depends upon some secret algorithm to perform commercial magic. More often than not, the calculations are obvious given the black-box behavior of the program. Even more often, there are several possible ways to do the same job. The value of a software package frequently lies in providing a convenient collection of functions with a sufficiently friendly user interface. Once you demonstrate the utility of a given package, you can be almost certain that they'll send in the clones.

You can protect valuable technology by limiting access to it. Require each customer to sign a license that grants only limited use of the intellectual property contained in your product. Have the license oblige the customer to protect your property from the assaults of would-be imitators. You may not actually prevent people from finding out your secrets that way, but should a competing product appear you have more ammunition to shoot it down.

You can argue in a court of law that the knowledge required to make the competing product is available only under license. Either the competitor has wrongfully obtained access to your proprietary information or one of your licensees has violated the terms of the license. One way or the other, you have someone to sue. If you understand just how costly and ineffective it can be to rely on the courts for protection, that may be small consolation. (See **Essay 1: Honestly, Now.**) But it's far better than no protection at all.

When I started my company, Whitesmiths, Ltd., ten years ago, one of the first things I did was go to a lawyer. I asked him to tell us how best to protect our software when we sold it so that we could stay in control of the products. He came back with a three-page license agreement. It promised the customer next to nothing, and permitted limited use of the licensed product for only fifteen years. I found the terms disgusting.

On the other hand, I couldn't think of a safe way to liberalize any of the clauses in the license. At least not without exposing my fledgling company to an open-ended liability from an angry and litigious customer. For a product as complex as a compiler, how do you define when it is working correctly? There are always bugs. How much maintenance support can you promise and be sure that you can deliver? The simplest looking bugs are often the hardest to fix.

I sat still for that license, and so did our first thousand-odd customers. Remember, this was back before the days of computer stores in every mall. You bought your software (if you didn't build everything yourself, or pay an arm and a leg for custom work) from just a handful of suppliers. There were no computer magazines selling software the way *Vogue* sells cosmetics. You took what you could get, on the offered terms.

As time wore on and the industry grew, however, we had to change our approach. The license got slimmed down, then slimmed down again. Eventually, IBM got in the volume software market. They used a shrink-wrap license (you open it, you agree to the terms) that fit on a single page. We figured that, since IBM doubtless pays lawyers more in a week than we grossed in a year, they knew what they were doing. So we imitated their shrink-wrap license and fell back on the protection of the copyright laws.

I want to emphasize that we weakened our protection out of commercial necessity. It was not just a matter of following the latest legal fashion. Getting those licenses signed was a real impediment to sales. We could no longer afford the extra one to four weeks in the sales cycle, compared to people who were willing to ship the same day on a telephone purchase order.

You can make your intellectual property arbitrarily safe. All you have to do is keep it from the light of day. If you do, however, you won't the rewards of your labors. A technological lead is not like a bar of gold. You cannot hoard it against a future need. It is more like a good harvest of wheat. You must live off it now, before it rots. Sell some and feed yourself on the rest. Use your added health and strength to prepare for future harvests.

For centuries, the more enlightened countries of the world have endeavored to overcome this natural tendency to hoard knowledge. A loyal subject with a bright idea (and the right connections in court) could get the king to grant "letters patent," that bestowed an exclusive right to exploit the bright idea in commerce. Armed with this protection from the highest reaches of government, the subject need no longer fear disclosing any trade secrets. Trade flourished and knowledge spread.

The U.S. has had a patent office since its earliest days. It was designed to give people exclusive use of an invention for a 17-year periods. (To keep the patent alive, you must make maintenance payments at 3 1/2, 7 1/2, and 11 1/2 years.) In trade, the inventor had to disclose enough information that someone skilled in the art could reproduce it. Nominally, it grants patents only to individuals, but that is a sham. An individual has the power to sign away rights to a patent. I don't know exact figures, but my guess is that the overwhelming majority of patents issued today are owned by corporations, and large ones at that. For the large corporations that I know about, you sign away your patent rights to your employer the first day you are on the job.

There is nothing sinister here. It costs a lot of money to support the kind of research and development you need to make commercially useful innovations. Just keeping up with your field, so that you don't attempt to patent something covered by an earlier grant, takes more effort than any individual can muster — particularly in a field as vital as computers. Filing a patent application is also an art form. Large high-tech corporations typically maintain a staff of lawyers who specialize in patent law, just to maximize return on the research dollar. This is a game for the big guys.

Chances are that you, as an individual or an employee of a small company, will not have occasion to pursue patent protection for the fistful of innovations you stuff into products every year. This field simply moves too fast for most of us to indulge in the leisurely pursuit of a patent. The process can take months of your time, cost tens of thousands of dollars, and spread out over years.

On the contrary, your worry should be that you do not inadvertently infringe on patents held by some large corporation. These outfits collect patents like Green Stamps, even in areas not directly related to their current business lines. Corporate patent factories like AT&T Bell Labs and IBM routinely trade bouquets of patent rights back and forth, so that they can go about their business without fear of reprisal.

They are also continually on the lookout for people (possibly you) who might bring a product to market without having secured all necessary agreements. Perhaps you have read about IBM demanding, and collecting, royalties from a variety of clone makers for use of patents on various aspects of their PCs. Nothing sinister here, either. IBM's list of innovations in the computer industry should garner awe, or at least grudging respect, from true-blue customers and competitors alike. So if you think you see a business opportunity in doing something cheaper than the big guys, check twice for hidden royalty costs.

Assuming you do have a piece of hardware that warrants a patent, don't let that make you too cocky. If you try to charge your competitors too much, you will only stimulate them to innovate you out of business in the area you think you own. I once heard the tale of a guy in the HVAC (heating, ventilation, and air conditioning) business who developed a duct with superior sound deadening properties. He found that a duct shaped like a sine wave, and suitably lined, was optimal in some ways for absorbing transmitted noises. Since this solves a perennial and important problem in HVAC design, particularly for expensive concert halls and broadcast studios, he felt he could charge a pretty penny for the right to install wiggly ducts.

His competitors found, however, that they could get most of the benefit he had discovered by shaping duct in the form of a square wave. Now, if you know anything about Fourier analysis, you know that a square wave can be represented as a sum (albeit infinite) of sine waves with multiples of the period of the square wave. The dominant term, the one with the largest amplitude, is the sine wave with the same period as the square wave. Perhaps a judge knowledgeable in both HVAC and spectral analysis, as well as patent law, could have been convinced that a square wave duct infringes on a sine wave patent. But that was not to be. Square ducts, to the unmathematical among us, look altogether too much like prior art.

No royalty.

If you come up with a bright idea in software, you face even greater perils. First off, it's much harder to convince the patent office to grant you a patent on software. You can't get a patent on a mathematical formula, or a bright idea. Besides being recognizably inventive, an invention must also be "reduced to practice." Patent courts tend to take a pretty mechanistic view of what constitutes reduction to practice. If you think Fourier analysis is lost on this crowd, try explaining some of the subtleties of computer software.

Arthur C. Clarke, the well known science-fiction writer, fell afoul of this gap in the patent law. Back in the late 1940s, he figured out that there were good uses for satellites orbiting over the equator 22,000 miles above the Earth. In such an orbit, a satellite appears stationary above a given spot on the equator. It is also visible over a large fraction of the surface of the Earth. What better place to hang repeaters for beaming telephone calls and TV broadcasts to the remotest corners of the globe?

Clarke invented the synchronous satellite, to be sure. But he could not get a patent unless and until he reduced the idea to practice. Since that was an enterprise well out of his financial reach (royalties for SF being what they are), he had to wait for the major nations of the world to do the job for him. Once they had done so, however, his chances for a patent evaporated. Hanging synchronous satellites in space then became prior art, which is not patentable. After some grumbling in print, Clarke resigned himself to owning just a footnote in the history books for his vision.

Nevertheless, a clever patent attorney can sometimes outsmart the system. Dennis Ritchie, for example, was granted a patent on the basic protection mechanism of the UNIX file system. The patent office decided that his set-user-ID bit was sufficiently inventive to warrant patent protection. (Fortunately, AT&T has been gracious enough to waive royalties for use of this clever invention. That has opened the way for much innovation in operating-systems design, not to mention the IEEE POSIX interface standard.)

I had occasion to read that patent. It described a mechanical device for storing information. The set-user-ID indicator was a mechanical toggle that the device could use to determine whether or not to yield up its stored information. Buried deep within the patent application was a paragraph of the "Oh, by the way" variety. It mentioned in passing that you could, of course, simulate such a mechanical device by programming a general-purpose computer to do all these things electronically. Naturally, the patent should cover this choice of implementation as well.

Very clever.

Chances are, however, that patent protection will prove to be inappropriate for any bright ideas you may generate in the course of writing programs. You should keep patents in mind for the hardware side of your enterprise, but don't waste too much time dreaming about being the founder of the next Polaroid or Xerox Corporation.

My personal opinion is that copyright protection is exactly the right shield for most of the intellectual property in computer products. That and trade mark protection, to keep others from misleading your customers into thinking that their products are connected somehow with yours. There is still a lot of contention, however, over where to draw the line in both of those arenas. I plan to address those areas of contention in the next essay. (See **Essay 4: What and How.**) □

Afterword: My feelings toward patent protection for software have become somewhat less benign in recent months. More and more, I hear of patents granted for silly bits of software technology. Many techies could demonstrate that these bits are commonplace in prior art, hence not worthy of a patent. Nevertheless, holding companies continue to exact royalties from software vendors for use of these questionable patents. It's often simpler to pay tribute than to seek justice.

4 What and How

I ran across a new slant on the old ruse for getting patents on software. In the previous essay, I told you about the clever way that AT&T Bell Labs worded their patent application on the UNIX set-user-ID protection mechanism. (See **Essay 3: Protecting Intellectual Property.**) The attorneys described a mechanical device that no one is likely ever to build, then pointed out in passing that you could program a computer to emulate such a device. Coverage for the mechanical device, they asserted, should extend to the computer program.

But now we have the case of Pennwalt Corp. v. Durand-Wayland, Inc. I read about it in a brief article by Joseph S. Iandiorio (**Ian88**). The case arose because a competitor produced a computer-driven conveyer system that does the same job as a patented mechanical system. The mechanical system determines sorting criteria (weight and color) for items on a conveyer as they pass a testing station. It then sends the information down a hard-wired shift register that is synchronized with the conveyer. At appropriate stations, items of a particular weight or color are kicked off the conveyer according to information provided from the shift register. The computer system does the same job using internally stored data in place of the hard-wired shift register.

The Court of Appeals for the Federal Circuit ruled that the software system does not infringe the hardware patent. The court evidently felt that there were sufficient differences in the way the two systems processed data. Since the differences identified in the suit are the inevitable differences between hardware and software processing, the ruling appears to have broad implications. And since this is the court that hears all patent appeals, the ruling appears to have clout.

If the precedent holds up, there is now a deeper schism between hardware and software patents. You can write programs to emulate patented hardware, or you can build machines that implement patented software, and have an arguable case that you are not infringing. Before you start raising venture capital, however, I suggest that you wait and see what happens. And don't take on AT&T or IBM on the strength of this one ruling.

N ow let's continue the discussion of various ways to make sure that others do not profit from your clever ideas at your expense. The sermon in this essay centers on copyright protection. For those of us in the software business, I believe that this corpus of law is the most appropriate form of protection. To see why, we need to identify more clearly just what we need most to protect.

I think it is fair to say that never before in history has intellectual property been so important to trade. Chip layouts, computer designs, and software packages simply *must* be protected. The profitability of the largest corporations in the world depends on it. Some would even argue that the future strength of the U.S., Japan, and most European nations is also at stake.

It is easy to decry the current litigious society, and to make rude jokes about lawyers, but the fact remains that we as a culture have a whole new set of rules that we have to work out. As the case above illustrates so well, the U.S. courts are the current battleground for the clash between old ideas and new needs. But it is also easy to get needlessly caught up in the skirmishing at the edges of patent and copyright law. Despite all this ferment, you shouldn't overlook the simple fact that many protections are already firmly in place. I can attest that you can run a computer software business for years with little fear that you will become the center of an interesting test case.

Great chunks of law exist that deal with the two fundamental components of a high-tech product:

- *What* the product does can be protected by trade secret or, in some cases, by patent.
- *How* the product does its job can be protected by trade secret or by copyright.

Despite all the current talk about look and feel, and whether such aspects of a product should enjoy protection, I believe that the distinction between what and how lies at the heart of the matter.

We discriminate between what and how all the time. Your boss comes to you with the specifications for the competitor's latest product. A spec sheet describes the *what* of a product. If you are told to match, or even exceed, those specifications with a new product, you would hardly take such orders amiss. Thousands of games of technological leap frog are going on in every corner of the computer business. Competition is a principal driving force behind the rapid advances of the past few decades.

But say your boss comes to you with blueprints for the competitor's latest product, or with source-code listings. These documents describe the *how* of a product. If you are told to imitate these details in a new product, you should smell a rat. Chances are you will be violating a trade secret, patent, or copyright in the process of duplicating such details. Never mind that some people do this all the time. Never mind that too many get away with it. This is not how you build a business, or a career.

So when we discriminate between what and how, we partition a design into two components. One is the black-box specification of the product, the part that is fair game for emulation (in the older sense of the word). Even if the *what* is protected by trade secret or patent, chances are that the specification can be stated at some level of abstraction that permits competition. The other component includes the details of implementation, the part that most of us agree is the intellectual property of the designer. Even if the *how* is not protected by trade secret or copyright, we feel a certain repugnance at simply knocking it off.

You may be surprised to learn that that sense of repugnance is a fairly modern conceit. The first copyright law on record was passed in Britain in 1709. Earlier history is replete with examples of intellectual borrowing unaccompanied by any apparent need for justification. There was little thought in the past that an artist or writer should profit from exploitation of his or her works. I learned about this from an excellent essay by Alvin B. Kernan (**Ker88**)

Copyright law in the U.S. was built into the Constitution (Article 1, Section 8). The protections offered owners of intellectual property have steadily and significantly increased over the years. Some would say that the balance has swayed too far in favor of the copyright owner. When I read about artists suing to prevent alterations to their works after they have sold them, I tend to agree. Others would say that the balance has not yet swayed far enough. When I see pirated copies of my books sold dirt cheap in countries that depend upon good relations with the U.S., or when I'm sent a publishing contract that would make Shylock blush, I tend to agree.

On balance, however, I'd say that the copyright law has been strengthened and clarified as it has proved to be good business to do so. Kernan's essay, which I cited above, ascribes the increased protections to a romantic view that art is somehow sacred. He sees modern technology as a serious assault on this view. I see instead a society with sufficient material wealth that it can (and must) give ever greater value to intellectual property. Prosperity requires that the merchants be protected from the thugs. Just as the U.S. Navy has long protected shipping from pirates, now the courts must protect computer programmers from copiers.

You might be surprised to learn, however, that you can't just copyright anything. You can only protect the expression of an idea if there is more than one way to express it. At one extreme, that means that you can't protect something if it is too simple. Or to put it another way, you don't infringe someone else's copyright if you express an idea in the only sensible way. Let me give you an example from personal experience.

In the process of working for three different employers, I have had occasion in the past to write the same set of functions. These functions performed 32-bit integer arithmetic on the PDP-11 family of computers. (A C compiler typically generates in-line calls to such functions when the operation is too complex to be performed directly in-line.) Being moderately honest and meticulous, I wrote the second and third versions of these functions without consulting my earlier work. I also, of course, avoided looking at similar function sets written by Dennis Ritchie and others.

I have since had occasion to compare those three implementations of the long-integer functions. Most of the functions produced executable code that was bit-for-bit identical. Moreover, most of the common functions were functionally identical to the ones that Dennis Ritchie wrote for the original PDP-11 C compiler. None of these discoveries troubles my conscience in the least.

If your goal is to write a function that performs a given job, if the job is small and precisely defined, and if you are constrained to do it the best (fastest and/or smallest) way possible, there is arguably only one right way to do the job. I may have drawn upon my memory of work done for earlier employers. I may even have seen Ritchie's code before I wrote my own. But I don't think so. And if I did, I feel I stayed well within both the spirit and the letter of the copyright law.

Compare that small potential transgression with what Franklin Computer once did to arouse the wrath of Apple. When you copy a design down to the contents of the control ROMs, it's hard to argue that you did it from memory. (Not that Franklin advanced such an argument, to my knowledge.) Apple did not have to stress the edges of copyright law very hard to convince the courts that its intellectual property rights were being compromised.

I mention the Apple v. Franklin case partly because it was reasonably clear cut. But one aspect of the case that received little publicity was far from clear cut. It shows the other extreme of the limitation on copyright protection, where complexity can be just as deadly as simplicity was in the case of my refried functions.

You're probably familiar with how to call upon system services under MS-DOS. You load various parameters into registers, load a service request number into the **AL** register, and execute one of the software-interrupt instructions. It is a moderately clean interface, sufficiently so that Phoenix Technologies and others have had good success at matching its black-box specification without having to peek inside MS-DOS or the ROM BIOS. The Apple II ROM, on the other hand, is not nearly so narrow an interface. You jump to absolute locations in the ROM to perform various system services.

Franklin argued that, because the interface was so diffuse, there was only one way to express the functionality of the Apple ROM. That was by copying the ROM contents verbatim. If there is only one way to express the function, then the expression cannot be protected by copyright. I understand that this argument gave the court pause. In the end, the court ruled that the ROM was protected because you could duplicate its functionality without duplicating it completely. But the hesitation was thrilling.

I have preached for years that you should keep interfaces clean for many good reasons. Maintainability and ease of use are two of the principal reasons. Until the Apple v. Franklin case, however, it never occurred to me that ownership protection was also an important reason. Just think, if a design is sufficiently ugly that you can't possibly replicate its features and bugs in any other way, then it can't be protected by copyright. Good design is building a clean fence between what and how.

One of the attempts at extending the reach of copyright protection recently received a setback. At issue is whether copyright law, or additional constraints imposed by a shrink-wrap license, can prevent a competitor from reverse engineering a product. The decision was handed down by the Federal Court of Appeals in New Orleans, in the matter of Vault Corp. v. Quaid Software (**LGU88**).

It seems that Quaid Software developed a copy program that subverts PROLOK, a copy-protection device sold by Vault. To do so, Quaid had to violate the terms of the shrink-wrap license protecting PROLOK (under Louisiana law). Quaid also had to copy the program into computer memory for other than its intended purpose. And Quaid used this knowledge to produce a product that can clearly be used to violate the copyright protection of other software products.

The court, however, found that Quaid had not acted improperly. The Louisiana shrink-wrap licensing law was pre-empted by federal copyright law in this particular case. Federal copyright law does not preclude anyone copying a program into memory for other than its intended purpose, nor was the court inclined to read such a meaning into the law. And the federal law does permit copying protected software for the purpose of making backup or archival copies. So long as there is a legitimate use for the Quaid product, the court ruled, Quaid is not just in the business of helping others infringe copyrights.

The net effect of all this was to once again clarify the distinction between what and how. Copyright does not protect your product from reverse engineering, no matter how badly software companies want such protection, and no matter how cooperative state legislatures are in endeavoring to provide it. Your competitors can read your secrets, if they are expressed in the product, to determine the *what* behind the *how*. So long as they avoid copying your expression, they can use the *what* to determine the specifications for their own product.

The center ring of the copyright circus, these days, is occupied by combatants on either side of the look-and-feel issue. We see Apple Computer v. Microsoft and Hewlett-Packard, with Apple claiming protection for the external appearance of its Macintosh software. We see Lotus suing and being sued over the external appearance of Lotus 1-2-3. (Some of the excitement in the Lotus case has been dissipated now that the court has ruled that Software Arts gave up its right to sue Lotus when it sold substantially all of its assets to Lotus. That may well avoid any determination of who originated the look and feel of 1-2-3.)

At issue, of course, is where specification leaves off and expression begins. Look and feel stands right at the interface between what and how. When there is more than one way to lay out a screen, for instance, the courts generally look askance at programs that exactly replicate the screen. When screen layouts, command sets, or other external characteristics derive in a similar way from common ideas, however, the courts generally find no infringement. A classic example is the "H" gearshift pattern used in many cars — it's a good functional solution to a common problem, and hence not protected. See Peter Waldman's article in *The Wall Street Journal*, March 21, 1988, for an overview of court decisions prior to the Apple suit (**Wal88**).

I'm not about to take sides when titans like these clash. All I care about is that the basic philosophy behind the copyright law survive intact. As one who has frequently reimplemented software products by working to a published specification, I'd hate to see competition compromised by excessive protection of the *what*. And as one who delights in expressing ideas both in code and in words, I'd hate to see a loss of protection of the *how*. At times like these, I'm glad I'm not a judge. □

fterword: Much has changed since I wrote this essay, but much has also stayed the same. Lotus won its lawsuit against Borland, possibly lending support to legal protection for look and feel. On the other hand, most of the Apple case has been dismissed against Microsoft and Hewlett-Packard. I wrote this essay as kind of a progress report on the education of the U.S. judicial system, courtesy of several informative articles I tripped across in quick succession. It's probably the sort of report that someone should produce every year or so for the foreseeable future.

5 Skin and Bones

I have devoted the past two essays to various aspects of protecting intellectual property, particularly when that property involves computer software. (See **Essay 3: Protecting Intellectual Property** and **Essay 4: What and How**.) This is the third and last installment on that topic, so let's begin with a brief summary of what has gone before.

When software is expensive, it makes sense to license it. You can limit usage in any way that suits your needs. You can avoid disclosing any trade secrets contained in the software. If your customers abuse your trade secrets, you can sue them (for what that may be worth). The problem with licensing software is that it takes longer to close a sale if you have to obtain a signed license before you can ship and bill. As prices come down, volume goes up, and competition intensifies, the cost, complexity, and inconvenience of licensing gets out of hand.

When a product is sufficiently inventive, you can patent it. The patent lets you disclose your secret invention (in fact, a patent *requires* disclosure) and ensures that you alone can profit from the commercial exploitation of your bright ideas. The problems with patenting are numerous, particularly for computer software. You can spend years and thousands of dollars obtaining the patent, which has a lifetime of only 17 years. And there are all sorts of ways to circumvent computer patents, by reimplementing hardware in software or conversely.

When the expression of an idea is more important than the mere idea itself, you should copyright it. Copyright law covers everything from sheet music to plumbing catalogs. The law has been recently updated to cover some of the specific issues related to computer software. The problem with copyrighting software is that you must be prepared to disclose your source code (by sending a copy to the Library of Congress) to obtain full protection under the law. And the corners of the law are still being illuminated by some pretty heavy-duty litigation.

Those are the basic forms of protection that you're likely to consider when making a computer hardware or software product. For another slant on the subject, read Glenn Groenewold's "Rules of the Game," *Unix Review*, October 1988 (**Gro88**). As both a lawyer and a writer, he spells out your options pretty clearly.

But let's assume that you've worked out the appropriate protections for your product. You've got the bare bones of a new money maker. It's time to put some skin on it, dress it up, and push it out the door. Compared to making a complex hi-tech product, you'd think that making up a name, designing the artwork for the box, and laying out the advertisements would be child's play. If you think that, you'd be wrong.

First there is the matter of a name. You want something that indicates what the product does. That limits you to naming rules similar to the ones that existing competitors have followed. On the other hand, you want to stand out from the crowd and present your product with an upbeat image. That opens up a new set of possibilities, but closes down many more. As Tom Plum has so aptly put it, "We want the absolute latest in cutting edge technology — that's tried and true and safe." Your job as namer of names is to convey that contradictory image.

Your job is also to come up with a name that does not too closely resemble that of any potential competitors. You can't call your new clone Joe's IBM PC (unless your idea of a good time is stepping in front of freight trains). Equally, you can't (or shouldn't) call it The Rosebud Colossus, because nobody will have any notion as to what it is or does.

So you find yourself pawing through books on mythology, looking for little-used names of minor deities. (Idris, after whom my company named an operating system, is the Persian god credited with having invented most tools and crafts, including the art of sewing things together.) Or you try predatory birds, mammals, fish, or mitochondria. The more desperate have been known to pull Scrabble tiles out of a sack and try rearranging them to make something pronounceable.

Chances are, however, that someone has beaten you to the punch. Whether you're naming a company, a piece of hardware, or a software package, someone somewhere has likely come close enough to your pet name to cause you trouble.

I thought of the name Whitesmiths, Ltd., for instance, as an obvious enough pun. If blacksmiths work on hardware, then surely whitesmiths must work on software. The extent of my research was to paw through the white and yellow pages of the Manhattan telephone book. It is well known that if you are looking for that one person in a million, there are eight candidates in New York City (and the one you want lives on the Upper West Side). Since there were no Whitesmiths in the phone book, I figured that I had created a genuine neologism, which is the best starting point for a trade name.

I later had occasion to browse through the Oxford English Dictionary, a dangerous but delightful pastime for those of us who are in love with words and their etymologies. I learned that a whitesmith is (among other things) one who polishes or finishes the work of a blacksmith. That proved to be a happy name for a software company, if an accidental one.

So I was still content, except for a nagging concern. The name of any trade that has survived in the English language for several centuries ought surely to be someone's surname. Sure enough, when we started selling overseas in quantity, we ran into a problem. It seems that there is an engineering firm in Manchester, England called Whitesmith (no "s") Limited, that also happened to sell the odd software package. There went any hope of locking up the name Whitesmiths throughout the European Common Market.

(Ed Yourdon claims that he first tried to call his new company Superprogrammers Inc. But the powers that be in New York State decreed a possible conflict with a Superior Produce somewhere upstate. Those folks were happy to give him permission to use the name he wanted — for a fee. So he called the company Yourdon inc. instead.)

Finding new names for software products has gotten much tougher in recent years. Partly this is because there are so many of them now. Partly it's because companies are more aggressive in protecting their trade names against the remotest possibility of infringement. And partly it's because the smart players have learned to tie up all of the obvious variations on names of successful products. (Have you ever wondered why nobody has named a programming language PL/2? Or why no multi-purpose PC package calls itself 4-5-6? Guess.)

My company tried and failed on two occasions, in recent years, to come up with clever new names for software products. We even tried contests among our staff, hoping that the often unbeatable combination of numbers, youth, and greed would succeed where we nominal leaders had failed. To no avail.

I was cheered to learn, however, that we are not alone in this difficulty. See Ronald Alsop's, "It's Slim Pickings in Product Name Game," *Wall Street Journal*, p. B1, 29 November 1988 (**Als88**). According to Alsop's article, federal legislation is in the works to limit the ability of companies to tie up unused trademarks. That can only help the current difficult situation for the makers of new products.

But let's assume that you've contrived a name for your wonderful new product. You've put skin on the bones, so all it needs is a new suit of clothes and it's ready to face the world. With its own unique name, and its own set of fingerprints, you need worry no longer about further identity conflicts. Right?

Wrong. There's another little matter of *trade dress*. People don't read the fine print on boxes. Often, they don't even read the large print. They see the colors, the artwork, and perhaps the type faces used. If enough of this stuff looks familiar, they assume they know who made it. That's a great way to piggy back the sales of your product on someone else's reputation. Except that there are laws against imitating the trade dress of a competitor.

Trade dress is a pretty encompassing concept. Lawrence Welk, on his way to becoming a band leader of some renown, at one time tried selling chewing gum. He called it Welk's, naturally enough, and packaged it in a green wrapper, as luck would have it. That was enough to attract the attention of Wrigley's, who felt their trade dress was being too closely copied. Welk eventually capitulated, and settled for making champagne music instead of gum.

On the other hand, I bought one of those children's plastic table and chairs for my son a few years ago. The logo on the side of the cylindrical table base was the word "Crayon" in Helvetica within an elongated ellipse. I'm sure I bought it because of the strong subliminal message that this was a Crayola product from Binney and Smith. Any company that doesn't change its logo in the near half-century that I have eaten its products, and that has resisted the urge to rename itself BSC Industries or some such, will get my business every day of the week. It disturbed me to learn that I had been snookered by a trade cross dresser.

When you package a software product these days, there are several "hafta"s you hafta obey. You hafta put the documentation and diskettes in a binder that fits in a box that sits neatly on a dealer's shelf (or on a customer's shelf, preferably). You hafta make the box appealing to look at, sturdy enough to hold up under use, and reveal some hint of its contents on the spine of the binder. All of those are reasonably functional haftas.

But you'd better not put IBM across the bottom of the spine in 48-point stripy block letters. In fact, you'd better not put anything on the spine in 48-point stripy block letters. You'd better not even pick one of those nauseous beige or interior-decorator greens beloved of everyone's largest competitor. Trade dress has its "what and how" just like software design.

But let's assume that you have survived the pitfalls of naming and packaging your product. Now all you have to do is advertise it and wait for the orders to come rolling in. What else can go wrong? Several things.

First, you have to protect that clever name you spent so much energy thinking up. Get it registered as a trade mark if you haven't done so already. That is a process that I have found to be not particularly time consuming or expensive. And it gives you some clout once you find that you are the established company and some upstart is tromping all over your hard-earned image.

Once you register a trade mark, make sure you use it right. The tales are legion of trade marks that have lost their reserved status because they have found their way into the language as common nouns. I'm told that the makers of Escalator-brand moving stairs hit the deck running (as it were) with an advertising campaign that doomed the name as a trade mark from the outset. The ads referred to "an escalator" as if it were a generic name for moving stairs. Perhaps the idea was to give the impression that this upstart product (at the cutting edge) had been around (and was therefore tried and true and safe), but the effect was to strip the proprietary clothing off the term and deliver it as a naked noun to the public domain.

I use florid language to emphasize a point. It can now cost you a serious investment of time and money to concoct a good trade mark. If you blow it by not caring for it properly, the people whose money you are spending will have florid faces to match.

You have probably noticed the recent trend toward defending trade marks. Robert Young orders Sanka-brand decaffeinated coffee, not just a cup of sanka. (As a businessperson, I would never intentionally weaken another person's trade mark. But as a writer, I could equally not put such words in the mouth of a fictional character. Robert Young will have to carry on the fight for General Foods without me.) Large companies have even taken to running ads in *Writer's Digest* to remind budding writers that their brand names have special status and demand proper care.

So the second thing you have to look out for when you write your ads is that you do not misuse the trade marks of others. I would never write, "Idris is the best UNIX you can buy." Or, "If you're looking for a UNIX, we've got just the thing for you." The first suggests that Idris is some form of the proprietary product called UNIX, which is not true. The second suggests that UNIX is a generic term for a certain class of operating systems, of which AT&T sells just one instance. Also not true.

If you've been living in a tree house for the past decade, or if you're really new to computing, you may not yet have heard that UNIX is the name of a proprietary operating system owned and licensed by AT&T Bell Labs. And AT&T has made it perfectly clear that they intend to keep UNIX under their control and out of the dictionary. Since UNIX has become a pretty important product, AT&T has my complete understanding and respect in this regard.

(The name UNIX was coined by Brian Kernighan, by the way. Ken Thompson had taken what he felt were the best ideas from the foundering MULTICS project and reimplemented them in miniature on an unused DEC minicomputer at Bell Labs. At lunch one day he asked for a name that would suggest the best of MULTICS for a single user. The rest is history.)

If you play fast and loose with the UNIX name in any of your ads, you will get a letter from AT&T. The letter will remind you that UNIX is a proprietary etc. etc. and suggest ways that you should refer to it in the future so as not to introduce the least element of uncertainty in the minds of readers of your ads. It is a very polite letter and looks good framed. It should also serve as a warning to you if you truly intend to misuse the name.

But I must let you in on a dirty little secret. You are not obliged to write that little superscript **TM** every time you mention UNIX. You don't have to tell the world repeatedly that UNIX is a trade mark of AT&T Bell Labs. All you have to do is not misuse the name in the obvious ways I cited above.

If you leave off the odd **TM** and AT&T sends you a letter, that's the end of it. They have a copy of the letter in their files to prove that they are assiduously defending their trade mark. You have a letter suitable for framing. The same goes for anybody else out there defending Sanka, Kleenex, or proprietary software.

Personally, I am tired of this recent mania for identifying trade marks in everything from scientific papers to help-wanted ads. A product that plays with half a dozen others can have so many pigeon droppings on the words (in the form of tiny **TM**s and ®s) that I can barely make out the sense of the main text. And all those footnotes in five-point type got lost on me shortly after my fortieth birthday. If any of this helped one whit in making commerce safer for honest business people, I would be all for it. But it doesn't.

So your third and final obligation is not to go off the deep end in defending your trade marks and those of others. Make your ads readable. Encourage others to mention your products as much as possible. Don't oblige them to license the right to mention your name when they talk in their sleep.

Perhaps the silliest extreme of trade mark mania was when the Department of Defense (a not-for-profit organization) decided to protect the name Ada for the programming language they paid to have developed. The idea was to discourage subsetting of the language. So DOD would only let you call your product Ada if it was validated as a full implementation.

Ada, in case you didn't know, was named after Ada, Lady Lovelace. She worked for a time with Charles Babbage on ways to put his analytical engine through its paces. So she was arguably the first computer programmer, and pioneered a practice which has since become widespread. That's not a great origin for a trade mark, but it will do.

When I read of DOD's incursion into the world of commercial trade marks, the habitual opposer in me woke up (as was too often the case in my misspent youth). I immediately set about planning a subset of Ada that I felt would yield most of the advantages of Ada while avoiding most of the cost. Since I couldn't call the product Ada, my plan was to call it Linda (after another lady named Lovelace who pioneered a practice that has since become widespread). Fortunately for all of us, I dropped those plans. Soon after, DOD dropped the trade mark on Ada.

I call it a draw. □

𝕬fterword: Techies tend to have little patience with mere matters of appearance. When the software business was new, we could mostly afford forgettable names and slipshod presentation. That has all changed now, but the word still seems to be spreading too slowly. It took me years to learn what I summarized here. I figured this essay could help others pay much less tuition than I did.

6 Product Reviews

𝕴've decided with this essay to branch out into the exciting world of product reviews. That seems to be the big thing these days in computer magazines, and I was beginning to feel a bit left out. It looks like a terrific racket, if you can pull it off.

In what other trade can you get vendors to part with their hard-wrought wares so easily? You get to play with all the latest toys, even keep a few of them from time to time, then turn around and bite the hand that feeds you. Like Broadway critics, product reviewers seem to thrive on finding bad things to say about works that they are themselves incompetent to produce. And like predators in other ecologies, reviewers have learned the advantages of squatting atop the food chain.

What set me down this new path was a clever product I saw mentioned in passing in one of the many magazines I slog through each month. I called the company that makes it and found myself talking to the president. All I had to do was mention my affiliation with *Computer Language* and I was able to extort a free copy out of him. (I'm sure I can phrase that more graciously, but probably not more honestly.) I can't help but wonder if Al Capone started out half as easily.

The product is called Nerd Perfect. It's produced by VaporSoft, Inc. (510 S.W. 3rd, Suite 400, Portland OR 97204) and it will set you back $9.95 plus $1.00 shipping, unless you can convince them that you are one of several thousand additional reviewers out there itching to give them free publicity. I also got a free poster of the Super Nerd on the cover of the manual, a $3.50 value to you people who have to pay full freight. (Admittedly, $14.45 ain't much in the way of extortion, but you have to start somewhere.)

So what is this Nerd Perfect? It's a charming blend of the novel and the traditional. Vaporware is hardly a new concept. Some of the largest software companies have been known to preannounce products by months or even years. One can't help but suspect that some of these announcements are merely trial balloons — the software gets produced only if sufficient interest appears. Meanwhile, the preannouncer has created an anticipation that often blocks the sale of real products, which never have the yummy specifications of a product that has faced no real-world compromises.

Nerd Perfect is vaporware to be sure. For your eleven bucks you get a manual and a 5 1/4-inch diskette. The diskette is not just write protected, it's not just copy protected, it's also read protected. The folks at VaporSoft achieve this triple level of protection by a simple innovation — they supply no magnetic medium inside the diskette jacket. Here we have vaporware raised to a new level. Not only do you get no software, the vendor still walks off with your money.

Whether VaporSoft gets the last laugh, however, depends upon your sense of humor. The manual consists of 35 pages of rambling satire. The humor is collegiate at best, sophomoric at worst, but it definitely has its moments. Your cubicle may well benefit from the cover poster with its stirring motto: "Software Before Its Time." The motto is allegedly trade marked, as is the name of the product, but you have already heard my position on promulgating the pigeon droppings that remind you of your putative duties to the owners of intellectual property. (See **Essay 5: Skin and Bones**.) You can at least clock some time at the coffee machine reciting some of the choicer bits to your peers.

The vendor calls this technology WYGIWYG, for "What You Get is What You Got." It is a refreshingly honest update of that old Latin standby, "Caveat Emptor." Either way, they've got your money and you've got what you've got.

The computer industry has a long tradition of letting the little guys prove in the innovations. Then the large corporations move in and take over the marketplace. I can't wait to see what the MBAs and corporate attorneys do to exploit this concept. Meanwhile, I wish the folks at VaporSoft all the best. May they never stop reminding us of our foibles.

Honesty compels me, however, to probe a little deeper in this, my first product review. Surely a comparative study is more revealing than a simple run-down on just one product in isolation. A novel product like Nerd Perfect demands to be put in perspective.

But what are the proper products to compare it to? I could stack it up against the twice-delayed release of Lotus 1-2-3 that is still not available. Or I could match it spec for spec against the 1,000 products that were supposed to be available by now for operation under OS/2. Somehow, that strikes me as being about as honest as debating an empty chair. Vaporware is a tough beat.

So let's focus instead on the more tangible aspects of Nerd Perfect:

- It supplies a modicum of humor.
- It provides you with an empty diskette jacket.

From that vantage point, two obvious competitors spring to mind:

- A box of 3M diskettes.
- Ventura Publisher 2.0 with Professional Extensions.

Now we can get concrete.

First let's look at prices. You already know about the eleven bucks list you have to shell out for Nerd Perfect. I haven't seen it discounted yet, but give it time to percolate through the channels. Rome wasn't burnt in a day. The latest box of 3M diskettes I bought has a marked list price of $37.10. I got it discounted for $17.81, clever shopper that I am. Ventura Publisher lists for about $895 these days, plus an additional $595 for Professional Extensions. If you buy it in one of those dress shops in the Fontainbleu Hotel in Miami Beach, you may pay that much. The rest of us go discount and slice at least a third off of list. (Too bad I hadn't honed my skills at extortion earlier. That's still a lot of cabernet sauvignon.)

As with any new technology, we find prices all over the map. You have to consider, however, the number of manuals and diskette jackets you get from each vendor. The 3M offering, for example, has no manual (more on that later), but it does deliver ten high-quality jackets. Ventura Publisher comes with extensive documentation as well as 22 jackets. So even if you ignore the manuals, you're looking at:

PRODUCT	COST PER JACKET
Nerd Perfect	$11.95
3M	$ 3.71
Ventura	$67.73

Much more sensible.

To make the comparison even more honest, you have to look at what's involved in getting the same final product. Nerd Perfect requires no additional work on your part. You get an empty diskette jacket just by breaking the shrink wrap. (Don't forget to read the licensing terms first.) The other products make you work. You have to read the license, remove the shrink wrap, then pull the annoying magnetic medium out of the jacket and discard it. This is hard for the average consumer to do without wrinkling the jacket in a most unsatisfactory manner. I trust the folks at 3M and Ventura will accept this positive criticism in the spirit in which it is intended and address this problem in future product releases.

I should point out before I go on that all testing for this product review was performed at Gedanken Laboratories. I favor them because they take an imaginative approach to difficult testing problems, they give quick results, and they are cheap. They also have an excellent reputation in the physics community.

In the humor department, Nerd Perfect has a definite edge. Admittedly, humor is a subjective matter. (The letters people write to *Computer Language* about "Programming on Purpose" are proof of that.) It's hard in this case to evade the objective facts, however. First of all, the box of 3M diskettes comes with no documentation. That eliminates most opportunities for a *bon mot* right off the bat. In this era of increasing attention to user friendliness, you'd think a major vendor like 3M would wise up and produce a proper set of manuals for their product. The possibilities for humor are endless in a five-foot shelf of documentation for a blank diskette. I think they're missing a real opportunity here.

As for Ventura, they have certainly provided lots of material. If you like your humor dry, you'll find any number of passages to chuckle over. I especially enjoyed the part about installing the extra Bitstream Fontware for automatic down loading to a PostScript printer. And the description of frame anchors is still good for a laugh ever since I tried to get Ventura to do what I wanted at 3 a.m. one morning. In many cases, though, you really had to be there to appreciate the humor in the text. So I would have to say that, on balance, Ventura errs too much on the side of trying to convey information. Some people just can't tell a joke.

Still another important point of comparison is weight. Nerd Perfect, as shipped, is 2.5 oz. The box of 3M diskettes is 8.0 oz. Ventura Publisher weighs in at a hefty 7 lb. That should tell you a lot right there.

If the significance of these numbers is lost on you because you lack the broad base of experience that we product reviewers have, I will deign to explain. The weight of a package has an obvious psychological influence, as has been well known in the proposal-writing business for many years. Simply put, the heftier the better for maximum impressiveness.

But there are other considerations that can lead to tradeoffs. One consideration often dominated by weight is terminal velocity. Unless the vendor has chosen a package that looks like a glider (or an Apollo re-entry capsule), a heavier package will generally fall faster.

That may not matter to you, but it does to some of us. You're probably still thinking about upgrading to a faster 80286 PC (or a Macintosh SE). We reviewers are ready to trade up from an 80386 PC (or Mac II) to something that's *really* new and fast. And I'll bet you're just getting used to using Fed-X and other next-day air-delivery services without feeling guilty at the cost. We reviewers are already pushing the limits of same-day air delivery.

You can see how important it is to keep the terminal velocity of a package as high as possible for same-day air delivery. Why bother to kick a package out the bomb bay at 5,000 feet if it's going to flutter slowly to the ground? That costs you productivity while you sit around waiting for it to hit. You want something that will really drop, and packaged software vendors had better wise up to this requirement soon or they're going to be left hanging in the air. So here are the terminal velocities of our three competitors:

PRODUCT	TERMINAL VELOCITY
Nerd Perfect	110 MPH
3M	115 MPH
Ventura	163 MPH

Here, Ventura Publisher has a clear advantage. That's the sort of perform-ance you can expect from a professional package.

But as I warned above, there can be tradeoffs. Just as important in delivering a product fast is a factor that we reviewers call *splatter radius*. On the face of it, it is an easily understood phenomenon. When the package arrives at your site via same-day air, it undergoes a rapid deceleration. That deceleration is invariably accompanied by a rearrangement of the contents of the package. If you circumscribe a circle around the final distribution of contents, the radius of that circle is called the splatter radius. (This is a slight oversimplification, but it will do for the lay reader.)

Assigning a figure of merit to a given splatter radius takes some expertise. If your goal is to use all of the material from the package at one site, then you'd like to keep the splatter radius small. If, on the other hand, you need to distribute empty diskette jackets to the various users connected to your LAN, then there is a clear advantage to a package that really splatters. Know your needs and don't be automatically swayed by large splatter radii. With that in mind, here are the performance figures for the products under test:

PRODUCT	SPLATTER RADIUS
Nerd Perfect	3.7 ft.
3M	1.3 ft.
Ventura	25.4 ft.

The data indicates that Nerd Perfect out performs 3M in this important dimension, but don't be fooled. The extra splatter is caused by the manual — with only one diskette jacket, there is no improvement in jacket distri-bution throughout a LAN. If anything, spraying the manual across your front lawn diminishes the humor somewhat. There is a definite loss of con-tinuity, which can be fatal to many forms of satire.

Again, you can see that Ventura Publisher is in a class by itself. The tests indicate a most satisfactory spread of diskette jackets. Moreover, the manu-als became even more amusing to read once their pages were thoroughly shuffled. If you own a LAN, this might be the solution for you.

So to summarize, each of these products has its individual strengths and weaknesses. Nerd Perfect does a good job of delivering on its stated promise. A box of 3M diskettes may not be very entertaining, but it is the cheapest way to obtain a stack of diskette jackets. And Ventura Publisher justifies its premium price in several ways. You can even do some pretty respectable desktop publishing with it, provided you load the software before you destroy the diskettes. On balance, however, I have to label Nerd Perfect a Best Buy. (They gave me the largest payoff.) But you can't go wrong with any of these offerings. It looks like the consumer is the winner.

espite what you may think after reading the foregoing, I take product reviews very seriously. As a product vendor, I awaited each review of my products with a queasy mixture of fear and anticipation. I am keenly aware of the influence they have on sales. As a consumer, I lean on them heavily. This is an important part of the computer software business.

At their best, product reviews serve several noble purposes. They inform consumers of the broad array of choices that we now enjoy, in a way that cannot be matched by product announcements and advertisements. Good reviews can put related products in context and in perspective. They are free of the hype that perforce accompanies any presentation by vendors of their own products.

The movie *Moscow on the Hudson* contains a telling scene. In it, Robin Williams portrays a Russian defector faced for the first time with an American supermarket. After years of waiting in endless lines to buy goods, and having few choices available when he can buy them, Williams must choose a brand of coffee from a score of offerings. He suffers an anxiety attack.

I suffer a similar paralysis when I have to buy commercial software or hardware these days. My natural stinginess rebels at the thought that I might shell out even $50 for a software package that is not the best possible choice for my needs. As a result, I skim ads endlessly, in search of the elusive details that will convince me my money will be well spent. A well crafted product review, like nothing else, can break my mental log jam and help me get moving again.

I'm sure that I'm not alone in depending heavily upon product reviews. And that places a heavy burden of responsibility on the writers of reviews. A poor review can cost vendors of good products many of the sales that they deserve. It can also cause many buyers to waste their money on suboptimal choices. And it tends to weaken everyone's faith in the whole process. An irresponsible reviewer is a loose cannon on a heaving deck.

I still bristle at the memory of one of the first reviews my company was subjected to. It was printed ten years ago, by a magazine that is still popular, authored by a reviewer who is still plying his trade. In that review, he indulged in a bit of offhand hyperbole. He intimated that the compile time of a test program on a Z80 was about half an hour, when in fact it was less than five minutes. For months afterward, potential customers would ask us why our compiler took half an hour to compile simple programs. We'll never know how many people just never bothered to call as a result of that irresponsible remark.

Another major magazine savaged one of our products several years ago. The reviewer characterized it as "written by sadists for masochists." As the sadist in question, I couldn't help but take the attack personally. The reviewer turned a blind eye to all the ways in which the product excelled.

He failed to mention that he had spent an hour on the telephone being obnoxious and irrational with our most polite and able customer-support programmer. He (and the magazine) also soft pedaled the fact that he headed up the users' group for a competing product. That magazine and that reviewer are also both still in business.

Fortunately, experiences such as these seem to be the exception rather than the rule. When reviews fall short of perfection, the causes are generally less pathological. In case you missed the point, I have been parodying the elitism that many veteran reviewers fall into. They lose touch with the criteria that we mortals apply. Often they fall in love with the latest and flashiest offerings, and forget to notice that they have little relevance to the real world. Honesty in a reviewer is paramount, to be sure. Intelligence also helps a lot. But a common-sense perspective is at least as important as brains in the making of a reviewer that I can depend on.

The last venal sin that I will carp about is being wishy washy. I want my reviews to arrive at a few simple conclusions. Maybe I won't agree with the opinions, but if they are accompanied by a brief set of reasons then I can happily decide for myself. Tables of numbers tell part of the story, but in the end it is the gestalt that I most depend on a reviewer to supply. If I trust the reviewer, then I trust that my overall reaction will probably be the same.

So let me end with just the briefest review of the reviewers. *PC Magazine* works harder at covering the exploding PC marketplace than any other magazine that I know of today. I have come to trust them from repeated personal experience. For the more specialized corners of our trade, I have a high regard for *Computer Language* and the other Miller Freeman publications. (Otherwise, I wouldn't be writing for them all these years.) I have found them to be consistently honest and meticulous. The various "computer shopper" magazines are a waste of time if you want to study comparative anatomy. They owe first allegiance to their advertisers, not their readers.

If I've left out your favorite source of product reviews, don't treat it as a slight. There are many good folks out there providing this essential service, more than I can read and far more than I can mention here. If you find a source you can trust, stick with it. And tell all your friends. □

Afterword: I can cheerfully report that the hyperbolic reviewer I mentioned in this essay has cleaned up his act. I now read his advice with (sometimes grudging) respect. Even more cheerfully, I can report that the magazine that savaged my company's product is no longer in business. If the reviewer himself is still writing for the magazines, I haven't noticed his presence lately. All changes for the good, in my opinion.

7 Awaiting Reply

My college roommate was a slob. At least by my standards he was. He could live for weeks in a dorm room paved with laundry, decaying through various stages from unused to unredeemable. He viewed waste baskets more as targets than as repositories. He made his bed every time his parents came to visit.

Pete's minimalist approach to housekeeping was awe inspiring. (He is the only person I know who can wash dishes without getting his hands wet. Think about it.) When it was his turn to straighten up, he believed firmly in objective specifications. He would preselect a vantage point, usually somewhere near the door. Then he would pick up, dust off, or rearrange as little as possible to set the scene. Once the room looked neat from his preselected vantage point, he defined the room as clean.

On the other hand, he almost invariably got better grades than I did. True, he is somewhat smarter than I am, but he was also much better organized. Pete knew just where to expend energy on organizing his notes, or his reading, or his experiments, so that he could indulge in a physics major at Princeton with a minimum of effort. I didn't like his strategy as applied to keeping our shared space clean, but I had to admit its superiority in the paper chase.

You see, as fastidious as I fancied myself when it came to housekeeping, in most other ways I was a slob. My first few years as a programmer, in FORTRAN and assembly language at that, forced me to develop tidier work habits. It was that or perish. Only after I drifted into the world of business, and became willy nilly an entrepreneur, did I let my creeping neatness spill over into my daily record keeping.

I learned to write notes to myself and leave them in places where I would trip over them in time. I used my physicist's training at making first-order estimates to anticipate cash-flow problems and to plan for taxes. I even learned to outline documents before I started writing, just like they teach in junior high school. In short, I developed the knack for looking organized from a preselected vantage point with the exertion of a minimum of effort.

Somewhat later in life, I learned another Great Truth. We are all slobs when you get right down to it. Those people who appear superbly organized and make us all feel bad about ourselves either are more adept at faking it or are so insecure they waste effort looking organized when nobody's watching.

(There may be exceptions to this general rule. One of my classmates at Princeton was one William Warren Bradley, a.k.a. Basketball Bill, or more recently Senator Bill Bradley, (D) New Jersey. He used to play superb basketball, get good grades, and teach Sunday school. If he was faking it, he sure had a lot of us fooled. I have to say the same for the likes of Ken Thompson and Dennis Ritchie as well.)

The basic message of this Great Truth is that you don't have to overhaul yourself completely to be more effective at getting things done. You just have to learn where to expend that minimum extra effort to up your efficiency in the areas that really count. The rest of the time you can continue being the good-natured slob you've always been.

One of the small tricks that I still use is to carry around half a dozen files in my briefcase. Every bill, every letter to write, every item to file permanently goes in one of those files. Quickly, before it gets lost. Periodically, I know to go through the files and pay bills, write letters, and get caught up on filing. A little time spent daily filtering mail and phone messages lets me be a lot lazier and still look organized.

My favorite file in this collection is the one marked Awaiting Reply. That's where I put a copy of any correspondence that requires an answer before I can lay the matter permanently to rest. Putting something in that file gives me the same sense of satisfaction you get when you lob the ball back over the net in tennis. You've demonstrated that you're still in the game and you've got a brief respite while the other person has to take action. This indoor version of tennis is otherwise known as *passing the buck.*

Most of the time, items stay in Awaiting Reply for a matter of a few days to a week or so. I usually truck around half a dozen to a dozen items at any one time, but the population changes continually. Some items, however, find their way into that folder and stick there for months at a time. When that happens, it almost invariably signals that the other player has dropped the ball. And when repeated reminders fail to dislodge an item from this folder, I know I have run afoul of a fellow slob who has not learned where to expend energy wisely.

Let me treat you to some of the items currently yellowing in my Awaiting Reply folder. I think they provide an illustrative cross section of the state of our industry. Since I am in a nasty mood, I will name names.

First we have the bingo-card black hole. Months ago I circled a bingo card requesting additional information about an ASCII to PostScript translator called Trading Post and a LaserJet gray-scale conversion package called Visual Edge. Nothing.

Now I know that bingo card processing takes time. The magazine wants to add your name and profile to its mailing list, since it makes good money peddling extracts from that list to various junk-mail generators. Then the labels go from magazine to vendor, who may choose to rekey the data for other nefarious purposes.

Eventually, however, someone should stuff relevant literature into an envelope and send it your way. If the vendor is sufficiently aggressive, you might even get telemarketed to qualify your level of interest and ability to fork over serious money. If you don't get any sort of contact within a couple of months, that tells you either that someone lost your name along the way or the vendor was just not prepared to pursue the leads generated by the ad you read.

Since I've long since received replies from contemporaneous bingo queries, I have to assume that the magazine is not at fault. It does not raise my faith in either of these companies that they cannot pursue a serious lead. If their sales effort is disorganized, what does that suggest about product support? Or even the original product engineering?

I confess that in the early days of running my company I let us get caught out more than once. We'd run an ad, then suddenly find ourselves awash with bingo card replies and no promotionals to send out. (In our earliest days, we were foolish enough to disdain reader service numbers. We felt that responding to bingo cards was a nuisance!) I have since learned to plan the promotionals at the same time as the ads, so everything is ready when needed.

As for the two requests for information that are still unfulfilled, I can't say who is to blame for the lapses or what caused them. I can only suspect that both vendors dropped the ball. Maybe I've got the wrong impression in either or both of these cases. But in this competitive marketplace, the onus is on the vendor not to let that happen. I can just go to another supplier, instead of just sitting around awaiting reply.

Another item in my folder is a note that I ordered a $50 software product called Axe from an outfit in Wayne, New York. It's supposed to do a nifty job of compressing your .COM files, to save disk space on your laptop. Zipadeedoodah. It could be that the order got lost along the way. If it got lost inside their order-processing department, I'm not excited about ever getting the product, for the reasons cited above. It could also be that the order is held up awaiting "a few software improvements."

Again speaking from experience, I can report that few internal tensions are worse in a company than that between sales and marketing, who have orders piling up, and development, who must make packages that won't get kicked back by irate customers. Sometimes you start advertising a product when it is "almost debugged." Come scheduled ship date, you're still shaking out bugs one at a time. Other times you ship a package for awhile, then get a report of a truly serious flaw. Schedules go to hell while you scurry to repair, repackage, and reship.

One of the hardest things for a salesperson to do is tell a customer that an order is in limbo for some unspecified time. Every conversation is an opportunity for the customer to cancel and go elsewhere. That's why you, as a customer, suddenly find your correspondence and phone calls going unanswered by the folks who normally love to talk your ear off. You sit around awaiting reply.

I don't know whether this is the case with my .COM compressor. I can only guess. I don't hear anything from the vendor.

Next we have two examples of what you might call "Holy Grail-itis." I have been trying for half a year to refit my Compaq DeskPro with a high-resolution screen and driver board. I want something that will ease operations with Ventura Publisher and be standard enough to work with newer graphics-oriented software packages. Every time I think I've covered all the bases with a given product, I discover one or two flaws. Were the marketplace less active, I probably would have picked something good enough months ago and settled for it. But since every feature I want is in *some* product out there, it's hard to resist shopping until all the good features come together in one place.

For that reason, I have interrupts pending for information on the newest video board from STP and the newest display from Microvitec. It is now well past the time when each of these enterprises assured me that their latest and greatest enhancements would be available, deftly sweeping away my remaining objections to purchasing their products.

As annoyed as I am for being strung along, I can sympathize to some extent. Sales people know that they can fill twice as many orders if only development would add a small list of enhancements. Developers wince at the length of the laundry list you get when you merge the wishes of as few as three different sales people. Doesn't anybody appreciate the need for design tradeoffs? Do you know how much this thing would weigh (or cost, or sprawl) if we put all that stuff in? Doesn't anybody want to buy what we've got, to subsidize making the next version?

All a poor salesperson can do with a customer like me is to hint darkly that the Next Release will have what I want. (Next Release is salesperson talk for Holy Grail.) When pressed for a date, a salesperson will quote the most optimistic date that can sustain a third-party audit, holding the phone with all fingers crossed. That leaves me sitting at home awaiting reply.

Another form of the Holy Grail is the preannounced product. There's this wonderful board called the Complete Communicator which is supposed to do triple duty as a fax board, a 2400-baud modem, and a voice messager. Only trouble is, it seems never to be quite ready to ship. I ask for technical details and I get glossies. (Wake up, America! You don't sell to us techies with pretty pictures and punchy prose. Give us numbers and specs every day. Either it sells itself or you're out of luck.)

Still, the product looks good. And it looks like it can fill a real need that I have and that I share with a number of my friends. I'd love to kick the tires, or at least have more fine print to read.

What worries me is that one of my calls to a distributor inadvertently got routed to an honest man. He told me that the product was aggressively preannounced. All he could do was feed me glittering generalities and take my name for future reference. That's all anyone else has done, but they haven't been nearly as forthcoming as my one refreshingly frank contact. Mostly I sit around (you guessed it) awaiting reply.

I am writing this essay on my latest toy, a Compaq SLT/286. It does just what Compaq advertises, I'm very happy with it, and I even got it at a good price. What it has cost me in place of money is aggravation.

I bought the laptop from an outfit called RP Systems in Oak Brook, Illinois. Let me say up front that their prices are wonderful, their people polite if harried, and their support all I could ask for. I did something colossally stupid with the 5 1/4-inch add-on drive, shipped it back to them, had them sort out my stupidity, and ship it back to me. The whole process took less than a week, they paid the shipping back to me, and they resisted the temptation to point out what a twit I was. Good service.

What keeps them languishing in my Awaiting Reply folder is the one-megabyte add-in board that I ordered with the machine, lo these many months ago. My impression is that this outfit started out on a shoestring, like so many mail-order houses, and is growing slightly out of control. They take orders for items that have never graced their shelves, then wait for them to come dribbling in from Compaq or other suppliers. As the items come in, the shipping folks hurriedly stuff them into baggies and boxes and send them on to impatient customers.

Because they can't afford an inventory, and because they evidently have zero clout with Compaq, RP Systems has been consistently unable to quote me honest delivery dates. They promise to call me with updates, but the calls only come when they have something to ship. I can understand that they're afraid I'll cancel. I just wish they would understand that I would much rather have an honest, pessimistic estimate than a dishonest, optimistic one. That way, I don't sit around awaiting reply.

I end this list with the prize gem in my collection. Many months ago I took delivery of a high-resolution monitor and board from an outfit called Elite Business Systems in Philadelphia, Pennsylvania. They promised super performance with Ventura Publisher for a mere $1,700. Satisfaction guaranteed or your money back.

Well, I got the thing and worked with it for several weeks. Mostly, it did what they said. It annoyed me that the driver board would not coexist with my EGA color board. (The Next Release is supposed to fix that.) I had some problems with display fonts not reflecting reality closely enough to support on-screen text editing. They tried hard to make things better by shipping me replacement fonts.

In the end, I decided that, good as it was, it got in my way too much to use every day. So I called up Elite, eventually got someone to agree to accept the return, and sent it back. The only problem is, they forgot to refund my money.

Now in case there is any doubt, I regard $1,700 as a serious amount of money. I have tried polite letters, firm letters, and nasty letters. No answer. The poor women who must answer the phone at Elite can only report that "everyone is out of the office right now." No one ever returns my phone calls. I am too pigheaded to let this matter drop, so I will keep escalating until I get satisfaction. That obviously involves throwing good time and money after bad.

In my latest letter to the ephemeral president of Elite, I said, "I suspect you are a typical small hardware company struggling with tight cash flow and an excess of competition. As the former owner of a small company, I can sympathize with your problems. I cannot, however, sympathize with your tactic of failing to honor your business debts."

The hardest thing in the world is to return a phone call to someone who is angry at you. It is particularly hard when you know you're in the wrong and fear that you cannot do anything to dispel that anger. What you have to learn is that not talking to angry customers is even worse. They can only assume the worst and get progressively madder. The one thing worse than an angry customer is an irrational angry customer.

I have learned to force myself to make those calls. There's a moral advantage in being the one to initiate the contact. And there's a tremendous sense of relief when you've finally laid all the cards on the table and can get on to working out a resolution, however uncomfortable that resolution may be. If you are indeed programming on purpose then you have customers. They may pay you in brownie points, internal funny money, or hard cash, but you have customers. Dealing with limited resources and dealing with irate customers both come with the territory. Get used to it.

As for your role as customer, let *caveat emptor* be your guide. I used to buy all my cameras from those Manhattan mail order houses. One of them once charged me over $200 for a camera they failed to ship. I never did get them to pay me back. I used to buy duty-free liquor whenever I flew home from overseas. A Winnipeg duty-free shop once failed to put my $40 worth of booze on the plane. Never convinced them to reimburse me. Those two failures obliterated most or all of the savings I had accrued to date by buying discount. I now buy much more from local merchants. It's often worth the markup to have a shin to kick.

I thought I had learned my lesson, but I guess not. Mr. President of Elite Business Systems, I am still awaiting your reply.

This column is not meant to be a diatribe against all the people who have caused me grief lately (at least not completely). Its purpose is to illustrate all the ways that you as a supplier of services can leave potential customers in the lurch. As tempting as it is to avoid the unpleasant, you must learn to make that extra effort to respond. Otherwise, you lose your customers. With customers, you can afford to spend most of the day being the lazy slob you want to be. Without customers, you may have to really get organized. □

Afterword: I got my money back from Elite. Shortly thereafter, they stopped advertising under that name, but I suspect they popped up in another guise. RP Systems also went bust. Even more revealing, I'm not using any of the products I was pursuing when I wrote this essay. Somehow others convinced me, by being more responsive, to buy from them instead. I was in a bitchy mood when I wrote this essay, but somehow I managed to deliver an important message along the way.

8 Soup or Art?

I was going to stay away from "look and feel" and the whole issue of software protection for awhile. I have already devoted several essays to the subject. (See **Essay 3: Protecting Intellectual Property, Essay 4: What and How**, and **Essay 5: Skin and Bones**.) The big lawsuits started by Apple and Lotus are still working their way through the courts. Since what the judges perceive is far more important than my myopic viewpoint, it appeared most seemly to wait until I could second guess my betters.

Unfortunately, stuff keeps happening. (I believe there is a popular bumper sticker that makes the same observation, albeit with more vulgar and direct language.) Several recent experiences have got me thinking on this subject again. You should know by now that the inevitable consequence is that you get treated to another 3,000-word essay on the topic.

The fundamental issues currently being debated are highlighted beautifully by Lily Tomlin in her one-woman play, *The Search for Signs of Intelligent Life in the Universe*. You might find more accessible the book of the same title by the playwright, Jane Wagner (**Wag86**). It begins with the bag lady Trudy describing her conversations with extraterrestrials:

We think so different.

They find it hard to grasp some things that come easy to us, because they simply don't have our frame of reference. I show 'em this can of Campbell's tomato soup. I say, "This is soup." Then I show 'em a picture of Andy Warhol's painting of a can of Campbell's tomato soup. I say, "This is art."

"This is soup.

"And this is art."

Then I shuffle the two behind my back.

Now what is this?

No, this is soup and this is art!

The parallels with our business are staggering. Have you ever tried to get a lawyer or judge to understand the distinction between software specification and implementation? It's like trying to get an extraterrestrial to distinguish between soup and art. It's not that they're stupid or they don't try. They just think so different.

Fictitious aliens generally come equipped with fictitious death rays. They can zap you because of a silly misunderstanding. Unfortunately, real-world judges come equipped with real-world powers. They can zap our industry if they misunderstand the issues.

Soup versus art is a recurring theme throughout Wagner's play. I believe she is emphasizing that art is nourishment to the spirit, just as vital as the soup we eat to nourish our bodies. While I agree wholeheartedly, that is not part of the parallelism that I celebrate here. I also won't disclose the charming way she has Lily Tomlin return to the theme to wrap up the play. Go see it, or at least read the book.

What I want to focus on is the relative importance of protecting soup versus art. Commercial food recipes are traditionally kept secret. Should you get your hands on a copy of the recipe, you cannot sell copies of it without risking trade-secret violations or copyright infringement. Should you reverse engineer the contents of a can of fish soup, however, nothing prevents you from selling the same mix of ingredients. Soup, being "usable," is not a mode of expression that can be protected by copyright.

Paint a picture of a can of soup and you have a different kettle of fish, as it were. Aside from the fact that it is not very usable for physical nourishment, it is also arguably a work of art. Andy Warhol managed to convince a number of people of this premise, at least. Should someone stuff your picture through a copier, you can demand a royalty on any sale of the copies. Should someone paint a similar picture, you have a case that the work is a derivative of yours.

Someone can even contrive to make your picture "usable," by making a window shade out of it, for instance. You still have a protected work of art, however, because it can be admired independent of its function.

Most judges eat soup, admire art, and appreciate the distinctions between the two as expressed by centuries of copyright law. They understand, in fact, that there is a continuum of works protectable by copyright. At one extreme there are purely aesthetic works, such as pictures of saints and soup cans. At the other there are fairly functional writings, such as engineering drawings and recipes for soup.

While the whole spectrum is protected, functional writings enjoy considerably less protection under copyright law than aesthetic works. Since the law does not protect the machine represented by the drawing, or the soup represented by the recipe, all it can cover is the unique expression captured in the functional writing. Many people could generate almost identical drawings or recipes in their zeal to describe the underlying function. So unless you can demonstrate that another drawing or recipe contains gratuitous detail that is also identical, you have a hard case claiming infringement of your copyright.

Fewer judges write software, design it, or appreciate the goals sought when Congress explicitly spelled out copyright protection for software only a decade ago. Just where software belongs on the continuum of protections is critical to determining what constitutes infringement when you reimplement someone else's highly successful product. If the courts broaden the current notions about what constitutes infringement, we'll all have to be much more careful.

So the question is, does a piece of executable software constitute a functional writing that captures an underlying unprotected set of concepts, and hence is protected only against fairly flagrant copying? Or is it an aesthetic expression that demands broad protections? Is a software concept soup, or is it art?

You'd think that the very use of the word "concept" would end the debate. Copyright law has long been clear that you cannot protect a concept, only a particular expression of the concept. Unfortunately, some courts have been known to judge infringement of aesthetic works based on similarity of "total concept and feel."

For an excellent discussion of this and other topics in this essay, see Pamela Samuelson's *CACM* article "Why the Look and Feel of Software User Interfaces Should Not Be Protected by Copyright Law" (**Sam89**). I am endeavoring to paraphrase some of what she says, but please remember that she is a lawyer and I am not. (I don't know law, but I know what I like.) Go read her article if you want to get the uncorrupted version.

Anyway, Samuelson cites a case in which McDonald's was taken to task for creating advertising characters that bore a strong resemblance to those from H.R. Puf'n'stuf. The court chose not to confine the comparison to the usual analytic dissection of similarities and differences. It went on to judge whether the total concept and feel were substantially similar, irrespective of details. Moreover, the established pattern in such matters has been to let experts do the dissection, but to rely on the untrained impressions of judges or jurors to decide similarity of total concept and feel.

I should emphasize that total concept and feel have not been recognized by all of the different courts in the U.S. Nor has it been applied to any cases except those involving aesthetic works. Nevertheless, there are those who are eager to stretch such notions to broaden the copyright protections extended to computer software.

An important first step in this direction was taken by Jack Russo and Doug Derwin in 1985. These two lawyers introduced the concept of look and feel, which avoids the dirty word "concept" while embracing the same goals. In doing so, they made a case for extending copyright protection to the user interface of a piece of software.

Look and feel does not cover just the aesthetics of how a screen is drawn. It also involves the patterns of interaction that the software supports and the underlying conventions that encourage those patterns of interaction. In other words, it covers the very things that everyone wants to knock off when they run across a very successful software product.

If you are the author of the successful software product, you understandably want all the protection you can get. Often, a large part of your value added is discovering what patterns of interaction help people make best use of the functionality the program provides. It is noticeably easier to reimplement (and improve on) an existing success than to achieve success in a new area. As someone who has reimplemented other folks' designs, and seen my own reimplemented in turn, I sympathize with the desire to control a market long enough to get a good return on investment.

There is a fundamental problem with protecting look and feel, however. How do you separate out your innovations from those you inherited from others? Apple benefited from work done at Xerox, and Lotus benefited from Visicalc. Even if these two beneficiaries have obtained clear rights to the obvious key concepts (and there is evidence that each has), both have also profited from many other sources as well. We all have, each and every one of us who has produced a commercial software product in the past twenty years.

If either Apple or Lotus prevails in their current legal efforts to protect look and feel, the courts will have opened Pandora's box. I can't imagine how a ruling can extend copyright protection to look and feel without leaving most of the industry wide open to claims of infringement from owners of older software products. And you can bet that Apple and Lotus will be prime targets for such legal aftershocks. Being zapped by a death ray might be pleasant by comparison.

Samuelson apparently regrets that software was ever subsumed under copyright law. She rightly observes that copyright protection, by its very nature, discourages the adoption of the kind of standards that software needs to improve usability. It forces each author to find a different way of expressing the same old concept. She points out that patent law is better equipped to deal not only with technology, but with technology that is continually enhanced by incremental improvements on existing protected works. And mostly I agree with her.

I lack Samuelson's faith, however, that software patents will be adjudicated any better than software copyrights. The trade press lately has been filled with reports of patents granted to companies for software concepts that many of us consider less inventive than does the patent office. Maybe the lucky patent recipients can collect some license fees until some company big enough and persistent enough can prove in court that the key concepts exist in prior art. Meanwhile, the patent grants just make everyone run a little scared. I favor the patent court's earlier reluctance to issue software patents, on the grounds that most software innovations are largely (unpatentable) mathematical concepts.

On the other hand, I feel that copyright protection is *exactly* appropriate for computer software. That's assuming that software has much more the status of functional writing than an aesthetic work. I wince when I see my clever programs reimplemented by a competitor. But to me, that's what competition in the high-tech business is all about. I scream in righteous indignation only when I see someone copy my source or binary verbatim, or perform just a simple obscuring translation on the code. That is where (and only where) I look to the law for protection.

But then, what do I know? Most of my encounters with the court system have ended up with me on the side that did not prevail. (Think about that before you ask me to testify as an expert witness. And never get in line behind me at a bank or a toll booth. I guess wrong there, too.) As I said earlier, albeit parenthetically, I don't know the law, but I know what I like.

More precisely, I think I know what the industry needs and doesn't need. It does not need to have a dozen big software companies get a lock on the look and feel of most popular applications. It does not need to have every would-be software startup merge with a law firm out of self defense. It needs protection from obvious rip-offs and encouragement to develop broader standards for interacting with computers.

We must not let people pretend that an accumulation of software concepts constitutes some form of art, so that it can be locked up in a private collection. This stuff is soup and we all need to be nourished by it.

What makes it soup, to me at least, is a fundamental concept that has come to be called *drivability*. For an automobile, the term is fairly obvious. It refers to those features that must be common to all cars so that a typical driver can operate it safely without retraining. All cars have steering wheels placed in front of a seated driver. They rotate clockwise to turn the car to the right. The driver's right foot falls naturally on the accelerator, with the brake to its left. Once you learn how to drive one car, you can drive many others without conscious thought.

Some items affect drivability only marginally. You may have to grapple for the headlight switch on a rental car. You may have some trouble finding the wiper control. And some items are downright arbitrary, or even aesthetic. You may not like the location of the hood release, or the shape of the horn buttons, but neither is likely to interfere severely with your ability to drive the car safely.

You can bet that the first automobiles were not drivable by such universal rules. It took the industry awhile to standardize on steering wheels and pedal placement. Even today we still see two major standards for pedals, one for automatic transmissions and one for stick shift. And you may well need special training before you drive a large truck or bus. Nevertheless, standardization is the rule more than the exception. It is a critical ingredient in the success of the automobile industry.

An obvious analog in the world of computers is keyboard layout. The world has standardized on the familiar QWERTY layout, even though the engineering reasons that led to its creation have long been subverted by other considerations. An occasional die-hard will still put forth a Dvorak keyboard, which sells mostly to other die-hards. A few more produce cheap or tiny keyboards in pure alphabetical order. All of the variants destroy the ability of a trained typist to "drive" the keyboard, reducing everyone to the same slow hunt-and-peck strategy of the untrained. (I personally yearn for the day when the brackets, backslash, and a few other nomadic keys settle down and take up farming as well.)

One of the significant successes of the Macintosh, of course, was the greater attention paid to the drivability of all its applications. The uniform use of the mouse for pointing, with pull-down menus and icons to click on, has helped many a beginner or casual user past the usual hurdles involved in getting started with software. It would be a shame, in fact, if the lessons learned at Xerox and Apple cannot be used to make all computers more drivable by the public at large.

Drivability issues abound in computer software these days. How do you navigate about a spreadsheet? Is there any compelling reason to do it different than Lotus does it? How do you manipulate the objects in a drawing program? Can you beat pointing and dragging with a mouse? Why not let everyone standardize on the same conventions for climbing over menus?

What is at stake here is the whole business of computer literacy. Literacy comprises a whole collection of common skills and shared meanings. Where you don't have literacy you need experts. And where you have a shortage of experts you have stunted growth.

I believe it was R.W. Hamming who used to lecture anyone who would listen about the days of scriveners and reckoners. Before there was universal literacy you wrote a letter by dictating it to a scrivener (for a fee, naturally). When you got an answer, you took that to the scrivener as well to get it read to you (for another fee). Similarly, you depended upon reckoners to do hairy calculations such as dividing up a crop into seventeen equal parts.

When the need for scriveners and reckoners became too widespread, society discovered the wisdom of teaching reading, 'riting, and 'rithmetic to all and sundry. That permitted most people to serve as their own scriveners and reckoners most of the time. It did not eliminate those professions completely. It simply elevated the level of competence needed to ply those particular trades. Today, we call such people copy writers and CPAs (among other things).

The same thing happened with postilions and chauffeurs at the turn of the century. The gasoline-powered automobile with electric self starter eliminated the need for such employees among a large class of people. They learned to perform the functions for themselves. Today most chauffeurs drive taxis and buses. But they're still around. Meanwhile, the rest of us have learned all sorts of things about traffic signals, self-serve gas stations, reading road maps, and so on and so on. Just try listing all of the synonyms you know for "automobile" and you'll see how much transportation culture you've absorbed.

The same thing happened with telephones. When the need for operators began to exceed the supply, along came the automatic central office. We still have lots of operators, but not nearly the astronomical number predicted early in the century. And we can all talk knowingly about dial tones, area codes, toll calls, and other arcana once understood only by an inner circle.

With computers we are still in the phase of learning what makes software more drivable. We are still lamenting the shortage of experts who can master the arcane skills needed to drive unwieldy code. We are still making dire predictions of the effect of such shortages on various important parts of our society.

This is hardly the time to begin stifling standardization. Or innovation. I believe that any company that pushes for control of a good user interface convention is being extremely short sighted. On the other hand, American business has demonstrated itself to be progressively more short sighted. All that counts is what maximizes profitability in the next six months. We can hardly expect individual businesses to be sufficiently altruistic, or even sensible, to work toward the common goal of making computers more widely usable.

That's why it's particularly critical that the courts understand the issues involved in protecting computer software. They need to know how to distinguish soup from art in our very technical field. Otherwise, they can zap our ability to make soup. And without soup, there can be no art. □

Afterword: The jury is still out on the protection of look and feel, as I mentioned in conjunction with the earlier essays on this topic. For that reason, I hope the points I raise in this essay get a hearing. We in the software business have to help the courts understand where software lies along various axes — practical to theoretical, mechanical to aesthetic. Until we accrete a fabric of sensible rulings, we face altogether too much excitement with each lawsuit.

9 The Seven Warning Signs

$\mathfrak{H}$ ow do you know when you're being had? Sometimes it's pretty obvious. The software you want to buy has wonderful specs, but the vendor refuses to give you a demo. And the technical literature isn't back from the printers. And all the satisfied customers insist on remaining confidential.

Sales and marketing types have only a few stale techniques like these to fall back on if they know the product is not up to snuff. All of these techniques are based on a theorem first enunciated by P.T. Barnum: "The flux density of credulous customers corresponds to a time-averaged creation rate of 1/60 per second." (He put it more bluntly, as I recall, but it sounds more elegant this way.)

Technical types have greater resources to draw upon, however. Wrapped in a cloak of innocent sincerity, they can tell a tale with a straight face that even a retread appliance salesman would blush to emulate. They can pull it off because they have already sold themselves on the wonders of the technology they have chosen to flog. Whether it is a software package, a programming language, or a new coding aid, you can bet that some techies somewhere will fall in love with it to the exclusion of all reason.

The human mind is truly marvelous. It seems that the more highly trained you are in cold logic and reason, the easier you succumb to emotion when logic yields only gray answers. This is the basis of yet another theorem, of uncertain authorship — "The fewer clear facts you have in support of an opinion, the stronger your emotional attachment to that opinion."

I touched on this phenomenon at the end of one of my April Fool's essay. (See my essay, "Programming on Purpose: The (Almost) Right Stuff," *Computer Language*, April 1989.) Proponents of object-oriented programming tend to repeat several pronunciamentos when pushed for confirming evidence that their discipline will massively revolutionize computer programming. I gave three quick examples, almost in passing.

That got me to thinking about other rationalizations I have seen techies fall back on in defending their latest religious conversions. I confess to having used most of them myself, back when I was less cynical and less humble. With a little soul searching, I was able to come up with an additional four perceptual lapses to which it is all too easy to fall prey. That makes a round seven stock defenses for positions that cannot be absolutely defended.

As a public service, I happily share those seven mind benders. The next time you hear one beamed your way, you should know to crank up your defenses. It should warn you that someone has chosen to substitute an excess of emotion for an insufficiency of reason. Remember that your priorities may vary from those of the speaker, and that you are being sold in the guise of being informed.

The first warning sign is the "bear with me" defense. The speaker explains to you patiently that the technology is incredibly new. It's going to take you av.hile just to absorb all the facts, then a bit longer to learn how to think in new ways. But you needn't worry, because the payoff for scaling the steep learning curve will be a dramatic improvement in your productivity. Eventually.

I once visited a startup software company that was preparing to revolutionize the process of developing computer programs. Don't ask me to tell you their plans, though. For one thing, I was acting under a nondisclosure agreement. If they turn out to be right, I don't want to be sued by anyone who can afford to pay high-class lawyers. For another thing, I had a lot of trouble understanding what they were saying.

The principals in this startup company kept reassuring me that I could grasp the profundity of their approach with enough study. I was (and remain) less sanguine. What fueled my doubts was that they themselves were not using their beautiful new system to design the complex software they were planning to sell to support the new approach. You see, it's kind of complicated to apply to simple problems. (The simple problem in question was weighing in at 100,000 lines of C++ code.)

On the other hand, none of the first fifty-odd programmers whom I saw switch to UNIX did so because he or she was forced to do so. Each found a number of simple jobs that were easier to get done in the UNIX environment and so switched over voluntarily. I saw people switch from FORTRAN and assembly language to Pascal and C for much the same reasons. You get feedback that is both positive and immediate in trying new technology that is good.

Brian Kernighan taught me to appreciate the need for giving potential customers quick rewards. He has a particular gift for implementing the most useful part of a complex system first. (His successes include the RATFOR language and the eqn and pic typesetting preprocessors.) With guidance from early satisfied customers, he then knows where to spend his time adding complexity. As a result, his products tend to be highly usable and remarkably simple.

I have learned to be suspicious of any technology that you can't ease into a bit at a time. If the "gulp factor" is too large, I despair of finding the time to gamble on an uncertain payoff. I also sympathize with cautious managers who refuse to risk projects and/or budgets on technology with a large front-loaded cost. Keep that in mind when you're busy adding whistles and bells to your latest product. You may be pricing yourself out of the market.

𝕬 variation on "bear with me" is "beware of old dogs." The enthusiast explains that the approach is so new, all you old timers are going to have to unlearn a lifetime of bad habits. If you present the same material to novices, they grasp the essence right away. That shows you how much more natural this new stuff is, and how ossified you have become. Baloney.

If I have learned one thing over the years, it is that programming is a nontrivial skill that must be learned. Like skiing, none of us is born with all the right reflexes for performing this somewhat unnatural act. Anyone who has had career successes as a professional programmer has skills that are not to be taken lightly. They are going to make a difference on the next project that requires computer programming.

If I have learned two things over the years, the second is that all programming has much in common. Whether you code in 8086 assembly language, Lisp, or Ada, you must express flow of control and operations on data with no small amount of precision. I have seen systems that try (and fail) to disguise the programming process behind helpful menus and lots of narrative description. When the statement of work gets complex enough, however, it takes a programmer to get it right.

The argument that a novice has an advantage in any sort of programming task just doesn't hold water. It is true that an intelligent novice can do better than an incompetent person working as a programmer. It is also true that a novice is more likely to replicate the simple examples that work right, rather than stress the edges the way we programmers do almost reflexively. You'd better not gamble the success of your next project, however, on innocence unchained.

What I usually find when I hear the old dogs being put down is quite the opposite. Novices are easily snowed. They lack the experience to know what is inherited technology and what is new and untried. They believe the enthusiasts when they're told how much better the world just became. Experienced programmers, on the other hand, home in on the weak spots. They know where to be suspicious and where to tread carefully. If that slows them down, then it should. I shouldn't have to remind you of the theorem about the relative velocities of fools and fearful angels.

𝕿hen there's the "wrong problem" defense. You ask the enthusiast how to perform some pedestrian operation that no longer looks so pedestrian. The enthusiast replies, "That's the wrong problem to address at this point. You want to look at the world entirely differently now." The English translation is, "You're right. My approach can't deal with that problem. But if you just content yourself with solving a loosely related problem instead, or if you'll buy this ornate circumlocution in place of the obvious solution, then I can still sell you something."

Back when software developers were so scarce they could call the tune, you had to listen to this song and dance all too often. But now that most good packages have several competitors, you can just keep shopping around. Eventually you will find some vendor hungry enough to want to solve *your* problem. You don't need to be told that you don't have the problem you clearly have.

The obvious example that springs to mind is programming in C on the Intel 8086 family. Those of us who wrote the first C compilers were appalled at the problems presented by this chip family. For a succinct discussion of those problems, see my *Computer Language* article "Son of PC Meets the C Monster" (**Pla87**). All we wanted to do was compile C for what is now called the "small" memory model. Function and data pointers are then all 16-bit entities, the compiled code is reasonably efficient, and you avoid all the nonsense involved in juggling segment registers.

Customers, however, wanted to write programs bigger than 64 kilobytes worth of code plus an equal amount of data. Even if the code got twice as big and ran half as fast, they wanted to manipulate an arbitrary number of 64-kilobyte segments, not just two. So we vendors swallowed our bile and gave 'em what they asked for.

Then they came back and asked for pointers of different sizes in the same module. We swallowed even harder, muttered a few laments about the dying Spirit of C, and complied again. Never mind that any C expert can explain that mixing pointer sizes is solving the wrong problem. That's what implementors wanted and that's what they now have. With all the good applications written in C that are now available for PC compatibles, it is clear with hindsight that the customer was always right. But then, the correctness of customer wishes is a well known tautology.

A subtler warning sign is one that I like to call the "spherical cow." The name derives from a shaggy-dog story that made the rounds of the nuclear-physics community many years ago.

It seems that a theoretical nuclear physicist at a midwestern university found himself without a supporting grant one summer. So he went to a prosperous dairy farmer not far from campus and talked him into offering the physicist a summer job. The farmer was dubious at first, but was finally swayed by the status of having a theoretical physicist on staff. Besides, all the guy asked for was an office in one corner of the dairy barn with a desk and a blackboard.

As Labor Day approached, however, the farmer's doubts returned. His fellow farmers began to suggest that he'd been had, since the physicist had done nothing to improve milk production (much less get his hands dirty on anything other than chalk). When the farmer delicately broached the subject, however, the physicist had a ready solution. He would give a seminar.

So on the last day of August, after milking, the farmer and all his hands arrayed themselves on the grass beside the dairy barn. The physicist stood up before them and, by way of introduction, drew a large chalk circle on the side of the barn. With practiced confidence he began, "Consider a spherical cow of uniform density."

Physicists can afford to poke fun at themselves for some of the simplifying assumptions they must make from time to time. They have a good track record for making progress that way, filling in the complexities only after they get the basics down pat. Software designers, however, tend to introduce spherical cows for less defensible reasons. Usually, they act more out of ignorance of the customers' needs than out of a real need to simplify.

We've all tripped over software packages that contain unrealistic oversimplifications. You have only fifteen characters to write a street address. You can't delete a customer account unless the balance is zero. An organization chart must be a pure tree with all management boxes filled. Spherical cows, every one. They may have a graceful symmetry, but they don't give milk.

Midway between the spherical cow and the wrong problem is the "Procrustean bed." Procrustes was a robber of note in the ancient Greek city of Eleusis. He is best known for his rather rigid notions of hospitality. He constrained his guests to lie in an iron bed. Short guests were stretched to fit, long guests were chopped short. (Standards are so much easier to develop if you have proper enforcement procedures.)

Perhaps you have heard Bob Newhart's routine where Abner Doubleday is trying to sell the sport of baseball to a modern day executive in a corporation that sells packaged games. The executive's first question to Doubleday is, "How many couples?" You can guess who gets stretched to fit the iron bed.

The techies of today are not quite so bloodthirsty as Procrustes. Nor do they have the economic clout of the games publisher. But they can be as rigid in their thinking as either of those worthies. They insist on defining the problem in their own terms instead of the customers' terms. They forget to meet the customer more than half way.

At the risk of beating object-oriented programming to death, let me give another example from that discipline. It is clear that many programs get cleaner and more maintainable if you identify and isolate the principal objects that the program manipulates. It is also true that you can make every datum an object and every operation a method. There is even a certain elegance in using the same descriptive machinery to define operator overloading that you use to disambiguate methods with similar names and properties.

The enthusiasts quickly conclude that a pure object-oriented language (such as Smalltalk) must be somehow superior to one that has the discipline pasted on (such as C++). The zealots go further and insist that only pure object-oriented languages provide acceptable support for writing good computer programs.

So what if you add one and two by sending the "add" message and the value of the "two" object to the "one" object? (Or is it the other way around?) You just stretch the short program with extra instructions to fit the pretty model. So what if a particular program does not benefit by being divided into objects? You just chop it up to fit anyway.

The long and the short of it is that computer programs come in all sizes. And they have highly varied needs as well. If you believe that one size fits all, you're living in a panty-hose commercial.

The spherical cow represents oversimplification and the Procrustean bed a rigid viewpoint. Still a third aberration is the skewed world view caused by "future shock" (to borrow Alvin Toffler's catch phrase). My favorite illustration of this lapse is yet another shaggy dog story that I heard years ago at Bell Labs.

It seems that a distinguished visitor was being given the usual tour of the labs. He made appreciative noises at all the innovations being paraded before him, at least until he came to the microcomputer lab. There he was shown a one-inch cube containing a 5 MIPS processor, 10 megabytes of RAM, and a multi-user real-time OS in ROM. He appeared unimpressed, to the surprise and disappointment of the engineers.

Outside in the corridor, the tour guide asked the distinguished visitor why he discounted this miracle of microminiaturization. The visitor snorted and replied, "I don't know why you'd want to make a computer so small. That just makes it harder to change the vacuum tubes."

I have seen menu-driven interactive software packages on mainframes that maintain data in 80-column blank-padded card images. I still trip over microcomputer software that is beautifully engineered, except that you invoke it by typing an ornate command line as cryptic as anything you'd find in RSX-11M land. Like the apocryphal visitor to Bell Labs, the software designers apparently forgot to update a few of their assumptions to match the rest of the technology.

I acquired a free copy of Carbon Copy Plus when I bought my Toshiba T1000 laptop. It turned out to be only half a gift, however. The documentation made clear that you were expected to buy a separate copy of the software for each machine on which you ran it. When you're shipping files between machines, it takes two to tango. If I wanted to use my freebie, I'd have to go buy another copy.

No, I am not terminally naive. Naturally I tried to install the one copy on two of my machines, if only to try it out. The software proved to be as paranoid as the manuals, however. It managed to thwart every attempt I made to install more than one copy. The authors evidently put more energy into protecting their investment from misuse than they put into convincing customers that it is worth using. So I stuck the box on the shelf, where it lives to this very day.

I bought a competing product called Laplink, instead. It contained no such archaic caveats or protections. In fact the newest version, Laplink III, can even download itself to a bare machine over the same cable you then use to ship files at blinding speed. As a result, I have convinced half a dozen of my friends to buy copies of Laplink. You decide whether minicomputer-think in software protection is consistent with microcomputer software marketing.

The last aberration on my list is called "the man behind the curtain." The name derives from the climactic confrontation in L. Frank Baum's "The Wizard of Oz." Dorothy, et al. are cowering before the great Oz until they espy a poorly hidden man working the controls that produce the impressive effects. In a futile attempt to cover up his discovery, the all too human Wizard of Oz booms out through the showy machinery, "Pay no attention to that man behind the curtain."

I always get suspicious of simple examples that contain inexplicable lumps of superstructure. The enthusiast showing the example usually says something like, "Never mind these lines of code here. I'll explain the reason for them later." (Translation: "Pay no attention to that man behind the curtain.")

You can be sure that those lines are vital to the correct working of the example. Otherwise why clutter a supposedly simple example with stuff that is hard to explain? You can be equally sure that you will have to learn a heck of a lot more about the subject before you can contrive similar "simple" examples. Magic lines have a habit of needing subtle changes when you change other parts of an example.

Remember what I said earlier about keeping the gulp factor low? If an enthusiastic proponent of a product can't show you an obvious way to use the product simply, that way probably doesn't exist. Techies can blind themselves to the difficulties they have swept under the rug, but you have to live with the lumpy carpet (or a man behind the curtain, to stick with the original metaphor).

Watch your step.

That's the list. If you have any favorites, I'd love to hear about them. I figure reality is a subtle enough concept, we need all the help we can get to hold onto it. (There's probably a theorem to that effect, but I don't know it.)

I end with one blanket caveat. If some guy tells you that his method, language, or product will increase your productivity by a factor of four to ten, listen carefully for any of these seven warning signs. And don't even *think* of believing him unless he drives a Maserati. □

Afterword: I enjoyed writing this essay. It let me summarize in one place a quarter century of accrued skepticism. It also underscored for me how faddish our supposedly rational discipline has always been. I have since found the taxonomy convenient for characterizing specious arguments more rapidly.

10 The Politics of Standards

𝕴 have devoted a significant portion of my professional energies over the past six years to the formation of a standard for the programming language C. During most of that period, I met quarterly with 50 other dedicated souls at various venues around the country. We would spend four and a half days meeting in a hotel conference room, discussing esoterica and haggling out wording. My duties as Secretary, subcommittee chair for the C library, and self-appointed technical gadfly consumed at least an additional four weeks a year back at the ranch. Helping make the C Standard has proved to be a much larger investment than I could have imagined when I first got into it.

Naturally, I have strong feelings about the C Standard in particular and the work of standards committees in general. It annoys me when I read sophomoric flames about our work over the various electronic-mail networks. It is much easier to toss off accusations of stupidity, or even greedy short-sightedness, than it is do the work. It really makes me angry when I see people delay the adoption of the C Standard out of an inflated sense of their own importance. (The temptation is overwhelming to accuse them of stupidity, or even greedy short-sightedness.)

As I write this, the draft C Standard is in the hands of the ANSI Board of Standards Review. It has been delayed nearly a year by the stubborn maneuverings of a *single individual*. He has managed to exercise every piece of statutory machinery on the books to press his lone opposition. The creakiness of this seldom used machinery, coupled with a zealous dedication to fairness among the standards administrators, has significantly added to the delays.

It's conceivable that there will be a formal ANSI Standard for C by the time you read this. It's most likely there will not be, however. I have no reason to believe that our nemesis has thrown in the towel. I have no assurance that the remaining avenues of appeal will be traversed with any greater dispatch. There must always be a balance between the needs of the majority and the rights of the individual. In this case, the balance still seems to lean heavily toward the individual.

Meanwhile, on the international front, a similar battle has been brewing. For reasons that now escape me, several years ago I assumed the role of ISO Convenor when Steve Hersee had to leave that post. My goal was and is to ensure that the ANSI C Standard will meet the needs of the international community so that the ISO Standard can be identical.

I charged into the role fairly dripping with enthusiasm and good intentions. The American C standards committee, X3J11, had already shifted gears to address international concerns. (We could have had a C Standard two years ago had we been willing to let ISO change C later to make it more international.) It is a well documented flaw in my character that I think I can win consensus through hard work and sacrifice. (If you share that flaw, get over it.)

ome people just have their own agendas. In this arena, there has been growing resentment that programming language standards too often emerge from the U.S. as God given. Americans are blessed with a single language and a simple alphabet. Europeans have had to live with English mnemonics and missing accent marks, to name just two deficiencies they perceive in hand-me-down programming tools. Now the Japanese are getting feisty as well, given their newly won economic clout. And they *really* have language and character-set problems.

The whole issue of synchronizing the development of computer standards to meet everyone's needs is a topic of hot debate within ISO. And well it should be. I have pleaded for guidance in this area at every opportunity. Like the appeals machinery within ANSI, however, the synchronization machinery within ISO has been more discussed than exercised. I've long since stopped counting the months of cumulative delay that C has suffered within ISO because I was given incorrect advice. (Or worse, no advice.)

Two countries are unhappy with the state of the C Standard. The U.K. has repeatedly asserted that the draft C Standard lacks precision. They have offered several rounds of comments to X3J11, many of which were accepted. (Some were rejected because they lack precision.) They still want to take another round or two before they are content to leave well enough alone.

Meanwhile, Denmark has asked for more support in C for ISO 646, the international character set based on ASCII. The problem is that C uses nearly all of the graphics in ASCII because it has so many operators and punctuators. Some of the important notation in C has been recycled within ISO 646 as letters with accent marks (among other things). X3J11 addressed this problem by adding *trigraphs* to C. For example, you can represent a left brace either as { or as ??< interchangeably.

The Danes argue that trigraphs are unreadable. Many people sympathize. They have proposed several alternate spellings of the more critical operators and punctuators. Several people have found flaws with their proposals. They have insisted that C is unacceptable unless their latest proposal is adopted (once debugged). Almost everyone disagrees.

The latest parliamentary maneuverings occurred at an ISO meeting in Berlin last September. I, in my naivete, went to the Embedded Systems Conference instead of attending that meeting. There the U.K. and Denmark roundly criticized the U.S. for being uncooperative in developing an international C Standard. Nobody else was present to offer an informed alternate viewpoint.

These two countries won the right to commence work on "normative addenda" to the C Standard from the U.S. These addenda, if adopted, will have the force of a standard. Hence, ISO can well end up with a different standard for C than the U.S.

I should point out that the U.S. is not alone in its desire for identical standards. Several nations have stated the same desire in no uncertain terms. The clarifications requested by the U.K. are not intended to alter the definition of C. It is very hard to change words in the C Standard proper without doing so, however. And the Danes are outspoken in their determination to "improve" the current draft. How we are going to resolve these tensions within ISO is something I cannot predict.

All I can say now is that an ISO Standard for C may be delayed indefinitely. I am trying hard not to take personally the remarks made in my absence by representative from the U.K. and Denmark. (It's not easy.) I am determined to keep working toward an international Standard for C.

If that Standard differs from the one we have labored on for so long in the U.S., so be it. All I require personally is that the members of ISO who vote for a changed Standard be properly informed when they do so.

The biggest lesson that I have learned from all these years of standards work is that standards involve more politics than technology. (I sort of knew this intellectually, now I *really* know it.) By that I mean that any number of different standards can be good enough technically. The one that wins in the end is seldom technically the best. It is seldom even close to the best. It is the one that is politically successful, by definition.

You may detect a plaintive note in some of my remarks. That is a reverberation from the last vestiges of my techie idealism. We techies like to believe that the technical issues are most important. Particularly in something as complex as a programming language standard, functionality and suitability must be paramount virtues. So much of our future productivity (and fun) depends on the elegance of the languages we use. We'd better get it as right as possible.

That viewpoint ignores an important truth, however. Each of us has his own notion of what constitutes the best technical solution. Put 50 techies in a room with a 300-page document and you'll get an amazing spectrum of opinions. Opinions about issues on almost every page. Just try to resolve each difference with a rational discussion aimed at achieving unanimity. I assure you the process will never converge.

The simple fact is, we techies are human. (Perhaps some of your coworkers are suspect, but I don't want to hear about it.) We have emotional attachments to certain ideas that are impossible to factor out. As I've often remarked, the fewer facts we can marshal in defense of a technical opinion, the more zealous we become in arguing that opinion.

Something has to give. Either the majority prevails by main force. Or a determined minority uses parliamentary jiu jitsu to its advantage. Or one eloquent speaker sways people long enough to hold the day. Those are all traditional "I win, you lose" ways to reconcile differences.

There are also "I win, you win" solutions. Someone can bridge opposing views by showing the way to a common ground. Someone even brighter can show the narrowness of both opposing views and suggest a creative alternative. Someone even more saintly can agree to back down in the interest of the common good.

All of this stuff is what our elected lawmakers call "politics." If that word strikes a cynical chord within you, it shouldn't. The problem with the word is that it trucks around at least three diverse meanings. Unless you have developed the ear of a politician, you may fail to tune into the appropriate one for a given context.

First we have "just politics." That's the maneuvering that I and my buddies do every day just to keep things moving. Sure, you have to pressure a little. Sure, you have to compromise a little. But you know that I am basically a person of good will, so you will forgive a bit of manipulation on my part. It's just politics.

Then there's "damned politics." That's what your opponents indulge in when they pull out all stops to keep you from getting your way. It's too bad the system can be perverted that way. It's too bad that some people are so underhanded that they take advantage of the checks and balances in the system. You and I know that these people are acting from base motives when they pull those tricks. They're resorting to damned politics.

Finally, there's "enlightened politics." That's where you and your opponents manage to soar above petty differences, if only for a moment, and achieve something almost noble. Both of you are willing to turn a blind eye to the maneuverings you indulged in to get there. Both of you are happy that you can compromise on something unimportant to achieve something important. Both of you are willing to concede that the other has at least a streak of nobility. Everyone is proud to participate in enlightened politics.

The next time you hear the word "politics" bandied about, listen more carefully. (We have congressional elections coming up, and a perennially unbalanced federal budget. You will have ample opportunity for practice.)

Supply the missing adjective to complete the conjugation. For predictable politicians, the pronoun will suffice:

- I indulge in just politics.
- You indulge in damned politics.
- We indulge in enlightened politics.

A few politicians, however, actually think before they speak. You will understand them better if you can hear the silent qualifier.

You will understand the process of forming standards better as well. Bear in mind that the best solution to your way of thinking may not meet someone else's needs. Remember that those needs encompass far more than technical concerns. (The most powerful needs have nothing to do with technology.) Try to believe that someone can disagree with you and still have defensible motives.

𝕬n important bit of tactical machinery in the world of politics is Roberts' Rules of Order. Ostensibly, they simply form a set of rules designed to keep a parliamentary body moving. The precedence of motions and majorities needed for each vote have evolved a certain elegance over the years. They ensure that the majority cannot keep a minority from being heard. They keep a minority from indefinitely thwarting the will of the majority.

But what really makes Roberts' Rules work is the culture that goes with them. You must not, for example, accuse your opponents of dishonesty during a debate. You are expected to display a modicum of politeness even to those with whom you strongly disagree. If you understand people, then you know that even a patina of civility is worth a lot. (At the least, it elevates bullying to a higher plane.)

The standards folk go even farther than Roberts' Rules, however. Committees may run their meetings by those rules, but final acceptance of a standard occurs in a different forum. For a standard to be accepted, either within ANSI or ISO, it must achieve *consensus* among all concerned parties.

That is an interesting word, consensus. It does not mean majority vote. That could oppress an important minority. No matter how large a fraction of votes you require to be yes, you run the risk of an industry ganging up on an individual company. Or academia ganging up on industry. Or conversely.

Equally, consensus does not mean unanimity. That runs the risk of letting the minority thwart the needs of the majority. The most likely outcome of a heterogeneous group that demands unanimity is stalemate. It is too easy for any individual to delay completion rather than lose.

So the standards process puts considerable emphasis on getting everyone to agree. If you disagree, you have a strong obligation to the whole. You must state as clearly as possible what changes will permit you to agree. Then you must not renege. If the majority agree to your changes, you must capitulate. You must not say, "Yes, but..." You must not introduce a fresh slate of issues.

This is still not sufficient machinery to ensure closure. The process must also tolerate the occasional die hard. If someone insists on changes to a standard that the majority simply cannot swallow, it must be possible to proceed anyway. In this case, the majority has a strong obligation to demonstrate (to a disinterested third party) that it has exercised due process. The minority viewpoint must have its day in court.

My colloquial definition of consensus is as follows:

- At best, everyone agrees.
- Barring that, the majority who agree also agree that the minority who disagree are being disagreeable.

The effect of requiring consensus in the end is to outlaw damned politics. Just politics works fine. It advances the standard toward that fine day when everyone has a concrete document to pass judgment on. People come to forget the petty maneuverings if the final product is acceptable. Enlightened politics is even better. It gives all participants a rosy glow that adds to the shine of consensus.

Damned politics borrows heavily against the future. When the time comes to make the final push for acceptance, the coercive majority and the tricky minority are both heavily in debt. They must run the gauntlet of obtaining unanimous support or defending its lack. And they must face people who are ready to cash in on their right to be heard.

In the early days of X3J11, we were all pretty unskilled in applying Roberts' Rules. As we began to understand them, a few people learned to use them as a blunt instrument. Some of those early minutes are full of motions to amend the amended motions and other such nonsense. Eventually, however, we all wised up.

What became apparent was that every parliamentary victory was Pyrrhic. It did no good to bludgeon folks into submission at this meeting if you had to earn their good will (and consensus) in the long haul. The interesting discovery, to me, was that it didn't even matter if the victor was right. Frequently, one or two meetings later, everyone agreed on the technical merit of a particular vote. But if the vote was in any way wangled, it would probably be reversed at least once along the way.

We learned that every new idea needs time to cook. Let the participants think about it and trace its implications. Let them take it home and talk it over with coworkers between meetings. Only after people get comfortable with an idea are they ready to come to true consensus. That's politics. (You supply the adjective.)

I cling to these basic principles in my current hour of frustration. At the ANSI level, I genuinely believe that we have formed a consensus. X3J11 thinks so. Its parent committee, X3, thinks so. Now ANSI must decide.

As much as I chafe at the delays, I take pride that everyone in authority has bent over backwards to avoid stifling dissent. The dissenter is one person. He has won no allies for all his arguing. That encourages me to believe that we are safe in agreeing that he is being disagreeable.

On the ISO front, I have several thoughts. I can sympathize with the Europeans who came late to the party. They haven't had time to build consensus the way we veterans have. They mistake our desire for closure for simple tiredness. True, we *are* tired. We also think we're done. We also (rightly or wrongly) dislike being second guessed by people who have not sat through all the discussions of the issues they raise yet again.

If X3J11, with its current control of the C Standard, is oppressing minorities within ISO, they have ample opportunity to demonstrate that to the rest of ISO. All they have to do is produce normative addenda that are compelling. If, on the other hand, a minority is blocking adoption of a good standard, then all they can do is delay. Eventually, the process of consensus formation will grind through.

I'm too close to the matter to know which is reality. What is just politics to me may well be damned politics to another. And vice versa. We all need to hold onto our faith that the process will converge. □

fterword: Well, we got ANSI to approve the C Standard, but it took most of a year from the time I wrote this essay. ISO adopted the same Standard within the year following. As I write these words, the normative addenda are still working their way through WG14, the ISO C standards working group. I find myself becoming ever more a political animal, within the standards arena at least. This essay is truer now than when I wrote it. If I had my way, it would be required reading of anybody who serves on a standards committee.

11 Setting the Standard

In the previous essay, I harangued at length about the politics involved in developing the C programming-language Standard. (See **Essay 10: The Politics of Standards.**) I endeavored to explain why politics, that much maligned field, must necessarily spill over into technology. Much as you might like to believe that only technical decisions should matter in forming a programming-language standard, the real world simply doesn't work that way. It takes the machinery of politics to work out many of the differences that inevitably arise.

I continue that discussion in this essay with a different emphasis. I want to impart some of the pragmatic lessons that I and other members of X3J11 learned in the process of producing the draft Standard for C. If you should find yourself involved in a similar activity, you can benefit from a few pointers. (Trust me.) Even if you don't get involved, you should learn to respect the efforts of those who do.

Making a standard is not easy. It is made worse by the fact that few people participate in more than one standards effort. (I have a theorem that a sane person moves between zero and one pianos in a lifetime. You may never have occasion to move one. But once you move a piano, you learn never to do it again.) That means that each committee must start afresh in learning how to build a standard.

Occasionally, an old hand will drift into a new venture. X3J11 was fortunate to have one or two veterans of FORTRAN and Pascal to give us occasional guidance. But we didn't use them enough because of another impediment to developing a language standard — there are no standards for making standards. That makes it very easy for each new committee to decide to ignore the past and do it "right" this time.

Look at the major language standards and you will see what I mean. FORTRAN is on its third iteration. It is evolving under control of a committee that feels obliged to reinvent the language every dozen years or so. COBOL is rather similar, except that it is broken into a dozen components each with different levels of support permitted. The last I looked, there were 4,096 acceptable configurations for a COBOL implementation.

Then you have PL/I, where the committee decided to invent a formal language to describe the semantics more precisely. It may be more precise, but it is much less approachable than the narrative descriptions favored for FORTRAN and COBOL. And PL/I is still more easily understood than the

Algol 68 Standard. That committee invented a language to describe a language to present a grammar that expands to a grammar that defines Algol 68!

C comes closest in spirit to the Pascal Standard. The latter was based heavily on the classic language description by Jensen and Wirth (**J&W74**). The Pascal committee worked it over, but left many parts intact. They also chose not to address the many commercial extensions needed to make Pascal a more pragmatic language.

Committee X3J11 began with the widely accepted definition of C given in Appendix A of Kernighan and Ritchie (**K&R78**). We worked the wording over quite a bit, but left the language remarkably intact. Our major additions were to describe the C operating environment and runtime library in detail. Neither of these issues was addressed in Appendix A.

We spent much of the first few meetings just learning how to proceed. One subgroup did a study of formal specification methods. After a bit of anguish, the committee chose to stick with a narrative description. The C Standard contains very precise notation for the formal grammar. Otherwise, it relies on reasonably precise English descriptions for constraints and semantics. A few people regret this decision, but it was generally agreed that the job would have been much harder had we tried for more formality.

To me, the most important early decisions we made bordered on the philosophical. For example, we accepted from the start that a standard is a *treaty*. On the one side you have the implementors. A standard dictates certain features that implementors must provide. It also provides latitude in how some features are provided. On the other side you have the customers. A standard promises certain features that customers can rely on. It also warns about permissible variations in some features.

Every statement in a standard must help delineate the meeting ground between implementors and users. Otherwise, the statement is dead wood. There can be areas intentionally left gray. It is a rare treaty that does not provide for some form of demilitarized zone where neither side can safely tread. But there must be no wishy washy clauses that constrain neither side.

It does you no good, for example, to have a standard say what an implementation or a program *should* do. The operative verbs are *shall* and *must*. Equally, a standard must not have constraints so weak that they are trivially circumvented. These provide rubber teeth at best.

Having said that, I must report that the C Standard has its wimpy moments. On several occasions, we describe what we intend to have happen, without really requiring it. Those occasions are places where C encounters a varied and sometimes ill-suited external environment. We did not want to say that an implementation is nonconforming, for example, because it lets you write to a printer that fails to expand horizontal tabs.

The C Standard is at its wimpiest in attempting to mandate certain capacity requirements on every conforming implementation. In the end, all we could agree on was that each implementation must demonstrate that it can successfully translate and execute a test program. That test program must contain at least one example of every translation limit being met. Each vendor is at liberty to contrive a unique test program. We all agreed that this is worse than rubber teeth. It is rubber gums.

On the other hand, the C Standard is not the only arbiter in the choice of C translators. There is a very competitive marketplace out there. You can contrive an implementation that manages simultaneously to conform to the C Standard and still be useless. That's a wonderful joke on X3J11 and an intellectual curiosity. But it is not a salable product.

We had to admit that *quality of implementation* was one vast area that the C Standard simply could not address. We couldn't mandate that C be compiled into efficient code, nor that C use the native data types of a machine in the obvious way. We couldn't even dictate that a given implementation of C be minimally useful. We could argue about where to draw the line (and we often did), but we all admitted that every issue has a line beyond which the C Standard must give up and let market forces reign.

Closely allied to these considerations was something we came to call *the as-if rule*. It reminded us that we could only specify so much in telling implementors where to get off. We could specify *what* an implementation must accomplish. We could not specify *how* it accomplishes it. This is true even when the language seems to require specific underlying machinery. All the C Standard can dictate is that an implementation behave *as if* the machinery were present.

A telling example is the requirement for separate compilation. Central to the design of C, and one of its strengths, is that it lets you translate a program in pieces and later paste them together. All sorts of concepts are artifacts of separate compilation, such as external identifiers, constant expressions, and libraries. Nevertheless, more than one company offers C as an integrated environment centered around an interpreter.

An interpreter has many advantages in developing and debugging programs. The C Standard does not outlaw such interpreters. It merely requires that they perform certain operations *as if* they had separate translation and linking phases. (They can produce smarter diagnostics in many cases, but they don't have to.) And it lets traditional compilers and linkers off the hook in several critical ways. The C Standard requires no diagnostics or other checks that are beyond the capability of traditional compilers.

Once we got comfortable with the as-if rule, we found it to be quite liberating. It let us describe semantics in several areas in terms of simple machinery. The machinery need not be efficient in its own right. It need not even correspond to any likely implementation. It merely has to give a clear and complete operational definition of compliance. So long as an implementation can do a good job and still behave *as if* it encompasses the simple machinery, it is blessed as conforming.

Treaty points, quality of implementation, and the as-if rule all are delicate concepts. They are easily misconstrued in the heat of debate. More than one discussion within X3J11 chased its tail until all the parties involved got in sync with the meanings of a few words. Surprisingly, once the issues were clearly delineated, they were often quickly dispatched.

Occasionally people found they all agreed. Sometimes there was a clear choice where a majority decision was acceptable to all. On a few critical points, several rounds of debate were needed to form consensus. Rarely did deep rifts appear that took years to resolve.

What this taught us was the need for precise terminology in certain critical areas. The two most critical areas involved how we determined the conformance of programs and how we determined the conformance of implementations. Neither area is as black and white as you might at first believe.

The problem with characterizing programs is one of sorting accusations. Say, for example, that a particular program contains a function call with two argument expressions. Correct execution of this program occurs only when the first argument expression is evaluated before the second argument expression. That requirement happens to conflict with a latitude that has been in C since Dennis Ritchie's first compiler. An implementation has traditionally been free to evaluate arguments in whatever order it chooses.

The committee chose to continue this license in Standard C. So here is a case where the treaty says that implementors have fewer obligations than programmers. The program is ill formed. The problem is, how do you characterize such a deformity?

If a deformity is serious and easily detected, it may be desirable to require each implementation to diagnose the flaw. (It's not easy to detect order dependence among function argument expressions, serious as it may be.) Or it might be preferable to require no diagnostic, but to require instead that each implementation document what it does. (It's not advisable to give programmers any assurance in this arena.)

The committee might also elect to let the implementors off the hook altogether. It might be desirable to permit each implementation to vary, but not require it to say what it does. (An implementation might even do something different as the barometric pressure changes.) Then the issue is whether the program is branded as flawed simply because it uses a feature that can vary. (In this case, programs call functions with multiple arguments all the time. A program should be flawed only if it is a sucker for order dependence, not simply because it contains order dependencies.)

What all this means is that every sin that a program can commit must be sorted into some bin. (Yes, we're talking sin bins.) The bin has a name that gives some hint as to the nature of the transgression. The bin also has a set of requirements that guides both implementor and programmer. Here are the bins that X3J11 eventually settled on:

Erroneous behavior is incorrect program behavior that must be diagnosed. Any C program containing the sequence **if if** must be erroneous. It is detectable with known technology by single-pass compilers with separate linkers. It is too serious to ignore.

Implementation-defined behavior is correct program behavior that can vary among implementations. Each implementation must, however, document what it does in this area. The code value for the character constant ' **a** ' is implementation-defined.

Locale-specific behavior is like implementation-defined, except that it is specifically permitted to vary among international locales. How characters collate is locale specific.

Unspecified behavior is also like implementation-defined, except that an implementation need not document what it does. The order of evaluation of argument expressions, cited above, is unspecified.

Undefined behavior is incorrect program behavior that an implementation can, but need not, diagnose. Arithmetic overflow during program execution is undefined behavior. On some implementations it is easily diagnosed. On others the cost of diagnosing every potential overflow would be prohibitive. So the C Standard puts the burden entirely on the programmer.

It took the committee awhile to determine all these bins, and a little bit longer to tweak them into shape. Even now, there remain minor disagreements over interpretation. Some people think you can document implementation-defined behavior, for example, by saying, "One of the following three things will happen." Or, "The computer will halt and catch fire." Others feel that these are copouts not in the spirit of the C Standard.

But let this not distract you from the overwhelming importance of the bins. By defining them early on, the committee had a specialized vocabulary with which to discuss the C language. Such a specialized vocabulary lets people capture subtle thoughts with fewer words.

That saves reinventing the same thought repeatedly, with a hundred variations. It also keeps the new ideas from getting lost in the welter of old debates about bins. We might argue about which bin a given lapse should occupy, but such arguments converge.

The arguments that do not converge are the ones rooted in fear. A sure recipe for heated debate is for someone to cry, "If the C Standard says that, it will break my program." That happens to be a C programmer's shorthand for a more long-winded statement:

"My program works fine right now, thank you, and I want to keep it that way. Require me to change my compiler to conform to this standard and the compiler will cough on my program. I'll have to change a million lines of code in unspecified places."

Now it so happens that the C Standard classifies the vast bulk of existing code as potentially nonportable. That's not news to anyone with experience porting C code. You may have code that works fine with ten compilers and that fails on the eleventh. A principal reason for developing the C Standard is to increase your chances of writing truly portable C code if you want to.

It also so happens that the C Standard "breaks" remarkably little code. Only where a practice has been made erroneous must every implementation cough on a program. (Many of these are clean breaks, as when one of your identifiers now collides with a new keyword. They are easily caught and cured.) Otherwise, existing implementations are generally at liberty to translate nonportable constructs just as they always have. The code is no more broken than it ever was.

I can't assert that all tail-chasing debates ceased once the bins got defined. But they sure helped. Creating the bins and sorting the programming gaffes into bins was probably one of the biggest contributions the committee made to clarifying C.

The other major problem I mentioned above was characterizing implementations. That problem centers around extensions. Everybody has them. Everybody wants to keep them. (Or you break their code, in the true sense of the phrase.) If a standard doesn't permit extensions, it will be ignored. If a standard permits too many extensions, it is toothless. How do you strike a satisfactory balance?

The trick we settled on involves a sexy little three-step dance. First we define a *strictly conforming program* as a program that uses no extensions. Furthermore it produces no output that depends upon behavior that is unspecified, undefined, or implementation-defined. In other words, strictly conforming is essentially synonymous with portable.

The next step in the dance is to define a *conforming implementation*. (The implementation can be either hosted or freestanding, but that is another matter.) A conforming implementation must successfully translate and execute any strictly conforming program. (The implementation can fail because the program exceeds one of its limitations, but that too is another matter.) So far so good.

The final step in the dance is the cute one. It defines a *conforming program* as one that is acceptable to a conforming implementation. The program need not be portable. It can take advantage of all sorts of extensions. It just has to translate and run.

At first blush, this looks like more rubber teeth. What's to prevent a C compiler from accepting COBOL and BASIC programs as extensions? Well, there are two important limitations on how an implementor can extend C.

The first comes from the definition of conforming implementation. You cannot extend C in any way that alters the meaning of a strictly conforming program. You can give meaning to undefined behavior, since no strictly conforming program can indulge in undefined behavior. You cannot, for example, redefine `if` or `printf`.

The second limitation comes from the definition of erroneous behavior. The C Standard lists as erroneous behavior any violation of the syntax rules or specifically stated constraints. An implementation is obliged to diagnose such violations. That makes it hard for an implementor to extend C to parse laundry lists and old programming languages.

The effect of this balancing act is to leave room for extensions. At the same time, the form and scope of extensions are curtailed. You can trust a conforming implementation to compile programs that you intend to be portable. You can also trust it to diagnose obvious nonsense. But you also know the areas where you can stumble across extensions.

And that illustrates the final bit of philosophy that committee X3J11 decided on from the outset. We knew that C lets you write portable programs that are surprisingly powerful. We wanted to increase the potential power of such programs. We also knew that C lets you write programs that are intentionally not portable. We wanted to endorse this practice and not penalize its practitioners.

Our goal was thus to give programmers a *fighting chance* at writing portable programs. Not a safe ticket by outlawing nonportable constructs. Not a free ride by requiring heroic measures of runtime systems. Just a fighting chance.

That's more than most languages give. That's all that most C programmers ask for. I think we gave it to them. □

Afterword: I still am amazed that X3J11 had to invent so much technology to write the C Standard. I am also saddened to see how poorly some of it is still understood by people working on C-related standards. The latest fad within ISO is to develop cross-language standards, and even standards for writing standards. Yet none of them deal with the shape of a standard, or the methods for developing a standard, at the level I discuss in this essay.

Software-related standards require far more "people" technology than any other, in my opinion. They are invariably complex, which makes them time consuming to produce. And they are steadily growing in importance, thanks to the rapid increase in the world market for computer software. Anything that can improve the process of making such standards is worth serious attention.

12 All the Standard Reasons

𝕴 promise that this will be my last essay about the C Standard, at least for awhile. I have produced two recent essays on the subject. (See **Essay 10: The Politics of Standards** and **Essay 11: Setting the Standard**.) You've heard me gripe about the politics that inevitably accompanies any group effort. You've heard me opine on the ground rules that helped bring the C Standard to closure. Now I want to look at some of the craziness that inevitably plagues efforts of this sort.

First, let me report gleefully that the ANSI C Standard is now official. Despite my pessimistic bleatings, the process converged sooner rather than later. The ANSI Board of Standards Review unanimously approved the efforts of X3J11. The protests ran down and stopped. People ran out of reasons *not* to have an ANSI C standard.

So before I start casting oily aspersions on troubled feathers (or whatever), let me just say thanks. Thanks to all those people who felt strongly enough about C to write diatribes for X3J11 to answer. Thanks to all those who participated in endless committee meetings. And thanks most of all to my fellow officers, Jim Brodie and Tom Plum, who gave fresh meaning to the shopworn adjective "tireless." The final product is a victory for us all.

I freely confess that there were times over the past six plus years when I didn't feel so thankful. Dennis Ritchie had the luxury of developing C when almost nobody gave a damn about the language. Many's the time when I wish that X3J11 could have enjoyed a comparable obscurity. If just a handful of us right-thinking folk could have been left alone for half a year, we would have cheerfully dispatched the standard without nearly so much *son et lumière*.

But as I pointed out earlier, that scenario was simply impossible. Seems there were a couple hundred other people who thought that *they* were the right thinkers. Those of us busy cobbling up words had it wrong and were busy ruining an otherwise fine language. It took years of haggling to build the shared meaning needed to achieve consensus.

Mostly, I didn't mind the haggling. I went into more than one discussion absolutely convinced that only I saw the true nature of the issue. It was a repeated annoyance to learn that other people could cling to differing opinions. It was a repeated shock to discover that their views, once I understood them, actually contained some compelling logic.

Any time that I found myself educated as a result of debate, I was elated. Any time that I could get disparate factions to align on my world view, I was pleased. Any time we could all understand each other well enough to hammer out a compromise, I was satisfied. Those are all good outcomes of a debate, at least to my way of thinking.

$\mathcal{S}$ome things drove me up the wall, however. Easily the worst was hysterical blindness. Some faction would become convinced that their special interest was endangered. They would go out of business should the majority hold sway. Threats of veto collided with accusations of selfishness and/or stupidity. In this inhospitable climate, reasoned dialog quickly withered. The only remedy that consistently worked was an enforced cooling-off period. Actually, it was more like the time outs that kindergarten teachers have to call occasionally. Everyone would go off to separate corners until the sniffles died down. When the incendiary issue came up again, it usually settled out with remarkably little debate.

The next worst, to me, was persistent myopia. The people who manifested this syndrome weren't being difficult to be self serving. They just couldn't see the negative implications of a feature that looked otherwise quite sexy.

Achieving a happy consensus was most difficult in the presence of persistent myopia. Incredible amounts of committee time were consumed in this process. Sometimes we even gave up before we resolved issues properly. The worst lapses in the C standard, I believe, arose from issues where people just got tired of arguing. For a summary of these lapses, see my column "Standard C: Wha Gang Agley" the April and May 1990 issues of *The C Users Journal* (**Pla90**).

The most commonplace lapse, however, was selective viewpoint. It seemed that people would first stake out an emotional position on an issue. Only then would they start searching for reasons to justify their particular stand. I found it grimly amusing that a highly intelligent techie could argue one issue from a given philosophical perspective in the morning, then argue another issue from the opposite perspective that afternoon.

About four years ago, in fact, I left a meeting feeling particularly overwhelmed. Sitting on an airplane going home, I drafted the following paper for distribution to X3J11. I called it "A Modest Proposal for Encoding Debate." It was a mini-hit at the next meeting. I got additional mileage out of it as a talk at one of the Software Development seminars. People still quote from it occasionally.

So I thought I'd recycle the paper one more time and share it with you here. It is a fitting complement to my more pompous musings on the process of forming language standards. For those of you not up on your C trivia, I have added some illumination. Remarks in italics are my editorial additions for the unenlightened.

We have had enough experience with the deliberations of X3J11 that I feel we can now introduce a number of abbreviations in place of frequently used arguments. An interesting discovery I made in the process of summarizing these popular arguments is that, like elementary particles, each is accompanied by its anti-argument; and the anti-argument has as much claim to being fundamental as its anti-anti. An equally interesting discovery is that certain members of the committee are adept at using both sides of a complementary pair, depending upon which flavor supports the desired outcome of a given issue.

So herewith are some suggested numeric codes, handed out in no particular order, and their complements. The assignment of + and – signs to members of a pair is likewise arbitrary, and should not be construed as favoring one argument over its opposite.

The base document was our starting point for drafting the C Standard. For the language, it was Appendix A of Kernighan & Ritchie's notorious opus, The C Programming Language (**K&R78**). *For the library, it was the 1984 /usr/group standard for a UNIX interface library, now the POSIX Standard IEEE 1003.1 (minus the part we stole).*

01+ It's in the base document.

01– It's a flaw in the base document that must be corrected.

02+ It's not in the base document.

02– It's an oversight in the base document that must be corrected.

Dennis Ritchie was the original author of the C language.

03+ Dennis Ritchie agrees with me.

03– Dennis Ritchie's opinion is irrelevant now.

C was born under UNIX. That made it particularly hard for UNIX enthusiasts to see the C language as anything but a UNIX utility.

04+ UNIX does it that way.

04– How UNIX does it is irrelevant now.

AT&T owns and operates UNIX. See previous note.

05+ AT&T isn't going to like this.

05– Who cares what AT&T thinks?

My company, Whitesmiths, Ltd., was the first serious commercial vendor of non-UNIX C compilers. Despite my shy and reserved manner, the interests of Whitesmiths were discussed all out of proportion to the size of its market share.

06+ Whitesmiths has done it that way for years.

06– What's a whitesmith?

See note under #04. The schism was made worse by the brashness of the MS-DOS contingent. They felt that they more than made up in numbers what they may have lacked in history.

07+ Most of the C compilers sold are under UNIX.

07– Most of the C compilers used are not under UNIX.

The second form is a direct steal from Adlai E. Stevenson. It was a sentiment he attributed to one of his political opponents.

08+ These are the facts upon which I base my opinions.

08– These are the opinions upon which I base my facts.

09+ I like it, it must be good.

09– I don't like it, it must be bad.

The greatest sin you could accuse anybody of within X3J11 was making a change in C that would "break" existing code. You break code when you cause it to misbehave or fail to compile under an ANSI C compiler.

10+ It will break working code.

10– The working code that breaks shouldn't have been written that way in the first place.

11+ It's an important addition to the language.

11– It's a major perturbation to an otherwise stable document.

12+ It only affects a small area.

12– It's a needless tweak to an otherwise stable document.

This is a specific application of one of my favorite theorems — Forty-two percent of all statistics are made up on the spot.

13+ It will affect a large fraction of existing code, in my opinion.

13– It will affect a small fraction of existing code, in my opinion.

Much of the work of the committee lay in resolving ambiguities and fleshing out lacunae in the base document. Where possible, we endeavored to identify current practice as the de facto standard.

14+ Current practice is right, the base document is wrong.

14– Current practice is wrong, the base document is right.

15+ Current practice is mixed in this area.

15– There's one obvious right way to do it, regardless of current practice.

The difference between zero and nothing is more than the stuff of idle speculation for philosophers. Why more programmers don't care about this is beyond me.

16+ Zero should behave just like any other number.

16– Zero is a special case, different from any number.

17+ We should stay out of the way of sophisticated programmers.

17– We should protect the innocent programmers.

18+ C is a quick and dirty language, that's its heritage.

18– C must become a safe language, that's its future.

19+ That's impossible to implement.

19– Anything can be implemented.

20+ That's inefficient.

20– Efficiency is not a consideration.

C is notorious for being a two-stage language. It's macro preprocessor is almost a pure string-substitution language. As such, it can do violence to the structure and readability of the underlying code. You can also lie like a legal brief with maliciously chosen preprocessor macros.

21+ That's impossible to understand.

21– Anything confusing can be hidden inside a macro.

22+ If my system can't handle it directly, it shouldn't be in the standard.

22– If you can lie to your system somehow, it belongs in the standard.

23+ The user community will laugh us out of town on this one.

23– The user community must be educated on this one.

24+ That's gone unchallenged for two years, why bring it up now?

24– That's been broken for two years, it's high time we addressed it.

No comment.

25+ Ada does it that way.

25– Ada does it that way.

$\mathfrak{N}$ow let me tell you about an incident that illustrates several of these creative forms of reasoning. For all the air time it consumed, it had only limited impact on the overall standard. That is fortunate, because it was a disaster in the philosophical arena.

C has a function called **malloc** that allocates storage for a newly created data object. It supports a heap discipline, which means you can allocate and free data objects in any order. You pass as an argument to **malloc** the size in bytes of the data object you wish to allocate. You get back a pointer to the new storage area if the storage can be allocated. Otherwise, you get back a null pointer. The function ensures that any storage alignment requirements are met.

That's all clear enough, except for one minor boundary case. What should be the effect of calling **malloc** with a size of zero bytes? If you're convinced that only one behavior makes sense, think again. We found two conflicting schools of thought in this small backwater.

One school holds that a data object of zero size makes eminent sense. Say, for example, you want to allocate storage for an array of all the outstanding debit records. On some occasions, there are no debits. You process debits in a **while** loop that executes zero times. It is only natural that the loop should process an array containing zero items.

This school views a zero-size dynamic data object as an analytic continuation of other reasonable data objects. You want **malloc** to return a non-null pointer because a null pointer conveys the wrong message. A null pointer tells you that **malloc** couldn't find suitable storage for the data object you requested. Under those circumstances, you usually have to shut down operations. Your program is starved for storage and may commence misbehaving in various strange ways.

Still another school holds a differing view. It sees a zero-size argument as suspect. Surely, you didn't mean to allocate such a creature. Surely, you want a good implementation to diagnose a **malloc(0)** call, not just bull ahead as if all were well. An array with zero elements should be handled as a special case anyway.

Were the C Standard to say that zero is a valid argument value to **malloc**, an implementation would be denied the right to diagnose this suspicious case. It would be labeled as nonconforming if it failed to return a non-null pointer. But if an implementation has the right to complain, then a program cannot depend upon the behavior of **malloc(0)**. You can't have it both ways.

As you might expect, people argued positions 16+ and 16– at great length. And as you might guess, I argued in favor of 16+. Here was a clear-cut case, I felt, where zero was simply just another value. It might be enlightening to walk through code that results in a **malloc(0)** call, but it should combine neatly with other reasonable situations.

The opposing viewpoint was championed by people with implementations that do lots of extra checking. Special debugging environments want to restrict C as much as possible. These folk would rather not have to disable many checks when conforming to the C Standard.

Such arguments were to be expected. What surprised and annoyed me were the arguments that were *not* presented. Someone should have uttered an occasional 4+, since UNIX has quietly fielded **malloc(0)** calls since the world was young. But the representative from AT&T, Larry Rosler in those days, was of the 16– school. He usually reminded the committee of the importance of keeping C in sync with UNIX. On this subject, however, he neglected to emphasize the prior art.

There was, of course, lots of 6+ and 6–. Whitesmiths' library was solidly in the same camp as UNIX on this subject. That was hardly surprising, since I had absorbed many lessons on robust programming during my years at AT&T Bell Labs, from the very folks who gave birth to UNIX.

There was even a little 3+, once the folks at Bell Labs woke up to the issue. Several of the wiser heads there saw fit to advise the committee that this was solidly a 16+ issue. Sadly, they shared my handicap. The proper answer was so clear cut to them, they saw no need to indulge in a long-winded explanation.

The debate spread across several meetings. That gave ample time for people to argue both sides of 9 through 13, 15, 17, 18, and 24. It also gave me time to marshal more convincing arguments. I was sufficiently persuasive that I converted Larry Rosler. Since Larry and I habitually canceled each other's votes on most major issues, I considered that a significant victory.

The victory was hollow, however, for a fundamental reason. We lost our audience. A small but ever more vocal minority got fed up with the whole subject. Some of us felt strongly that this was a fundamental philosophical issue that should not be compromised. (And we were right.) The loud minority felt that this was a minor issue that was taking time from more important areas. (And they were right too.)

I don't remember how often the committee reversed its position on the issue of **malloc(0)**. The final outcome was one of those compromises where everybody loses, however. In the end, the committee voted to label such a call undefined behavior.

That means that an implementation can return a non-null pointer, but the programmer cannot depend on it. It also means that an implementation can diagnose such a call, but the programmer cannot depend on it. So the programmers who were happy allocating zero-size data objects are in the same boat as those who want their fingers smacked. They can't depend on the behavior they enjoyed in the past.

I went over this escapade in detail for a reason. It was not to make fun of X3J11 or to argue the one right viewpoint yet again. It was to show how hard it can be to hammer out technical details in the teeth of conflicting philosophies. Despite my strong bias in favor of 16+, I respect those who argued 16– and their reasons for holding that position.

Now consider that X3J11 had to deal with perhaps a thousand technical details in full committee. How many more were quietly handled off line is hard to estimate. If only five percent of those details require protracted debate, you still have 50 opportunities to make bad compromises. The miracle is that the C Standard has nowhere near that many lapses. And we got the technical work done in only five years.

I began this series of essays by talking politics. That is human interaction at its most strategic level. Then I discussed the ground rules that X3J11 settled on for forming the standard. That is the tactical level.

Any veteran soldier will tell you, however, that both strategy and tactics are irrelevant when you get down to the basics of combat. That's where the grubby details become important, not what the generals talk about.

The C Standard, like any standard, was hammered out by dedicated people. In the end, they happened to do mostly the right things. Along the way, they happened to do those things for many crazy reasons. It wasn't exactly combat, but sometimes it felt like it. □

Afterword: This completes my trilogy of essays on what I learned from the making of the C Standard. It was the most whimsical of the three, but probably also the most effective. Several people active on other standards committees tell me that my modest proposal was quoted frequently. I figure that if I can at least make people aware of a few of their foibles, I will have encouraged more rational debate.

13 The Physicist as Programmer

This essay marks my forty-eighth consecutive installment of "Programming on Purpose." Had you told me four years ago that I would still be writing for *Computer Language*, I would have been mildly skeptical. Had you told me that I would not miss a single issue in all that time, I would have been certain you were daft. My flirtations with deadlines are notorious among the editors at Miller Freeman.

Nevertheless, I have made it this far. And the job has gotten to be more fun as time goes on, not less. I can't say it has gotten any easier. I put a lot of effort into each essay, and I hope it shows. But the job is at least as rewarding as when I first started.

My perennial fear is that I will run out of things to say, or repeat myself excessively. I vowed that I would quit if either of those fears became sufficiently real. Yet somehow, I always have two or three ideas in the pipeline. And somehow, I can find new slants even when I do revisit old topics. My current plan is to keep writing "Programming on Purpose" for the foreseeable future.

That is consistent with my latest career as a free-lance writer (read "unemployed"). When I began this column, it was a minor sideline to my principal role as head of Whitesmiths, Ltd. Then I sold the company to Intermetrics Inc. and helped them with the transition. Now I have the freedom to write as much as I have always wanted. It will be interesting to see if I continue to enjoy that freedom as much as I have always dreamed.

My first love remains computer programming. I want to see the state of the art keep improving. I enjoy learning about anything that helps people program better. I enjoy explaining to others what works and what does not. Whether I practice much more or merely preach, I can think of lots of things that need saying.

That love of programming goes way back. I got into this business in 1963, when I was a sophomore at Princeton. By then I had already started down a different career path. Stubborn as I am, it took me many years to wise up and focus on what I do best. It also took an outside nudge or two, as you shall soon see.

Along the way, I earned a doctorate in experimental nuclear physics. That may seem like wasted training for a putative expert on computers, but it is less so than you think. To learn physics, you have to pick up quite a number of analytical skills. These are generally applicable to many fields.

To earn a doctorate, you have to develop quite a lot of self discipline, and self confidence that you can complete major projects. Those attributes are even more widely useful.

It is not unusual for a student of physics to acquire expertise in another field. Experimentalists usually pick up a useful trade or two along the way to acquiring academic credentials. They learn how to design and build electronic circuits, detectors, vacuum systems, and/or magnets. They learn how to write computer programs.

𝔓hysicists are particularly arrogant about their ability to charge into other fields and make useful contributions. Generally, I have found this arrogance to be justifiable, except for one serious handicap. The process of earning a doctorate does not acculturate you to solving other people's problems, as most employers would want. Instead, it encourages you to keep elaborating on your thesis research. At least it leads you to believe that all the world's a research laboratory, equipped for your personal benefit.

I had to overcome that acculturation. It cost me my first job out of graduate school learning how to shift gears. Few enterprises want to pay you to solve *your* problems. They want you to solve *theirs*. The trick lies in learning how to have fun solving problems thought up by other people.

I still take pride in being educated as a physicist. I maintain my membership in the American Physical Society. I endeavor to keep up with the latest goings-on in physics research. (I confess, however, that much of elementary-particle theory and cosmology goes over my head.) And I bristle a bit when someone calls me an engineer, even though I also hold memberships in ACM and IEEE.

The Department of Physics and Astronomy at Michigan State University invited me to give a talk recently. I was pleased at the prospect of returning to my graduate school alma mater. I was also a little trepidatious about what I could say. Certainly I was in no position to lecture on anything in physics.

I decided instead to describe my personal evolution from nuclear physicist to computer programmer. For any students interested in making a similar career transition, I figured I could give a few useful pointers. For anyone afraid of being lured away from physics research, I figured my life could serve as a cautionary tale. Watch what you do, this could happen to you. I began my talk by explaining what I mean by "programming on purpose." This being an anniversary of sorts for the column, it doesn't hurt to review the term for the entire class. Pencils ready?

𝔗he first requirement to be programming on purpose is to have a *focus.* You have a use for the code you write. It is not an idle exercise. You are not simply hacking. That potential use imposes some *specifications* on what you write. Those specifications give you a touchstone to know what must go into the final program and what can and should be left out.

Those specifications also give you a way of testing for when you're done. If the program doesn't do everything required, keep working. If it does everything you need, quit and get onto the next project. You need to know when you're done because you also have a *timetable*. The intended use cannot be postponed forever. If the program is not ready in time, it's useless.

The second requirement to be programming on purpose is to have a *customer*. The direct customer might be you, but you can usually identify an indirect one as well. Your advisor, boss, or coworker is depending on you to do something and the program will help you deliver. More often, there is a clearly identifiable customer other than yourself whom you must satisfy. It is remarkably unimportant whether the customer is someone inside your enterprise or an outsider. Your purpose remains to convince someone else that you have met specifications.

A characteristic of customers is that they pay you. That is an important part of your reward for programming on purpose. (I ignore, for now, the additional reward you get from knowing you have done a good job.) The reason I say that the nature of the customer is unimportant is because payment comes in many forms. An external customer will probably pay hard cash. That is the most direct measure of accomplishment that our society recognizes.

Within a large organization, however, you might see only funny money. Your internal account benefits from your success as a programmer. Within a smaller group, you might simply earn brownie points. These are seldom quantitative, but they can be redeemed for prizes at a later date. Don't sneer at either of these latter two forms of payment. Both are worlds better than no payment at all, and neither is taxable.

The final requirement to be programming on purpose is *follow through*. A program alone is incomplete, only part of a solution. You must provide some form of *documentation* to make the program usable. Don't tell me about self-documenting programs. I agree that all programs should aim to minimize the need to refer to manuals while you're using them. That does not, however, eliminate the need for documentation in various forms.

You need to capture for posterity a number of important facts not easily retained within either the source or executable code. This includes information on: how to install the program, what it's for, what a novice needs to know, how to do the commonest operations, and subtle facts an accomplished user might need to know.

You also need to capture a similar set of facts to support *maintenance*. If the program is any good, it's going to be complex enough to have bugs that must later be removed. A bug is not necessarily a botch caused by an inept designer or programmer. It might simply be an infelicity, or a shortcoming that arises when usage patterns change.

If those patterns change enough, we all agree to stop calling the changes maintenance. Instead, we label them *enhancements*. Unless you code cleanly and with future changes in mind, it will not be easy to add them. You will also find that the code quickly silts up with maintenance changes and enhancements. Once a program gets too expensive to change, it is effectively dead. Your job is to give your programs a reasonably long life expectancy.

A program does not become a product for a customer unless you touch all these bases. You must focus on what is needed. You must get the customer to admit that you have met specifications in a timely manner. And you must provide sufficient follow through that the program retains its value. *That,* my children, is programming on purpose.

What I have described here is a recipe for being professional about computer programming. I find that you have to spell the recipe out in greater detail for programming than for other trades. Why? Because it is harder to tell when you're dealing with amateurs, or with amateur products. It is also remarkably easy to get away with amateur behavior yourself and still make a living.

A program consists of a lot of complexity hidden inside a black box. It can take a lot of poking and prodding to determine how well a program meets its specification. It can take even more to determine whether the program is maintainable or enhanceable. While you are busy poking and prodding, the amateurs who made it can scamper off to the next project.

Of course, not everyone who works with computers wants to be a professional programmer. Not everyone *should* endeavor to be one. Believe it or not, there are other things to do in life besides writing quality code.

What I told all those physics students is the same thing I tell many people. Decide what level of involvement you want to have with computers. Then learn the behavior appropriate for that level of involvement. And stick with it. I can identify at least three levels of involvement in computer programming:

- The *reluctant programmer* is a person who views computer programming as a necessary evil. Programming is a distraction from the real business at hand. But you just can't buy everything.

- The *determined programmer* is a person who views computer programming as a useful tool. Sure, programming is a nuisance and a time eater. But you can do so many more interesting things if you're not afraid to use computers.

- The *enthusiastic programmer* is a person who views computer programming as a delightful challenge. It's nice that the job has so many interesting problems connected with it. That creates such great excuses for playing with computers along the way.

$\mathfrak{L}$et's say that you classify yourself as a reluctant programmer. I don't know whether you're reading *Computer Language,* but I'm glad if you are. You needn't apologize for not wanting to get caught up in computer programming. Even I have had periods in my life where I've felt that way. The most important thing for you is to remember the cardinal rule for the reluctant programmer:

Don't program.

You must defend your amateur status at all costs. For one thing, computer programming is too complex to do by halves. You must be prepared to invest serious time in it, because a half-hearted investment is too often wasted. And once you get caught up in doing it right, you can easily find yourself evolving into a determined programmer. You don't want that to happen, now do you?

When you need a computer program, you have several choices.

- If at all possible, buy it. That gives you someone to yell at if it has bugs.
- Next best is to borrow it from a friend. Please note that I didn't tell you to knock off an illegal copy. The last thing you want to do is starve out anybody who actually *wants* to write code instead of you.
- If all else fails, bribe a determined or enthusiastic programmer to write it for you. (If you are a manager or faculty adviser who holds power over such a programmer, you can note that "bribe" is a euphemism.)

You should confine your reading to product reviews. Publications like *PC Magazine* or *MacWorld* are safe enough. Avoid articles in this magazine that have snippets of code in them. Stan Kelly-Bootle is generally a safe bet, if you can understand his puns. Just be careful you don't learn too much.

I end my advice to the reluctant programmer with an appropriate inspirational quote — "To err is human. To really foul things up takes a computer." (Anonymous)

$\mathfrak{N}$ow let's say you classify yourself as a determined programmer. You are probably at home reading *Computer Language,* because you can pick up tricks of the trade without having to program all the time. You should also be properly horrified at the tales of large projects that end in disaster. Those tales underscore the cardinal rule for the determined programmer:

Never program anything big.

As I remind people periodically, computer programming is an exercise in mastering complexity. If you are on your way to becoming a professional programmer, you will find yourself tackling ever larger projects. Inevitably, you will get in over your head. You will misjudge the size of a project and the complexity will master you. If your goal is to stop short of becoming a professional, you will want to avoid this trauma at all costs. It is a painful rite of passage.

If a job starts looking too big, consider buying someone else's solution. (See above.) Resist the urge to write a better version yourself. If you must write code, remember K.I.S.S. (Translation — "Keep it Simple, Stupid.") Remember that your first love is your application, not the act of writing code for it.

Besides *Computer Language*, you should be reading good trade books on the development software you use. A little investment in learning your favorite programming language and operating system can save you from needless distractions. In short, be as good as you have to be to do what you want. But no more.

My inspirational quote for the determined programmer is attributed to Bill Wulf, though I don't know the exact source — "More computing sins are committed in the name of efficiency (without necessarily achieving it) than for all other reasons combined, including blind stupidity."

Finally, let's say you classify yourself as an enthusiastic programmer. I make no secret of being in that category. I believe that many readers of *Computer Language* are as well. We may not make the world go 'round, but at least we keep it from hanging up quite so often. Our job, more than anybody else's, is to be professional about what we do. The cardinal rule for the enthusiastic programmer is:

Never give away anything you can sell.

If you're going to pursue programming with enthusiasm, you won't have time for another profession. Make sure you get paid for what you do. Computer programming has the virtue of being worth a lot of money to people who have money to spend. They too will be more comfortable if they believe you're getting enough loot to stay focused on the job. Trust me.

You should also avoid writing programs that are available and cheap. Even if your (ambitious) goal is to displace an existing market leader, confine your energies to making code that is wonderfully new. There's just too much to do for you to be reinventing wheels.

You should of course be reading just about anything that will improve your skills as a programmer. Find an academic journal (or two) that has a good impedance match with your level of education, then read it (them) religiously. And don't forget trade publications, such as good old *Computer Language*.

My inspirational quote for the enthusiastic programmer is aimed at others who chose to switch careers. I heard it often from R.W. Hamming, who delighted in repeating it in my presence — "Computing is full of second-rate physicists."

And that brings me back to my personal history. I promised to tell you earlier how I finally wised up and stopped pretending to be a physicist. Credit for this transition goes to Prof. Edwin Kashy of Michigan State. I first met him as a sophomore at Princeton. He taught us a mean course in electricity and magnetism. Tough taskmaster that he was, I chose him as my junior-year advisor. When I graduated, I followed him out to MSU. He was my Ph.D. research advisor as well.

Kashy is an enthusiastic physicist the way I am an enthusiastic programmer. Enough of his enthusiasm rubbed off on me to keep me going. Nevertheless, I faced a real quandary when the time came for me to choose my first job. Seems I could earn twice as much as a computer scientist at Bell Labs as I could staying in physics research and teaching. It was time to take a hard look at my identity.

I like to tell people that Kashy convinced me to switch by making a simple statement, "I have seen you do physics for eight years. Take my advice and get out of physics."

It's tempting to end on that note, but it's not the whole truth. What he really said was more like, "I've seen you work for eight years. Anytime I've given you a problem in physics, I've had to hold you into it until you get some momentum. Then you do a decent job of solving it. But anytime I've suggested a problem involving computers in your presence, you've had an answer later that afternoon. Now, you decide what you like to do best."

More recently, he reminded me of something else he said at the time. "I think you're a competent physicist. I think you can become a pretty good physicist. But you're much better as a programmer. You can become very good, even great, if you focus on that."

I realize that Kashy and Hamming were saying much the same thing, each in his own way. I don't mind being called a second-rate physicist. It's probably true. So long as I can aspire to being a first-rate programmer, I'm happy. □

fterword: I don't know which is worse, getting caught up with computers when your heart lies elsewhere, or not getting caught up with computers when that's what you really want to do. I've seen people suffer from both mistakes. Much of my motivation in writing this essay was to help a few people choose more deliberately.

14 Shelfware

$\mathfrak{J}$t is probably the dirtiest open secret in the software business. I'm not talking about schedule slippages or cost overruns. I'm not talking about excessive bug levels. Nasty as they are, those are all things that can be overcome in time. Software can suffer a much worse fate than taking too long, or costing too much, or even being too hard to debug. It can fail to capture and hold your interest after you buy it. When that happens, you purge it from your disks. You remove its diskettes from the handy carrier and its manuals from the back corner of your desk.

If you're really annoyed at the software, you dump all traces of it in a trash can. More likely, you retain some painful memory of what you paid for it. So you feel obliged to retain some hope of resurrecting it in the future. You pack diskettes and manuals into a cohesive lump and stow them somewhere not too handy. Probably on a top shelf just out of reach.

Once a product makes this transition, it is no longer software. It has acquired in recent years a more derogatory name. It is called *shelfware*.

No self-respecting programmer sets out to write shelfware. We all have higher ambitions than that. We want to make products that change people's lives for the better. We want to write software that people will use every day and recommend to their friends. We want to acquire a following that eagerly awaits each new release we contrive.

Even if your ambitions are purely mercenary, shelfware is bad business. Computer software is more than one-shot publishing, like a book or an audio recording. It requires on-going maintenance and enhancement. Put another way, it gives you, the software vendor, numerous opportunities to sell back to your client base. You can sell maintenance if the product is complex. You can sell new releases of any software not dipped in epoxy.

A marketing person will tell you that selling to happy customers is about the easiest sell you can enjoy. That helps make it one of the most profitable sells as well. And that pays the rent, and orthodontists' bills, year after year. Unless you are in the business of going out of business, like the infamous shops in Times Square, that's the kind of business you want to build.

I confess to having written my share of shelfware. Some of it found its way to the top shelf by a reasonably honest path. It got old. Perhaps I could no longer justify supporting and enhancing it for the few remaining customers. Or perhaps I sold the rights to it and the new owners chose to remainder it. That sort of thing happens a lot in our rapidly evolving field.

Other software I wrote became shelfware for less defensible reasons. I refused to listen to customers and make the changes they needed. Or I guessed wrong about which customer feedback to respond to. Or I simply got blown away by the competition because I didn't work hard enough to keep up.

I found it hard to see the causes for my own shelfware. It was not until I started acquiring commercial software in serious quantities that I wised up somewhat. I could see other people's failures much easier than my own. Funny how that works.

To help you see some of the origins of shelfware, I have tried to characterize some of the principal causes. What follows is a series of caricatures. Each emphasizes some shortcoming that can push a product over the line. Or, more aptly, onto the top shelf. True shelfware often suffers from a combination of shortcomings. But lets keep it simple for openers.

The *orphan* is a product that has lost its support. It may have been a mainstay two years ago, but it hasn't seen an upgrade since. Meanwhile, the products it works with have been improved. The orphan knows nothing about the new file formats, so it keeps crashing.

You call the service hot line. If it hasn't been disconnected, you get a support person who's not really sure about the behavior of such an old product. No patches are available. Questions about new releases get met with embarrassed evasions.

Soon you figure out that the once wonderful product is trapped in a time warp. If you want to stick with it, you'll have to discard anything newer than your Sinead O'Connor CDs. Otherwise, you'd better kiss it good night and shelve it.

I cited above some reasons why a product gets orphaned. You can't expect a company to keep enhancing your CP/M word processor. And you can't bring a company back from the dead if it goes out of business. But you can gripe if a company simply moves too slow, or puts its energies into products less important to you. That's when you vote with your feet by climbing on a chair to reach the top shelf.

The *nest of vipers* is worse than the orphan. It sops up all your gumption trying to get it to work the way you want. Every time you think you have it under control, it finds a new place to bite.

The problem is not lack of support. Every time you call the hot line — even after eight at night — techies are there to lend you a hand. Typically, they are the actual folks who developed the product. They are always willing to help you try one more patch, or another clever work around. You can avoid buying diskettes for a year just by recycling the quick fixes they ship you.

As you might guess, it is this freewheeling approach to software that caused the problem in the first place. I know of one software company (no longer major) that took pride in the continuing program of product enhancement conducted by several of the techie principals. Every shipment embodied the very latest version of the product, often only a day old.

After two years of booming along this way, the company found itself completely mired in supporting existing customers. Some of their customers tried to help each other, until they found that no two had exactly the same product. Up to the very end, though, that company was happy to provide patches.

The customers left because they couldn't afford all that assistance. What they needed was a product with fewer bugs. Barring that, they at least needed one with better version control. No amount of first aid will save you from repeated injections of venom.

The *amnesiac* doesn't poison you so much as it annoys you to death. You might have a product that does just what you want. It has all the parameters you could possibly imagine, so you can tailor its behavior to perfection. There is only one small problem. It flatly refuses to remember any of your detailed conversations from run to run. You have to renegotiate the desired behavior every time you want to use the product.

If you're lucky, you can wrap such forgetful critters in a cocoon. Command scripts are great for capturing invocation lines that contain a dozen-odd unmemorable parameters. That's where the modern trend toward menu-driven interfaces does you in. Not all of them provide keystroke alternatives to pointing and clicking with a mouse. I have yet to see a really good system for capturing mouse movements in a script.

The writing analyzer I favor is barely usable, at least to me. I spent a day jiggering search paths, tailoring command scripts, and configuring whatever I could. That got me to the "doit file" style of invocation, with just an occasional gratuitous return to reassure an asinine query.

I am now trying to convert completely to Windows 3.0. To say that I am back to square one with this product is treating it with too much kindness. Its principal competitor now comes in a special Windows version. However reluctantly, I am tempted to turn an old standby into shelfware.

The *chatterbox* shares many of the same problems with the amnesiac. It is a product of the "Don't be scared" school of user-interface design. No matter how adept you get with this product, it refuses to wise up. That sucker is going to talk to you, and ask you questions, until long after the cows come home.

I am all in favor of an occasional "Are you sure?" The less I use a product, the greater my chance of saying something rash. It's nice when a product checks with you before it obliterates half the banjo players in Cleveland.

Still, every such checkpoint should come with a "Trust me" override. I'll use it at my peril, but please let me use it. I certainly need it to write scripts that run unattended. I want it whenever I get tired of clicking **OK** buttons. (If you want to be puckish, how about an occasional "Were you sure?" once it's too late to undo the damage?)

Brian Kernighan and I preached the gospel of software tools for many a year (**K&P76**). Our basic sermon was that programs should not be designed differently for automatic and interactive operation. You should be able to automate any interaction. You should be able to interactively debug any automation. That calls for I/O that is at once clear and to the point.

I fear that the industry has lost sight of this laudable design principle with its new-found love of user-friendly software. I just plain don't want to interact with much of the software I use. I want to tell it what to do, go get a cup of coffee, and digest the output when I get back. If it insists on chatting, it can talk to the packages beside it on the top shelf.

The *fortress* is more worried that you will steal it than that you will put it to good use. You invoke it and it paws at drive A for a key diskette. No diskee, no washee. Or it asks you to prove you're the rightful owner by entering esoteric information from some document that makes copy machines cough. I always feel like I'm renewing a loyalty oath when I reassure one of these paranoid products.

I am all in favor of people getting paid for fair use of software. Illicit copying was a concern when I owned my own software company. Abuse of intellectual property is an ongoing concern to all of us who earn a living capturing ideas in words and bytes.

I am also all in favor of customers getting fair value for their money. Treat us like potential felons and you lose our sympathy. Put too many impediments in our way and you lose us as customers. You can protect a product so well that it ceases to be a product.

I like to think that our industry has grown up over the past few years. Don't ask me to show figures — it's just a feeling. No longer is the Underground Computer Club of Dubuque the principal source of (illicit) software for that fair city. Sources of reasonably priced software abound. No longer can employees plead ignorance if a niggardly manager buys one package for simultaneous use on 20 machines.

I personally can't afford either the time or the inconvenience of trafficking in pirated software. For good software, the vendor has me on documentation, support, and upgrades. For mediocre software, the vendor doesn't hold my attention long anyway. I suspect that much of the market is more like me than not.

I railed about one fortress package in an earlier essay. (See **Essay 9: The Seven Warning Signs**.) It was a communications package that refused to run on more than one machine. You're supposed to buy a separate copy for each end of the communications link.

𝕵 wasn't about to do that until I was sure the package did what I wanted. Every attempt I made to install the same package on two communicating machines was cleverly foiled. The package was great at protecting itself, but lousy at winning hearts and minds. It quickly ended up on the shelf, replaced by a package that *encouraged* your installing it on multiple machines.

More recently, I became addicted to a program that plays bridge. Yes, I know this is not "programming on purpose," but I procrastinate occasionally just like the rest of you. I found it perfect for sharpening my game and idling away an unproductive mood.

Only problem is, it comes on two diskettes, one of which is a key diskette. To make it usable, you have to copy the contents of both diskettes onto a hard disk. To actually use it, you have to have the key diskette in drive A when you start the program.

That means I have to tie up disk space, yet still be anchored to the diskette drive to use the program. Worse, the diskettes are available only in 5 1/4-inch format. My laptop has such a drive that I hook up to when at home. On the road, I have to leave it behind.

What I really want is a single 3 1/2-inch diskette that holds all the files for the bridge program. I can make one, but it won't work because the vendor is certain that I'm trying to steal an extra copy. I'm even willing to buy a second copy for the road, but the vendor chooses not to sell one in the form I need.

I can no longer afford to devote hard disk-space to this minor indulgence, so it has recently gone on the shelf. It's one thing to shelve packages related to work. But when I'm reduced to shelving procrastinationware, you know I'm annoyed.

𝕿he *disk hog* believes that you can't get enough of a good thing. It comes on fifteen diskettes, all of which you have to copy onto your hard disk. But that's not the end of it. Some of those files are compressed. They puff up like popcorn on their way into your system. Next thing you know, you've given away megabytes of precious magnetic real estate. I won't even discuss applications that generate three-megabyte temporary files with little or no warning.

The designers of disk hogs forget that you have other uses for your system besides running their package. They figure you'll really appreciate all the extra whistles and bells they thought up while developing their pride and joy. They cheerfully lade on examples, tutorials, help files, and cute little utilities that you might have a use for some day.

I think all those things are great, mind you. Put each group of related files on a separate diskette. Provide a separate guide for each and a separate installation procedure. Where possible, show a way to use the extras right off the diskette. At the very least, you want to be able to pick and choose the parts you want to keep.

What generally happens instead is quite the opposite. The installation process pumps everything you could possibly need onto the hard disk. Files have such cryptic names, and little or no documentation, that you don't know which are used for what. I have paralyzed a large software package more than once trying to trim its diet for disk space. Chuck the wrong file and you get fruity behavior. Seldom is the package smart enough to say, "Hey, what happened to C:\GOOBER\PEANUT.SHL?"

When I acquired my battery-operated laptop with a 40-megabyte disk, I thought I was set for years to come. After all, didn't I produce hundreds of thousands of lines of commercial software on a machine with a tenth as much storage? Yeah, I sprawl a bit more with advancing age, but not all that much. I thought I was in pig heaven.

Then I got elbowed aside by a few disk hogs. It never occurred to me that a *typical* PC application eats half a megabyte or more of disk space. The big ones demand five to ten times as much space. It wasn't long before I found myself purging the disk on a weekly basis to avoid those nasty "disk full" messages. Have you noticed that they usually occur half an hour into a major run that cannot be resumed?

I soon learned that the quickest way to liberate disk space was to remove the largest packages I could live without. Being a disk hog is the best way to rise to the top of my hit list. It's worth reinforcing that top shelf to take the weight of the package. Vendors, take note.

The *way of life* is my last target. I apply this term to a broad spectrum of packages. Their common denominator is denial. They want you to forget you are running in your environment of choice and heartily embrace the one they provide. They want you to do things the One Right Way.

I have seen C made to look like Algol 68, MS-DOS made to look like UNIX, UNIX made to look like VMS, and VMS made to look like UNIX. Each was a tour de force, in its own way. But each was also a perversion. You can never completely turn a silk purse into a sow's ear, or conversely.

One problem in dealing with a way-of-life package is that it tends to snub its neighbors. If you don't match the protocols and file formats of the interloper, you can't talk to it. That makes it hard to combine packages to get a job done. In this day and age, that makes it hard to solve a problem cost-effectively.

Another problem follows directly from this inevitable isolation. The cost of buying into a renegade package is necessarily high. You have to be willing to invest in special versions of many tools and applications. You also have to be willing to turn your back on a larger marketplace and shop in more specialized boutiques. Or you have to learn to build for yourself what you cannot buy.

My company had pretty good success selling compilers, but we never did nearly as well selling operating systems. I finally figured out why. Almost any engineer can get permission to buy a compiler and tuck it in some corner of the development system. People can use it or not as they see fit. They can often contrive some way to mix and match code from different compilers and assemblers.

You don't just buy an operating system and tuck it in a corner, however. Such creatures tend to take over the whole machine. They define the set of applications that can run on the machine. That is a commitment with far-reaching consequences. You don't just buy an operating system, you get married to it. It becomes a way of life.

We even tried packaging our operating system in a less intrusive manner. We made it run as a guest under several popular systems. That made it easier for a single engineer to tinker with it. It stayed out of people's way. But it still suffered from a dearth of applications written for it. You wrote your own or did without.

I still trip across MS-DOS packages that endeavor to impose a unique way of life on the MS-DOS environment. I use them where I must, but less and less. It's not that I love MS-DOS — far from it. I've simply learned the necessity of having a homogeneous environment where diverse products work together. Those that don't end up sharing the top shelf of my book case.

That's my menagerie. I'm sure you have your own beasties that belong in this zoo. We can all feel sorry for software that lacks staying power. But we should also endeavor to learn from such failures. I don't want to make any more shelfware, and I certainly don't want to buy any more. My top shelf is almost full. □

Afterword: This proved to be a popular essay. I was asked to present it several times at conferences, after it appeared in print. I can also report that some of the vendors I mentioned here have begun to see the light (not that I can take credit for it). Carbon Copy now has a more reasonable license, though it is still fussier than most. My favorite bridge program is no longer copy protected. And large applications now provide more tailoring and space estimating at installation time. Still, a significant fraction of the software I buy turns into shelfware.

15 It's Not My Fault

$\mathbb{J}$ always get a kick out of watching historical and sci-fi movies on the late show. The game I play is to guess when they were made. Cleopatra has shoulder pads and a Veronica Lake hairdo if ancient Egypt is revisited from the 1940s. Buck Rogers sports a crew cut and a smug self-assurance if he's filmed in the 1950s. Black cowboys confidently integrate Nineteenth Century saloons thanks to the revisionism starting in the 1960s. In short, a movie always tells you more about when it was made than when it was made about.

For that reason, I was particularly struck by a recurrent theme in the second of the *Star Wars* epics, "The Empire Strikes Back." Here we have several rugged individualists charging about and defying a galaxy-wide fascist state, usually surviving by the skin of their teeth. That takes oodles of courage and unadulterated chutzpah. Nevertheless, these unapologetic rebels fall back on the same excuse whenever their schemes stretch thin. Over and over you hear them bleat, "It's not my fault!"

From a 1970s perspective, I found that drone string jarring and unpleasant. It didn't fit my image of Han Solo or Luke Skywalker. Having watched the 1980s run their course, however, I realize how much in tune with our times that particular sentiment has become. If any one theme can characterize the American attitude in the 1990s, it is a persistent unwillingness to take responsibility for one's less admirable behavior.

Gone are the days when a public official feels the need to apologize for getting caught out. Athletes renege on deals and behave rudely to women reporters with unabashed confidence that their human worth is reflected in their salaries. Business leaders and lawyers cheerfully espouse the ethics of carrion birds — and get away with it.

Such behavior is hardly confined to the putative leaders of society. Your average American has developed a knee-jerk reaction to any loss. Someone should have protected me from my own stupidity. Someone, preferably someone with money, should be obliged to shoulder the blame and compensate me for my loss. Whatever I may have done to contribute to the problem, it's not my fault.

That's how we can produce such a preposterous series of courtroom charades. When my car hit the school bus, the kids didn't die — it was the fire and smoke that did them in. If your only evidence of my crime is my freely given confession, maybe I didn't give it as freely as it appeared. That ten-foot rowboat shouldn't have capsized when I stood up in it in the middle of a storm. And so it goes.

As you must have guessed by now, this attitude is a sore point with me. I find it injurious not only to society, but to the equivocating individual as well. Consider — if you are not to blame when you fail, who should get the credit when you succeed?

If you have struggled for years to make a relationship work — and I hope for your sake that you have — you have probably learned a most important lesson. Each party must take complete responsibility for successful communication. That way, on those days where one of you can't pull off more than a 30 per cent effort, the other willingly supplies the missing 70 per cent. If you each commit to no more than a 50 per cent effort, you will have many days when the gap looms large. If the relationship fails, it hardly matters whose fault it is.

Years ago, I took one of those California-ish seminars designed to help you get your mind right. It was a mishmash of pop psychology and seat-of-the-pants therapy, but it mostly worked. One of its strongest points was the attitude it demanded about responsibility. You may as well assume that you are responsible for everything, because given half an excuse you will rationalize away any blame. I find that attitude a useful anchor. And by accepting my gaffes, I can revel in the occasional victories as well.

I will now climb off my social soapbox and climb back on my programmer's soapbox. I hope you will come to see the obvious parallels. We live in an exciting era, one where computers are improving the quality of life on a thousand fronts. Every one of those fronts also introduces a risk. Short-sighted programming can fail to improve the quality of life. It can lower it, or cause economic loss, or even cause physical harm. In a few extreme cases, bad programming practice can lead to death.

Just a few years ago, we programmers had a simpler constituency to satisfy. We trafficked in calculations that only an engineer or an accountant could love. Such customers are trained to be wary, particularly of new ways of doing business. Give them good numbers and they are suspicious. Give them bad ones and they are quick to discard anything that smacks of nonsense. Your botches might have cost you the confidence of sophisticated customers, but you seldom faced a lawsuit. The customers mostly kicked themselves for ever trusting you and went away.

Your customers today are at once more numerous, more diverse, and more litigious. You can't rely on camaraderie, sophistication, or understanding to save you when you blow it. You now have a greater obligation to yourself as well as to your customers. You can't afford to code by the seat of your pants anymore, if you ever could.

This is not all bad. Despite my earlier examples of silly defenses, I accept the reality of distributed responsibility today. Genuine abuses still exist that are only now being rectified. A manufacturer who knowingly makes an unsafe product, an individual who recklessly puts others at risk — both must be held accountable for their behavior.

When I was much younger, I learned how to cut weeds with a sickle. It is a wicked instrument that can be very effective in a trained hand. It can also sever arteries and remove digits with a moment's inattention. Grow up on a farm and you learn the pros and cons of sickles, scythes, threshers, and a score of other cutting tools. You don't think to blame the manufacturer for selling you sharp edges.

A few years ago, I bought my first gas-powered weed wacker. It came festooned with caveats. The manual told me not to do several obviously stupid things. It also told me how to refuel the beast, restring it, and service it safely. Since it is one of several *hundred* gadgets that I use just a few times a year, I find this more cautious packaging entirely appropriate today. I can't depend on oral tradition and several days of close tutelage to teach me the modern culture of wacking weeds. The manufacturer prudently saw to my minimal education on the use of a potentially dangerous product.

In some ways, I regret this loss of innocence. The first serious camera I owned I learned literally inside and out. I lovingly dismantled it and put it back together. I read the manual until it became dog-eared. I memorized the list of accessories and recited it before every gift-giving occasion. That camera was a wonder and a wellspring of joy to me.

Today, I am awash with the toys that come with wealthier adulthood, yet I am starved for that simple joy. I barely have time to master the basic operation of the light mechanical devices that now surround me, let alone become intimate with their many secrets. Please understand, I would no more go back to a life dominated by a single prized possession than I would go back to cutting weeds with a sickle. But I do appreciate the price you pay in lost innocence when you have sophistication inflicted on your life.

As we inflict sophisticated computers on more and more lives, we must learn to be more responsible. We must meet them far more than half way. We must document the obvious and shield the sharp blades. We must make our code ultra reliable and fail safe. We cannot fall back on the old excuses that circumscribe the role of software in the usability of the finished product. We cannot simply say that it's not our fault.

Whatever excuses we had in the early days of computing have worn thin. We can't argue that we lack the horsepower, the know-how, or the development tools. There's plenty of each to go around, should we choose to make use of what's out there.

ere's another of those analogies that's not quite right. Think of the evolution of the airplane. What the Wright brothers first put into the air was grossly under powered. You can buy garden tractors with more horsepower than the engine that carried the first human being aloft. You can hardly fault Wilbur and Orville for failing to enclose their cockpit.

An enclosed cabin is pretty much a necessity for commercial aviation. Sure, a few hardy souls paid good money to travel in open biplanes, but they were doughty pioneers, not your aunt Martha. As engines became more powerful and airplane design became more of an engineering discipline, passenger planes became much safer. And almost comfortable.

As late as the 1950s, however, stiletto heels were punching holes in the thin aluminum floors of the biggest aircraft. The 20 Kg limit on baggage was no joke. And in-flight movies were still an unfulfilled promise. In the end, all these limitations sprang from a common root — aircraft engines hardly had power to spare. Note that the commercial airplanes of today are not 600-seat biplanes with open cockpits. With increasing power and better materials came greater safety first, then greater comfort. Sure, capacity went up, but not as fast as it could have.

Back to computers again. The first computer I programmed had the smallest resident control program I have ever seen. One hundred 36-bit words were set aside for recording the current date, counting down the program's allotted time, and rebooting the batch control program from magnetic tape. Many of us programmers begrudged even this tiny tax. We wanted all the computer power we could get our hands on.

Then came multi-user systems that ran user programs in protected mode. No single program could crash the entire system, which was a definite improvement. The cost was a much larger resident and more insulation between the user program and low-level I/O. We sacrificed tens of kilobytes of precious memory, and direct access to I/O devices, for greater system integrity.

Today, the resident code imposed on us often measures in the hundreds or thousands of kilobytes. Application programs work through standard graphic display drivers, network interfaces, database access methods. We may have 20 times the memory and processor speed, but we don't necessarily run programs 20 times bigger or faster. Instead, we spend some of that increased horsepower on improved file-system integrity, more reliable data transfers, and so forth.

I warned you earlier that the analogy is not quite right. Analogies between conventional engineering and software development seldom are. It is much easier for an impartial observer to distinguish improvements in the reliability of tangible things. Hence, it is much easier to measure hardware reliability.

Software quality is much more elusive. You can judge some of it by reading code. Other aspects you can determine only by developing a nontrivial suite of tests. Such testing is often a significant fraction of the cost of developing the code proper. And in the final analysis, no amount of bench testing tells you what you need to know — will the code work properly in the field?

You can breadboard a piece of hardware and test many parameters of its behavior with confidence. Make a production version and it usually behaves even better. You can prototype a piece of software and test only a few useful properties. Make a production version and you're back to square one with regard to reliability testing.

That means that the accretion of working code is comparable in importance to the accretion of software-engineering knowledge. Making 50 bridges from one basic design is no big deal. Making 50 useful programs *is* a big deal. Each is bespoke, a custom item, a useful addition to our cumulative lore.

There is another difference. If a bridge falls down, an investigator can quickly determine whether the engineering or the construction was at fault. Less and less often are engineers caught out. They can rely on well known properties of construction materials and generous safety factors. If a program fails, however, it is a harder call. The conceptual distance between software engineering and program construction is much less. It is not so easy for any one player to assert confidently, "It's not my fault."

Software development is a maturing discipline, notwithstanding all these caveats. We do have more horsepower to spare and we are using it to make a more reliable product. We are getting smarter at developing reliable products and we understand the importance of making them safer and easier to use.

The "we" in the preceding paragraph is the computer industry in general. I find that too many individual programmers have not yet internalized this attitude, however. Altogether too much code is still produced like the Wright brothers' first flier — by hand, in a bicycle shop, with inadequate materials and technology. That may be fun for the home tinkerer, or the classic hacker, but it ain't professional. It's not "programming on purpose."

I have preached at great length about the microscopic details of writing more reliable code. (For an early essay, see "Programming on Purpose: Writing Predicates," *Computer Language*, August 1986.) If you keep reliability and testability in mind all the time, you are less likely to write spongy code in the first place. You are also more likely to debug it successfully in the end.

𝕴 still believe that good coding techniques are important, but that is not the brunt of this essay. A chain is only as strong as its weakest link. You can forge many strong links, and you should, but that is merely necessary. It is not sufficient. The way to improve overall system reliability is to avoid delivering chains of components. You may not be able to speak for the strength of the weakest link.

For all the promise of distributed computing, only a few forms have proved generally successful. Those involving loosely coupled but otherwise autonomous systems have fared the best. They can afford to be suspicious of their links to other systems, and to invest in checking and retry logic. Closely coupled systems, on the other hand, tend to fail like our proverbial chain.

The more reliability we need in a computerized system, the more we need parallelism, loose coupling, and reconfiguration strategies. The need in hardware has long been obvious. The need in software is more slowly becoming apparent.

A highly critical system like the space-shuttle guidance easily warrants any expense that improves reliability. It makes sense to code the same software with two independent teams, then fly with both versions checking each other. Controlling a few dozen traffic lights is also important, but not on such a scale. Designing for fail-safe behavior and coding for reliable operation are the least we should expect from the software developers.

I do not mean to suggest that nobody in our field is coding responsibly except under duress. I merely want to emphasize that we are entering yet another era in the application of computers. More are being used as appliances, rather than as tools for sophisticated users. More are appearing in places that can cause loss or harm to unsophisticated customers.

You can look on defensive coding and reliable design as an exercise in ass covering. Nobody buys insurance out of a love for insurance companies. We do so to limit our exposure to extreme losses. More than a few doctors still view diagnostic tests as protection against malpractice suits. Whether your attitude is negative or positive matters less than your actions.

We programmers are well past the point where we can command the tolerance afforded to back-yard tinkerers. If we want to be treated like professionals, we'd better assume responsibilities commensurate with those assumed by the other professions. Otherwise, we'll wake up one day and find ourselves:

- over regulated
- under insured
- in hot water
- out in the cold

Or all of the above. If we do, we'll have no one to blame but ourselves. □

Afterword: This essay was my attempt at a call to arms for programmers. I still find that many otherwise conscientious programmers look on reliability and quality assurance as nuisancy requirements imposed by management. Just let me code it and debug it my way, in my own good time. That should be good enough for everyone else. We'll never develop adequate technology for making responsible software until we develop the widespread attitude that nothing less will do.

16 Customer Service

The software business differs from others in several interesting ways. It is also more like other businesses than many programmers want to admit. The business of business has one universal invariant — customers. Without customers you have no business, whatever you're selling.

You'd think, therefore, that every business would put heavy emphasis on customer relations. Sadly, this is not so. The world is full of surly shop clerks, receptionists, and wait people. My fellow middle-aged adults bemoan the lack of good manners among the nation's youth. That may or may not be truer now than when we were surly youths. But it is not the true source of bad customer relations.

Every enterprise has a distinct personality. Often, that personality derives from the beliefs and attitudes of a founder or chief executive. It is maintained by an ever renewing coterie of managers and loyal employees who have bought into the culture. Those are the folks who, in the end, determine whether rudeness toward customers is tolerated.

I have heard managers say that you can't get good help nowadays. What they're really saying is that they refuse to demand enough from their employees. And pay enough to keep the ones that will meet the demands. Be indifferent to your employees and they will be indifferent to your customers.

I have also heard managers say that you can't afford to be polite these days. Too many customers are argumentative or even litigious. What the managers are really saying is that they have a greater stake in being right than in being considerate. "The customer is always right" is not a grovel. It is a pragmatic observation. Customers don't have to be right, but they don't have to be your customers either.

Of course, the worst offenders are the enterprises who think they have a monopoly. You have to remain a customer whether you like it or not. Theirs is the only news stand in the subway, or the only print shop in town, or the only diner open after midnight.

What these outfits fail to realize is that their arrogance still costs them business. You buy only what you have to when you begrudge the vendor a profit. These outfits are likewise quick to sink as soon as any form of competition sails over the horizon. If customer loyalty is a life raft, customer dissatisfaction is lead overshoes.

𝔐any companies fail to see the profit in caring for customers. It is typical of today's short-sighted economies to focus on the bottom line. Any branch of the business that doesn't contribute in an obvious way invites cutbacks. Managers often lose sight of the reason for doing business while optimizing bean counts.

Indeed, the "customer service" department is an afterthought in many enterprises, if it exists at all. Some managers see it as an arm of public relations. You need a few people to answer silly questions and calm ruffled feathers. The budget gets lumped under general marketing overhead. That's about as far from the bottom line as you can get.

Here is where the software business begins to diverge. Customer service is not an incidental part of what you sell. It can be as important as the product itself. That's because software, by its very nature, is complex stuff. Customers are more likely to need hand holding for a spreadsheet program than for a Buick, even if the latter costs 50 times as much as the former.

Sure, Buicks are pretty complex in their own right. But our society has had decades to build infrastructure for maintaining automobiles. Tens of thousands of people are prepared to tune or repair your Buick. You have to go back to General Motors only for original parts or warranty service.

We are building a similar infrastructure in computer software. Lots of people are prepared to educate you on the more popular software packages. You don't have to go back to Lotus, or Borland, or Microsoft, for help with your spreadsheet program. Don't count on similar support for the less popular packages, however. The infrastructure is not that well developed.

The conclusion is inescapable. If you hope to be a vendor of a successful software package, be prepared to support it. That means staffing a telephone with folks competent to help customers with technical problems. It means providing bug fixes and workarounds. It means producing regular upgrades to stay ahead of the bugs and the competition.

For an inexpensive product, you have to do all of this stuff for little or no money. That makes cost/benefits analysis painful. You know you need to offer customer service. You don't know how to measure the return on investment. So you can only guess what level of expenditure is appropriate for software sold at a given price. And you can only guess how much, if anything, to charge for software maintenance.

As an entrepreneur, I struggled with these issues throughout the past decade. As a consumer, I see companies continuing to wrestle with the parameters of appropriate customer support. I don't pretend to have definitive answers, but I do have a few observations.

𝔗he first observation is that arrogance is a waste of time. Techies delight in recounting the foibles of the unwashed. Partly, this reinforces the sense of superiority that any specialized group enjoys. Partly, it is a way for the overworked to commiserate. Neither goal is well served, however, if the price is making customers feel ill at ease.

You've heard all the cute anecdotes, probably several times over. A novice rips the diskette out of its protective sleeve before stuffing the wreckage in the drive. Or the diskette ends up in that little gap between diskette drives A and B. Or a customer complains that the keyboard lacks a key marked **ANY**, so how can one "Press any key to continue"?

I confess to having committed equally ignorant acts. As a lad, I borrowed a camera from my father. (Naturally, it had no documentation.) I threaded the first roll of film on the wrong side of a pressure plate. All the pictures came out black, shielded as they were from any light passing through the lens. My father thought I was particularly stupid at the time. I had sense enough to know I was merely ignorant and momentarily confused.

After the third time I stuffed a diskette between the drives of my Compaq Deskpro, I taped over the gap. Sure, I knew better. But I didn't realize I had done something silly until DOS typed its familiar message at me several times. I have never hunted for the **ANY** key, but I can recall early confusion over the dubious synonyms **RETURN, ENTER, LINE FEED**, and **NEW LINE**.

Never mistake ignorance for stupidity. The first is a temporary condition that is easily corrected, should the ignorant be properly motivated. The second is a more permanent affliction. It takes more than motivation to cure. If you persist in making ignorant people feel stupid once you know better, you are being stupid, not ignorant.

Don't think your attitude doesn't show. Even across several thousand kilometers of telephone wire, I can detect a condescending techie. I have sufficient self confidence in my technical abilities not to be intimidated by such arrogance. But it does annoy me, and it makes me rather less eager to do business with the company in question.

Even simple impatience can be off putting. I bought a rather good package called UULINK about a year ago, from an outfit called Vortex Technology. It lets me send and receive UNIX-style electronic mail from just about any PC compatible. Together with the commercial UUNET service operating out of Virginia, the package opens the world-wide Usenet to those of us who can't or won't work under UNIX all the time. It just takes a little tenacity to get the communication scripts working right.

I struggled for a day or two before calling Vortex. Lauren Weinstein, the author of the package, answered the phone. That proved to be a mixed blessing. While he was extremely knowledgeable about the code, he was also rather defensive. Any suggestion that the package might be less than perfect caused him to bridle. He was also impatient if I didn't get his explanations completely on the first recitation. I got the distinct impression that any failures were pilot error, pure and simple.

I was inclined to agree, but that was beside the point. Software is no good to us ignorant pilots if we can't figure out how to fly it. In fairness to Weinstein, I must say that his advice was a help. I eventually got the package going. Moreover, Weinstein called me unsolicited a day or two later to see if I still needed help. That ranks as better than average customer service.

This incident illustrates my second observation. The folks who develop the code do not always make the best customer support types. For one thing, their inevitable defensiveness gets in the way. For another, they don't always have the best skill set for the job. What makes a good code developer doesn't necessarily make a good code supporter.

When a company is young and small, it may well have to ignore this observation. You can't hire specialists while you're still making one dollar do the work of three. You should at least be aware, however, of the subtle price you pay. If that cost is not in bad public relations, it pops up in other places.

In the early days of Whitesmiths, Ltd., we had development programmers do double duty. All of us had to sign up for regular stints as Techie du Jour. On the days when you were *it*, you fielded all telephone calls requesting any kind of technical assistance. Pre-sales calls were from potential customers who wanted more details than the order desk could provide. Post-sales calls were for installation assistance or ongoing maintenance.

I did my stints as Techie du Jour along with the rest of the crew. I can attest that it is not an easy job. A typical day for one of us involved two dozen calls, and it was exhausting. Half were pre-sales, half post-sales. Of the latter, about a quarter were installation problems. Another quarter involved difficult-to-use features and occasional bugs in the product. Fully half of all post-sales technical calls were only incidentally related to the compilers we sold. Mostly, they were people requesting advice on programming problems in C or Pascal.

We did our best to answer all calls as politely and completely as possible. I confess that we often gave technical support even to people not under maintenance, just to keep customers happy. I also confess that a stint as Techie du Jour seldom ended with close of business. Each day's calls invariably resulted in another half day of follow-up work. We had to verify bugs, make workarounds, and call back customers. All in all, it was an expensive way to use development programmers.

When we finally got around to building a customer-support staff, I was dubious. I couldn't see how anybody could support the code without being intimately involved in its development. Boy was I wrong. Our developers did a good job as Techies du Jour. But the folks who ended up doing it for a living did as well or better.

A willingness to help is the primary prerequisite for a good technical-support type. A love of problem solving is also important. Some technical training is necessary, of course, but not as much as you think. Customers are willing to hear, "I don't know, but I'll get right back to you with an answer." Particularly if the staffer is telling the truth. And not being arrogant in the bargain.

Customer-support types need access to the developers, of course. But that access can and should be limited. Bug reports and a bug-tracking system are vital to any software enterprise. Managers should use this machinery to structure the interface between designers, coders, and customer-support personnel. Do it right and you will minimize distractions and hard feelings. (Do it really right and you won't have customer-support people asking to transfer to development all the time. That means paying the poor blokes on the phones enough to offset the enervating working conditions.)

I as a customer prefer working with support types who are not overly technical. Once upon a time, I called for support on Ventura Publisher. (I pay good money for maintenance on this package.) Seems that the circles I drew on screen didn't appear on a PostScript printer. The techie on the other end of the line knew about the problem. He felt moved to point out, however, that "the insides of the circles are fine — only the outsides don't print." Since I was trafficking in white circles with black rims, as is my custom, I was unimpressed. It did me no good to know that the white insides were printing as white as they should be. That's the kind of distinction that only a hard-core techie can delight in.

My third observation is that a company can go too far the other way. Some customer-support desks are little more than animated answering machines. They are all smiles and friendliness, but they don't know squat about the product. You describe the problem, they write it down. Maybe one day they get back to you. Try to get past them to a real techie and you drown in warm, friendly molasses. Outfits like these think their purpose in life is to pat customers on the head until they go away. And to insulate the company techies from any contact with the real world.

One of the worst offenders in this regard is Compaq Computer Corporation. Understand, I love their products. I gladly pay the premium they command for a reassuring level of quality and reliability. My brand loyalty borders on the canine. I even bought hardware religiously from Digital for two decades, despite the best efforts of their extensive sales-prevention force.

But I cringe every time I need technical information on a Compaq product. If it ain't printed on glossy stock by the marketing department, it ain't available. Compaq has this interesting belief that dealers should provide all technical support for their products. Then they supply the dealers with infinitesimally more technical information than you can read in their ads. Turn up a bug in a ROM, or a software incompatibility with their hardware, and you're simply out of luck.

I've lost count of the number of different channels I've pursued into Compaq. The only enterprises with more Byzantine phone systems are the consumer-credit departments of major banks. Not once have I tripped across a techie in any of my probes. I don't think they're permitted telephones. (Voice-mail systems can be fun, by the way. Ignore the instructions and dial digits at random. Or pretend you're playing Hunt the Wumpus on a very small computer.)

The net result is that my Compaq computers are not as useful to me as they should be. Microsoft Windows 3.0 does several fruity things on their hardware. Naturally, the friendly folk on the Windows support desk can only point an accusing finger at Compaq. I could work around the problems with just a little inside information. As a youth, I might have spent three days disassembling ROM code and performing experiments. As an adult, I would pay list price for some decent customer support.

My last observation is about customers who call looking for support. You as a vendor must remember that these folks are not at their best. If they're installing your package, their ignorance is profound. They don't know your terminology yet. They don't know whether the product is any good yet. They are feeling befuddled, embarrassed, and more than a little insecure. It is an act of courage and desperation for most folks to yell for help. Remember that, and you might find additional reservoirs of patience and compassion in fielding their calls.

Customers who have been using your package are only slightly better off. If they can't find what they need in a manual, they will be frustrated. If they think they've tripped over a bug, they will be annoyed. If they're dead in the water, they may well be frantic. You can hope that they've had time to build some faith in your company and your product. But don't expect them to be very tolerant by the time they get around to calling for assistance.

After all, how tolerant would you be? □

Afterword: I wrote this essay as more than a gripe session. My intention was to impart some real and useful information on how to provide customer support. The evidence is that it worked. Several people have since told me they modeled their customer support on the advice in this essay. (With good success, by the way.) Some adopted the Techie du Jour scheme for a short spell. Others used these words as inspiration to set up a proper customer-support department. I have also been happy to see a general improvement in customer support by computer companies of all sizes. Even Compaq lets you talk to an occasional techie these days.

17 Heresies of Software Management

Ⅼn a recent essay, I presented several principles of software design that may at first appear heretical. (See "Programming on Purpose: Heresies of Software Design," *Computer Language*, February 1991.) I did so to stimulate thought in an area that is not noted for consistent successes. I figure any field that cannot reliably turn out a product needs a jaundiced glance or two.

That material derives rather closely from a seminar of the same name. I first presented the seminar at Software Development '90, sponsored by Miller Freeman Publications. The other seminar I gave at that conference was a similar approach to the management of software projects. I recycle that one in this essay to complete the set.

Before I do, however, I need to provide a bit of background. What inspired this essay was a personal failure I experienced many years ago. It was on the occasion of one of my first attempts at consulting in the field of software management. There's nothing like getting off on the wrong foot to acquire an overdose of humility.

A major computer company, which shall remain nameless, was soliciting outside advice on a new product. It was a product of intense interest to me, so I contrived to get myself invited as one of the outside experts. I really wanted this project to succeed, since it promised a new plateau of hardware and software integration.

The product was a new line of minicomputers, complete with all new software to match. You could hang multiple processors on a single bus. They could share memories, disk drives, and other peripherals. You could edit FORTRAN code interactively. (This was before the days of C dominance.)

If the compiler caught an error, it bounced you right into the editor at the appropriate spot. You could see the diagnostic and the offending line both at once, use the former to fix the latter, and retry the compile in a trice. All this magic could happen even when the editor and compiler ran on different CPUs.

To those of you accustomed to today's integrated development environments, this may not seem such a great deal. But this was about ten research projects and 50 interim products back. All those concepts were more dream than reality in those days. To tackle advances on so many fronts was most ambitious.

That was exciting enough, but it wasn't the end of the story. It seems that the hardware and the software were being developed in parallel. The software folk had limited access to a target simulator that ran at a tiny fraction of the proper speed. They had essentially no access to the lone prototype. The hardware types were busy shaking down all the peripherals and the distributed bus on that.

The project plan did provide for a period of integration at the end. Two or three months were set aside to shake down all the hardware and software components after they were brought together for the first time. That was about all the marketing folk would allow before they unleashed a major promotional campaign.

I recall sitting through a morning of presentations by various front-line managers. Each reported the usual small successes and the usual delays. They explained where they could make up time, mostly during the integration phase. In many cases, the code for a chunk of software was "90 per cent written, with just a few more bugs."

Most of us are sophisticated enough today to see that this was a disaster in the making. I was a bit precocious at the time, or perhaps simply infected with a rare insight. In either case, I drifted through the morning's presentations with growing unease.

Finally, I tried a simple experiment. I wrote down the ten most common reasons I could think of for the failure of some past programming project. Then I went through the presentations and noted places where one of these reasons seemed to be present on this particular project. The result was disheartening. The project scored a solid 7.0 on my mini-Richter scale. A major upheaval was on the way, by my reckoning.

So far so good. I had useful data for this company, the kind that only a knowledgeable outsider can sometimes provide. It looked like I was going to justify my presence at this presentation. Then I proceeded to blow it. Big time.

What I should have done was talk privately to the vice president running the meeting. I could have taken him aside during lunch and aired my concerns. That would have given me the opportunity to elaborate on my reasons for smelling disaster. It would have given him the time to perform a few sanity checks. And it would have given him the latitude to intervene in several non threatening ways to avert the worst of the disaster.

That's not what I did. Instead, I let lunch go by without acting. At the start of the afternoon session, the V.P. asked for comments from us outsiders. It was clear that the assembled managers were expecting enthusiasm and praise. And several of the outsiders were willing to oblige.

When my turn came, I laid my cards on the table. I explained about the common causes for software disasters and what I saw on this project.

Silence. I realized suddenly — but much too late — that I had done entirely the wrong thing.

One by one, the front-line managers explained why my conclusions were wrong. I didn't really have a proper picture of the project status from the brief overview I had seen. There were mitigating circumstances to explain away every apparent problem. Enthusiasm was high enough to overcome a few shortfalls.

Pretty soon, it was me against the room. The V.P. was conciliatory, but he was pretty much forced to back his managers. By the end of the day, I had to allow as how they might be right. My superficial outsider's view was probably no match for their detailed knowledge of the status of the project.

You can probably guess what happened next. The project was indeed a disaster. A subset of the product came out several years late. By then, it had lost its competitive edge. Exactly how they muddled through, I'll never know. I was never allowed to see the inside of that company again.

One of the managers in that room went on to head a startup company that has since become a major player in the computer business. He was kind enough to pass on to me, through a third party, a bit of intelligence. He wanted me to know that I was right and that essentially all of my predictions had come to pass.

Hearing that made me even sadder than before. It was bad enough that I was right but ineffective. It was worse that this highly competent manager didn't seem to understand the depth of my failure. Being right is small consolation if you do not make a difference.

That experience taught me several important lessons. You do have to be right. If you don't understand the forces at work when you manage software projects, your successes will be based largely on luck. But you also have to apply what you know in ways that will work. It does no good to form antibodies against ideas that will help a project to succeed.

I also learned how hard it is for managers to hear. That's not because they're stupid, but because they're often under stress. It's too easy for them to hide behind a chain of "yes-but"s when they're hemmed in on all sides. As an outsider, you must often resort to heroic measures to get those folks to hear you. Particularly when they need to hear you the most.

And that, my friends, is why I'm not afraid to indulge in heresies. If they grab your attention the least little bit, they have served a useful purpose.

That particular minicomputer project was hardly an exception. Managing software projects is a field that has a checkered record of successes, just like designing software. Hence, I find it just as worthwhile to examine a number of heretical management principles, even though heresies generally deserve their bad reputation.

The rest of this essay takes an open-minded look at software management principles both in and out of vogue. The goal is similar to the one for my design essay — to formulate an approach to management that works, for whatever reason.

A heresy is a belief that opposes the common view. Some people gravitate to heresies simply because they like to oppose. They (erroneously) assume that opposition is the mark of the independent thinker. Others do so because they have lost faith in the common view. They (erroneously) assume that a heretical view must be right because it differs from a view that is wrong.

The common view generally becomes common, however, because it is mostly right. Heresies are worth examining only when the common view has a poor track record. In that situation, even erroneous heresies serve a useful purpose. They force you to think.

With that in mind, let's trot out a few heresies:

Heresy: **Every software project must be just slightly out of control.** We all pay lip service to reducing software development to an engineering discipline. Making another system should be just as predictable and reliable as designing yet another highway bridge. That may be a laudable goal, but it is unattainable. What puts it out of reach is a simple fact — the only computer program that you know exactly how to write is one you have already written.

Engineers can make a good living applying the same algorithm to building dozens of bridges. Software developers, on the other hand, are in the business of capturing algorithms in executable code. Do that once and there is little need to do it again. The only need comes when you need to rewrite it to take advantage of something new, in which case you have something new in the equation.

Put more cutely, the only programs that are commercially worth writing are the ones you don't exactly know how to write. If it's easy, there's no market for it.

Notice that I said a software project must be *just* out of control. If a program pushes the state of the art too much, it is a research project. The unknowns are so great that you can't afford to bet your company on success. The commercial balancing act is always to find software projects that are hard enough to be worthwhile but not dangerously hard.

If you don't like uncertainty, get out of the software business.

Heresy: **Your goal as a manager is to make software projects boring.** Never mind all that junk you hear about challenging your programmers. If you stay properly at the edges of control, they will have plenty to make their work interesting. Your problem is to keep projects from being so "interesting" that you and your boss get ulcers.

So the idea is to get the researchy bits out of the way up front. Let your bright programmers have their freedom, by all means. They will solve problems for you, innovate, and generally add value. The skill you must develop is to know when they have innovated enough to achieve the project goals. Then clamp down.

At some point in every project, management must declare a moratorium on adding clever new features. If you don't, you'll never achieve closure. If you do, the bright programmers will get quickly bored. Then their only hope to get on to interesting stuff once again is to push this project out the door.

Mature programmers will not only put up with such crass manipulation, they will welcome it. They know what pays the bills.

𝕳eresy: **Your obligation to your programmers is to answer their telephone calls.** Seriously, the best thing you can do for a hard-working group of programmers is to protect them from interruptions. Creative people need several hours at a stretch with no fear of distraction. Otherwise, they never achieve the depth of concentration required to do the tough bits. And they need days at a stretch of staying on the same task. Otherwise, they spend too much time getting back up to speed. See *Peopleware,* by Tom DeMarco and Tim Lister, for an excellent discussion of this topic (**D&L87**).

If you think managers make high-level decisions and issue orders to minions all the time, you're in the wrong business. (That's true no matter *what* business you're in.) The best managers spend much of their time doing grundgy chores. That frees up their subordinates to get the real work done. The managers handle the interruptions and knock down obstacles to productivity so the workers don't have to.

Don't worry about getting credit for doing grundge work. Nothing looks better on your record than heading a project that succeeds. For whatever reason.

𝕳eresy: **Your indispensable programmers are your greatest liability.** Sooner or later, we all fall into this trap. One person on your staff becomes the reigning expert on a particularly abstruse bit of software. Everyone else breathes a deep sigh of relief. Soon, the expert is raised to sainthood by general acclaim. It is easier to dole out praise than risk dealing with the hard stuff yourself.

This is a dangerous situation. What if your reigning expert quits? Or walks under a bus? Or just loses interest in maintaining yucky code? Or isn't the expert that everybody likes to imagine?

Hard liners tell you to fire indispensable people. My approach isn't nearly so Draconian. (I have experienced a few recessions, and watched my friends grow older, even though I haven't. I no longer take it as axiomatic that you can always get another job.) I prefer to make them document what they know. If necessary, teach them how to write. Put someone else on maintenance and put the expert in the role of mentor. After a few months of this, force the expert to use up some vacation time.

I know this approach works. I've dethroned myself as reigning expert several times now.

Heresy: **Teaching BAL programmers C++ is a waste of time. You're better off buying them a Coke machine.** One of the concrete findings in software engineering is that software organizations evolve through various stages. Some shops have barely begun to understand the basic lore they bring to bear on each task. Others are comfortable using one or more design methods (a.k.a. methodologies). Only the most advanced plan for testing and maintenance as part of the analysis and design phase.

It is important that you know the stages of evolution. It is even more important that you have an unclouded picture of where your shop fits on the evolutionary scale. Armed with that knowledge, you then know what technology your shop is capable of using to advantage. Anything more than one level removed from where your shop now stands will be useless, or even detrimental. The Software Engineering Institute, for example, is attempting to delimit the stages of evolution more precisely (**Hum89**).

I do not demean BAL programmers when I say they shouldn't bother to learn C++. Rather, I emphasize that they must advance through a few intermediate steps. You don't appreciate the need for object-oriented languages until you're comfortable with high-level languages in general. You need to master control flow and data structuring along the way.

Skip steps and you only engender cynicism and confusion in the ranks.

Heresy: **Staying within budget on a software project is more important than making a profit.** I realize this is the purest of heresies. After all, if a company is not profitable, it will not long endure. Surely that must be your highest goal. Well, it is the *company's* highest goal, but it is not *yours*.

Management comes in three layers. *Top management* is answerable to the shareholders. They must make a good return on investment by choosing wisely what goals to pursue. They are profit minded.

Middle management is answerable to top management. They are given goals and budgets. They win only if they achieve their assigned goals *within budget*. It is the job of middle management to oppose change. Change threatens budgets. Middle managers lack the discretion, or the inclination, to alter their own budgets to pursue unexpected opportunities.

Front-line management talks to the troops. As a front-line manager, your obligation is to do your job. You are answerable to a budget-conscious middle manager. Stay within budget and you make your boss's job easier. You also look more like middle-management material. You must trust that doing your job will help the grand scheme of things.

If you lack faith in the managers above you, go get another job. Or try starting your own company.

Heresy: **Writing software must be fun, but not too much fun.** Once upon a time, programmers worked for companies because computers were too expensive. Now, the average programmer can well afford a comfy program-development environment at home. You will keep many of your programmers because they prefer a salary to the thrills of independence. You will keep a few more because they like to work on large projects or as part of a team. But it is harder than ever to keep programmers if the work isn't fun.

Just as you must keep your boss happy by staying within budget, so must you keep the troops happy. You do that with programmers by giving them fun things to do. The trick comes in balancing the fun against the needs of the project. Programmers must be challenged, but not to the point of certain failure. They must have freedom, but not to the point of project anarchy. Err to either extreme and you lose.

To me, this last heresy is probably the most important. Here is where programmers and entrepreneurs have a commonalty of interest. What makes software development so exciting is that it has to involve a certain amount of fun. Otherwise, it's not worth doing. There's no pleasure in it for the programmers and no money in it for the entrepreneurs.

That may be delicate grounds for an important partnership, but somehow it works. □

*A*fterword: *This essay has a companion on software design. (See "Programming on Purpose: Heresies of Software Design,"* Computer Language, *February 1991.) Both were written only 0.2 in jest. Too often, both programmers and managers subscribe to the same nonfunctional beliefs about software management. Programmers see themselves as managed by Philistines. Managers see themselves as herding cats. Neither caricature helps get a difficult job done. An unvarnished view of reality can, however. The resultant rules are cast as heresies, but I believe in them religiously.*

18 Watching the Watchers

𝕴 like writing complex bits of software. Over the years, I have turned out an assortment of compilers, operating systems, and various software tools. It hasn't always been easy. I haven't always been as successful as I'd hoped to be. But it has been fun.

One of the least fun aspects of writing complex software is testing it. Some folks have a knack for it, but I don't. Over the years, I have developed an adequate skill in this area. Still, I prefer to let others write the more thorough test packages.

Those test packages often rival the software they test in overall complexity. True, a typical test suite consists of many small tests. Each is simple enough in its own right. But it takes lots of tests to add up to a comprehensive suite. And those tests have to play together in sensible ways.

There is no virtue in large numbers when it comes to testing. Any jerk can write a program that performs the same stupid test a billion times. A clever tester can span a thousand varied but sensible combinations with a different program. The former program does not make you feel a million times more confident than the latter. Quite the contrary. I have learned to respect the test-designer's art.

Testing has become an important sub-industry. With the explosion of software customers — and vendors — has come a new phenomenon. Customers now have a choice. In the past, often your only choice was which company to trust to write your custom package. If you wanted something off the shelf, you had a choice of at most one. Now it is not uncommon to have three to 30 vendors to choose from, all with software that nominally meets a common specification.

How do you choose? If you are lucky, you can find someone who has done the relative comparison for you. *Computer Language* and other magazines devote considerable real estate to comparing compilers and other essential development products. The service can be invaluable. (See **Essay 6: Product Reviews**.) All you have to do is calibrate the reviewers. If you trust their criteria and their methods, you can usually trust their results.

If you have to do your own testing, you face a second dilemma. You now must choose among test programs as well. Want to validate a C compiler for conformance to the ANSI/ISO Standard? Several vendors offer you test suites to do just that. Want to verify that a corpus of C code is highly portable? All sorts of commercial tools will pass judgment on the stuff line by line. You will even find an assortment of useful public-domain offerings that purport to help. You simply have to decide which to invest your time and money in.

Unlike compilers and operating systems, however, you can usefully adopt more than one set of tests. There is a difference between repeating the same test pattern a million times and performing two sets contrived by different authors. Even if the two tests purport to check for the same things, their coverage is bound to differ. You catch more problems with multiple test packages. Your limitation with testing, as with so many things, is the personal resources you can afford to invest in this particular area.

I'm not talking just money. The large commercial test packages aren't cheap, but they are often worth every penny you pay. You get a well-engineered test harness and some hand holding in setting up and using the package. The "free" packages are often harder to get on the air. They may contain bugs. (See **Essay 19: Washing the Watchers**.) You must be prepared to invest an open-ended amount of support time if you choose to save money here. Other testing costs include disk space, the time to run all those tests, and the time you spend evaluating the results.

The testing sub-industry provides a useful service, but it also creates yet another dilemma. How do you know if a validity test is itself valid? A bad suite can miss serious flaws and encourage you to buy a defective product. Or it can falsely diagnose problems and discourage you from buying a good product. In either case, a few terse messages from a complex piece of software can carry considerable clout. It would be nice to have some confidence that the messages are valid.

Well, that's what testing is about. But who tests the testers? Do you shop around for yet another validation suite to validate your validation suite? That seldom happens. Instead, vendors of test packages try to convince us that there's safety in numbers. They point to all the compilers they've passed judgment on. Or they cite astronomical numbers of lines of code that people have laundered with their product. If you think about it, that's exactly the sort of blather we compiler writers indulged in before validation suites came along.

The question remains, who watches the watchers? I'll spare you the Latin, but not the reminder. That question has been with us for millennia. We have learned in politics never to trust blindly in the judgments of a small group of people. Particularly if the group is self appointed. We need to be equally cautious in the technical arena. So stand by for a little watcher watching.

My first experience with a comprehensive validation suite was back in the days of Pascal. Seems some blokes at the University of Tasmania saw fit to paste together a set of tests. You could get them fairly cheaply and run them in a few hours at most. They poked at the dark corners of your

Pascal translator and gave you reams of output to pore over. With enough patience, you could learn quite a bit about the strengths and weaknesses of a given translator.

I got the Tasmanian suite to test the Pascal compiler I wrote. Pascal was definitely not my favorite language, so I was not steeped in the lore of the language. The suite introduced me to much of that lore, if only through the back door. I was amazed to learn what some of those vague sentences in Jensen and Wirth (**J&W74**) were commonly held to imply.

Part of the suite was a very comprehensive set of tests for the math functions. I have since learned that they derive from work done in FOR-TRAN by William Cody, Jr. and William Waite (**C&W80**). Those tests do a superb job of unearthing problems. I learned just how ignorant I was about the subtleties of approximating functions on a computer. (See "Programming on Purpose: Approximating Functions," *Computer Language*, June 1991 and "Programming on Purpose: Economizing Polynomials," *Computer Language*, July 1991.) As a result, I was able to improve considerably the functions that we shipped with our C and Pascal compilers.

The suite also had its idiosyncrasies, to be sure. It was pedantic about testing some of the really dank corners of the language. It placed a premium on run-time checking, to the annoyance of this old-line C programmer. It also had a few bugs. But it was only an informal offering, so what the heck. No government agency or corporate purchasing department could take us to task if we chose not to pass the more esoteric tests.

Then along came the ISO Pascal Standard and the situation changed. The Pascal Validation Suite got more capital letters in its name. It was updated to reflect the niggling alterations made in standardizing the language. The price went up a bit, as I recall. Worse, people started talking about official certification.

You'd think I would welcome such certification. I should have. After all, we had a good product (or so I felt). We had been tracking the Tasmanian suite for a couple of years. We were in a good position to achieve complete compliance with a Suite based on that suite. It would be something to brag about in our ads. All we had to do was find out:

- how much it cost to get certified
- what the criteria were for certification

I was astonished to find that I couldn't get either question answered unequivocally. The guy setting up the certification process didn't seem to understand about portable software. He quoted a price to come certify a single Pascal compiler running on a single operating system. We had Pascal and C running on five computer architectures, under two dozen operating systems. He sort of felt we should pay full price for each target, but he wasn't sure. He never did quote an exact price for multiple certification.

Fine, I was willing to certify our most popular combination. I'd worry about the others later. *So what do we have to do to pass?* Well, the guy really wanted to reserve judgment on that. *Huh? Look,* said I, *the tests come in two lumps. One lump directly addresses conformance to the standard. The second tests "quality of implementation." I assume we have to pass all the tests in the first lump?* Of course.

What about the tests with bugs? What bugs? *We can show that some of the tests are buggy.* I'll have to get back to you on that one. *Then what are the rules for passing the quality tests?* I dunno yet. *Beg pardon?*

What eventually emerged was that this guy believed strongly in Pascal as a "safe" language. He didn't approve of the proliferation of commercial implementations that omitted any of the run-time checks. Not even when the checks were optional. Hence, he was disinclined to certify any implementation that exhibited certain profiles on the quality tests. Only problem was, he couldn't quantify his criteria. He wanted us to lay our money down first, then he'd decide whether we did a nice enough job. Baloney.

Admittedly, we caught the Pascal certifiers just as they were setting up shop. Other companies, with a heavier investment in Pascal, had the patience to work with this guy and his minions in establishing reasonable test criteria. But I lacked both the patience and the resources to deal with such an un-business-like attitude. No way would I commit to pay for a certification process when I couldn't assure a successful outcome.

Fortunately for us, Pascal was already on the decline commercially. We could afford to walk away from this snafu. Our business depended less and less on credentials in the Pascal marketplace. Had the same thing happened with C at the time, I can assure you that the fight would have been bloodier.

What has emerged with C has, in fact, been a different kettle of fish. Several vendors have seen fit to develop commercial validation suites for the C language. Most have tracked the language from the days of Kernighan and Ritchie (**K&R78**) to the modern world of Standard C. You don't have to rely on AT&T, the original developer of the C language. Nor do you have to hope that some computer-science department will see fit to build a suite with student labor. You have a genuine commercial market-place to shop.

Many people agree that the Plum Hall Validation Suite is technically superior among these suites (**Plu91**). I am fortunate to count Tom Plum as a close friend for many years. He beat on the compilers I sold to prove in his suite. That gave me lots of useful feedback on subtleties I had overlooked in tracking the C Standard. I believe that both compiler and validation suite got better as a result of this protracted testing.

I was pleased when both BSI in the U.K. and AFNOR in France (the two standards bodies for those countries) agreed to adopt the Plum Hall suite for validating C translators in Europe. For once, official government agencies were following the market instead of trying to dictate it. They were not writing their own suite or canvassing the universities for a free one. They were not hitting up a major vendor with a vested interest for a donation of software and labor. They were actually choosing a market leader with a profit motive behind delivering and maintaining a good validation suite.

Government decisions don't always turn out so right. Some watchers are easier to watch than others. You can boycott a poor commercial product. You can take free software with a grain of salt, or not take it at all. Once the government gets into the act, however, you have many fewer options. In some cases, the only act that can follow is an act of Congress.

For historical reasons, the validation of programming languages for U.S. government purchase lay with the National Bureau of Standards (NBS). Its current instantiation is now called NIST (pronounced "nasty"). I have long been impressed with many of the achievements of NBS in the development of physical standards. My experience with NBS and NIST in the area of programming standards, however, has been less comforting.

NBS/NIST are the folks who issue FIPS standards. You want to comply with a FIPS standard to sell software to the U.S. Government. Otherwise, the paperwork can be enormous instead of merely huge. That gives NIST considerable clout in the marketplace. A FIPS standard is supposed to follow an existing U.S. standard, but it doesn't have to. NIST has the discretion to make changes, and it does so.

I attended the first meeting or two at NBS concerning the development of a FIPS standard for POSIX. POSIX is the nominally vendor-independent specification of the UNIX system interface. I had already gotten embroiled in the issue of whether the U.S. Air Force could require UNIX as a "vendor-independent" software standard. I was disturbed that the POSIX effort was being swept aside in the communal zeal to close a potential multi-billion dollar deal. I became even more disturbed at the easy way the people at NBS were apparently willing to ignore the work of other standards bodies.

The original POSIX standard was designed to cover an assortment of implementations. To do so, it intentionally left certain details unspecified. For some aspects of conformance, a system could comply in one of two (or more) ways. That makes it harder to write certain portable programs, but it is a practical necessity in a commercial marketplace. You can't always deny a serious product the cachet of standards conformance, or require it to change, just because the designers found a different solution to a moot design issue.

But the folks at NBS considered these choice points to be mere lapses in the POSIX standard. They were prepared to "fix" them by nailing down the choices once and for all. They were happy to accept free labor from one or two concerned vendors to help them make their choices.

I admit that cooler heads were beginning to prevail even as I left this process behind. (I saw the handwriting on the wall and realized that my commercial interest in the POSIX standard was rapidly waning.) It was the tendency toward precipitate, and unchecked, action at NBS that bothered me then. And it still seems to be there, at least from my perspective.

More recently, NBS decided to make a FIPS standard from the ANSI C Standard. They left the language essentially unchanged, thank heaven. But they saw fit to lob in several extra requirements in the area of translation-time options and error reporting. Committee X3J11 debated such requirements while making the ANSI Standard. We omitted them for good reasons. I don't know of any attempt by NBS to consult us about those reasons before they chose to override them in making the FIPS Standard.

Most recently, NIST has chosen to adopt a different C validation suite from BSI and AFNOR. They did so despite a handshake agreement to follow the lead of BSI, who first performed a careful study of competing products. They seem to have done so because they got a better business deal. That's not a good reason to part company with the international community on the important issue of C validation.

You may want to test your compiler against various suites, but you don't want to *have* to in order to sell to major customers around the world. ISO makes a point of requiring member nations to accept each other's certifications. Otherwise, a small company can go broke obtaining multiple certifications.

I still don't know the status of BSI certification in the U.S. My bet is, however, that no self-respecting bureaucrat is going to take on the paper work to prove that it's okay. International treaties go out the window when red tape meets commercial hunger. Equally, I suspect that FIPS certification will not be received with unqualified joy in the international community. ISO member nations are rightfully distrustful of second guessing by the U.S. government.

I can't comment on the technical merit of the suite chosen by NIST. The vendor has threatened litigation against people who offer to discuss the evaluations. Nobody has told me that the chosen suite is superior to the Plum Hall Suite. Obviously, I can be accused of bias in favor of Plum Hall. I make no bones about that.

My concern with NIST predates this flap, however. I have spent years of my professional career writing software products. I have also spent years helping develop good standards for such products. Both efforts are compromised when official certification gets out of step with the community at large. If that happens once, it's regrettable. If it happens repeatedly, it's worrisome. In my book, here are some watchers who definitely need watching. □

𝕬fterword: I wrote this essay and the next (See **Essay 19: Washing the Watchers**.*) because standards have grown so much in importance. A decade ago, you conformed to a FIPS standard to sell to the U.S. Government. Now you must conform to ANSI and ISO standards to sell to countless customers around the world. Standards are seen as an important mechanism for assuring a level playing field in international trade. Both companies and countries complain when the standardization process gets perverted. Beat that against changing market forces and shrinking government budgets and you have numerous opportunities for conflict.*

19 Washing the Watchers

$\mathfrak{J}$n the previous essay, I discussed the business of validating complex software products. (See **Essay 18: Watching the Watchers**.) I focused on my experience with validation suites for Pascal and C compilers. I expressed concern that official certification can be based on standards, and software, not widely accepted by the community. When that happens, it can be hard to rectify. Government agencies under attack combine the best defenses of turtle, porcupine, and skunk.

I continue my harangue in this essay, but on politically safer turf. My focus is on technical issues this time. I describe my experience using a variety of testing and validation tools. Some are public domain, some are commercial. All are useful in various ways. But all have also caused me problems.

I have spent entirely too much time lately finding and fixing bugs in other people's software. That's not unusual, except that this software is supposed to help me find and fix bugs in my software. And that's why I call this essay "Washing the Watchers." Sometimes you have to wash the magnifying glass to get a clear view of your own problems.

Over a year ago, I decided to write the entire Standard C library in Standard C. My primary goal was to write a book that concentrated on the C library (**Pla92**). I figure the world doesn't need yet another book explaining the C language proper. I also figure there's nothing like working code to illustrate how something works. If the narrative doesn't make a point clear, you can at least see what one implementation does.

A secondary goal rapidly evolved. There seems to be a market for the code. One corner of that market is among companies who sell C compilers. True, most have a library of their own. But the C Standard has mandated a number of additions. A thorough implementation should support multiple locales — collections of cultural conventions — and let you switch among an open-ended set. It should support large character sets such as Kanji. And it should have a top-quality math library. The code I wrote implements the Standard C library in all its excruciating detail. It also offers these special added features.

$\mathfrak{E}$arly in this project, Tom Plum put me in touch with Compass Inc. of Wakefield, Mass. They needed a full library for an Intel 860 C compiler they were developing. They were prepared to test thoroughly whatever they bought from me. We soon agreed that I would license them the code.

They became my first customer. Plum Hall Inc. has since rounded up several additional customers, even before the first release was ready to go out the door. Willy nilly, I was back in the business of developing software.

It was nice to have somebody run the Plum Hall Validation Suite against my library for me. I conned a fresh copy out of Tom Plum, but I didn't want to invest my then limited disk space and CPU cycles in running my own tests. Better that a serious customer should do so in conjunction with a serious product.

What was really nice, or so I thought at the time, was the additional testing that Compass planned. These folks are serious about their math libraries, have been for years. We agreed up front that my math library must yield sane answers for whatever arguments you throw at it. In the world of IEEE 754 floating-point arithmetic, that includes accepting and producing infinities and various flavors of NaN (for "Not a Number"). Even more stringent, a finite result must agree with the best internal representation of the correct result within two bits of precision. That's essentially the state of the art for high-quality math functions.

The Compass compiler runs in a mixed FORTRAN/C environment. So they obtained the ELEFUNT (for "elementary function") tests written in FORTRAN by Bill Cody. (Mail the request "send index from elefunt" to **netlib@research.att.com** to get a copy.) This is the granddaddy of the math tests I first ran across in the Tasmanian validation suite for Pascal, as I mentioned in the previous essay. They derive from the book by Cody and Waite that I also mentioned there (**C&W80**).

I cheerfully sent Ian Wells at Compass my first batch of math functions. He not so cheerfully reported back that the precision stank. ELEFUNT reported horrid loss of precision all over the place. That helped me find any number of bugs. It also taught me a fresh respect for some of the tedious safeguards recommended by Cody and Waite in their excellent book. I stopped cutting corners.

Still, certain functions kept reporting serious loss of precision. I rewrote them. No better. I rewrote them again. They kept getting cleaner and more elegant, but they weren't getting any more precise. Deadlines came and passed, both at Prentice-Hall and at Compass. (There were other reasons for the overruns, to be sure, but the math library was a major time eater.)

The worst offender was the **sin/cos** function. For small arguments it was just fine. For larger arguments, however, the relevant ELEFUNT test was reporting a loss of 12-15 bits of precision. The problem clearly involved how I reduced angles greater than 2π to their equivalent smaller angles. (See "Programming on Purpose: Economizing Polynomials," *Computer Language*, July 1991, for a few more words on this topic.)

Now here was my quandary. Even the stupidest approach to reducing angles should give better accuracy than this for the tests in question. Cody uses a triple-angle relationship to compare sines near 2π to related sines near 6π:

```
sin(x) = sin(x/3)(3 - 4*sin(x/3)*sin(x/3))
```

It is a nasty test, but one carefully contrived to test the function properly. I spent days analyzing the test results. One whole day went into computing 64-bit floating-point values *by hand* to check my code. The code was producing exactly what it should to the nearest bit. Only problem was, the fifteenth-nearest bit was not what the test demanded. Where was I going wrong?

In sheer desperation, I finally did what every programmer dreads. I read the documentation. Cody and Waite end each chapter of their book with a description of their test methods. Under **sin/cos**, my eye caught a remark about "purifying arguments." You can't just pick any old **x** near 6π and expect to get a satisfactory **x/3** to go with it. Not in the eerie world of floating-point arithmetic. You have to perform a clever dance step to adjust **x** slightly. In FORTRAN:

```
Y = X / 3.0
Y = (Y + X) - X
X = 3.0 * Y
```

This code sequence ensures that both **x** and **x/3** are exactly representable in the chosen floating-point format. Otherwise, the test shows you the error in the argument pair, not in the function itself.

Fine, ELEFUNT does that. But how it does so contains a caveat. My eye caught an even briefer remark about how you must write the purification code. Cody and Waite cite an article by W.M. Gentleman and S.B. Marovich (**G&M74**). The code relies on an expression that truncates intermediate results to the final stored precision. On a machine that keeps intermediate results to higher precision, you have to rewrite the dance step:

```
Y = X / 3.0
Y = Y + X
Y = Y - X
X = 3.0 * Y
```

The test machine was a Sun 3 workstation with a Motorola MC680X0 processor. It performed floating-point arithmetic with a Motorola MC68881 math coprocessor. That follows the IEEE 754 Standard for floating-point arithmetic. It even supports the 80-bit extended-precision format for intermediate results. Aha!

Unfortunately, I was now in Australia for the year. The source for ELEFUNT was back in Wakefield, Mass. All I had to go on was the one value for **x** that Ian Wells had sent me with the ELEFUNT results. Fortunately, my computer is an Intel 80386 with the Intel 80387 math coprocessor. It supports the same IEEE 754 formats, but with different byte order in storage. I checked the purification of my nasty test case. **X** changed by one bit. The fifteenth bit of the result fell into line.

I had been spending months of my life rewriting code that was correct. And all because of an implementation bug in a piece of free validation software. A careful perusal of Cody and Waite turned up the same caveat in several other places. One by one, other persistent test failures also proved to be bogus. Had I thought to challenge the test reports sooner, I could have been done months earlier. That was yet another important life lesson learned the hard way.

Please understand, I think the ELEFUNT tests are wonderful. They have taught me a lot. They have saved me from shipping many a bug. They perform an invaluable service to people who buy software. But even the best piece of code needs maintenance and support. Without it, "free" software can prove to be very expensive for all concerned.

I can gripe about other packages as well. W.M. Kahan has written a nasty little item called PARANOIA. (Mail the request "send paranoia.c from paranoia" to `netlib@research.att.com`.) It does a wonderfully malicious job of stressing the floating-point arithmetic in a C implementation. That's fine. It is also rather opinionated about how good is good enough. That's less fine.

PARANOIA complains even about single-bit errors. It will write out an extreme floating-point value, for example, with `printf`. If `scanf` doesn't yield exactly the same bit pattern, the program gripes. That may be desirable from a user's standpoint, but it's not always easy to do. Two papers that illustrate this point are in the *Proceedings of the ACM SIGPLAN '90 Conference on Programming Design and Implementation*. See William D. Clinger, "How to Read Floating-Point Numbers Accurately," for one side of the issue (**Cli90**). Also see Guy L. Steele, Jr. and Jon L. White, "How to Print Floating-Point Numbers Accurately," for the other side (**S&W90**).

I said earlier that a maximum loss of two bits of precision is state of the art. That's almost true. For certain functions, you can expect a maximum loss of one bit, at least over certain intervals. Square root is in that category, as are sine and cosine for small angles. Nevertheless, PARANOIA complains about single-bit errors for other functions too.

And it contains bugs. Or at least it is a sucker for bugs in floating-point hardware. Compass sent me a gripe that my `sqrt` function was botching the square root of the smallest representable number. I couldn't reproduce it on the PC. Ian Wells verified my conjecture — the Motorola floating-point hardware was incorrectly setting the squared result to zero. Naturally, PARANOIA blamed the software, not the hardware. That is much less fine, in my book.

I have some other open issues with this program. Right now, it looks like the MC68881 gives inferior results compared to the 80387. I can't confirm that, however. It could be operating-mode problems or code-generator errors for all I know. My major gripe is that the program trumpets peccadilloes with the same intensity as serious errors. That makes it hard for a customer to properly weigh the seriousness of a diagnostic. And that makes it hard for a poor vendor like me to defend my craft.

I have passed my library code through several compilers to test for portability. My original plan was to turn on every test imaginable and rewrite the code until all the critics went silent. I soon gave up on that goal. *Every* compiler I used has bugs in its error checking.

Most get some aspect of Standard C type compatibility wrong. (The new rules are admittedly subtle, particularly to old-line C programmers.) That includes products that claim conformance to Standard C. It also includes products that claim "lint-like" error checking. The program lint, in case you didn't know, is an early product of the compiler folk at AT&T Bell Labs. It substitutes for the usual code-generator back end an extended checker that generates no code at all. Instead, the lint back end looks for portability gaffes and other questionable usages to kvetch about.

What you have to do to quiet these deranged products is introduce gratuitous type casts. Even if they optimize away to no code, such type casts are a nuisance. They make the code harder to read and understand. They also weaken the type checking considerably. Old C compilers let you type cast practically any scalar type to any other. Standard C is more restrictive, but still generous compared to the restrictions of most other contexts. You give up a lot of hard-won ground when you have to indulge in unnecessary type casts.

Nearly all of the compilers I used issue spurious complaints about uninitialized data objects. Some are downright stupid about the flow analysis they perform. One I used didn't even understand the order in which expressions execute in a **for** statement.

The best of them were easily thrown whenever I use a pair of scalars in tandem. If the first scalar has some funny value, such as zero, I know not to access the value stored in its companion. Invariably, these half-smart analyzers warned me that the second scalar might be used before it is initialized. I can quiet them only by adding gratuitous, and misleading, assignments. The state of the art of flow analysis is none too good.

Fortunately for me, I can ignore spurious messages from these compilers. Some shops have adopted more stringent rules. All code you write must keep the compiler quiet for a given set of testing options. You have to write silly or suboptimal code sometimes to shut it up. Even more fortunately for all of us, nobody has promulgated official standards for source code. At least not yet. Given the state of the art, I hope that day does not come soon.

This is not directly related to testing, but I should also point out the widespread capacity problems I encountered. When I first wrote the library, I paid no heed to any size limits. A few functions weighed in between 150 and 250 lines. Most were 100 lines or smaller. I soon found, however, that *every* compiler I used choked on at least one of the functions. (Different compilers choked on different large functions.)

I had to carve these functions up artificially to get them to go through all the translators of interest. Along the way, I made a virtue of this necessity. I decided to ensure that all functions could be displayed in my book on a single page or on a pair of facing pages. That took just a bit more carving beyond the initial butchery. In the end, I ran across one testing tool that still coughed on one of the largest remaining functions. I don't intend to dice any finer, however.

I mention this surprising limitation because it is a significant impediment. Both translators and test tools should nowadays handle source files that comprise 1,000 lines at least. I confine my attention only to host computers that have 32-bit addresses and many megabytes of usable memory. In reality, I see no reason why the upper limit should not be 10,000 source lines or more.

As a final user report, I must say that I also found several bugs in the Plum Hall Validation Suite. Fortunately, that is a commercial product supported by a motivated vendor. All I had to do with those was report the problem or, in some cases, the suspicion of a problem. It also helped that Tom Plum spent a month visiting me in Australia. (Our wives are twin sisters.) He and I spent a couple of intense days reducing our respective bug lists to zero. Admittedly, not everyone can get such direct support from software vendors.

Let me emphasize once again that all these various testing tools are most helpful. I don't mind a few false negatives if I get enough true positives to improve my product. To paraphrase an old country-and-western tune, even a bad test is better than no test at all. The hard part is explaining to a customer why the nasty messages that appear should be taken with a grain of salt. Customers are naturally suspicious of any apparent attempt to sweep problems under the rug. With or without salt, to thoroughly mix the metaphor.

I recite this history primarily to pass on useful lore. I also hope to raise the general level of skepticism about software that purports to test other software. Remember, the testing software was also written by people as error prone as you and me. □

𝕬fterword: Testing the math functions for The Standard C Library *probably required the biggest use of outside validation suites of any project I have undertaken. Were I not so finicky about the code, I could have glossed over any number of errors. I'm glad I didn't, in the end. Along the way, however, it was one of the more frustrating periods in my career as a programmer.*

Sadly, I must report the demise of Compass, Inc. Their parent company, Softech, laid them to rest during the recent recession. I like to think that their using my code did not deal the death blow.

20 Who's Always Right?

There's more to a computer-based business than the software. However complex or novel, software is but one component of a larger enterprise. The goal of that enterprise must be to perform a useful service to some base of customers. If you don't serve your customers, you lose them. If you lose your customers, you don't have a business. If you lose your business, it doesn't matter how wonderful your software may be.

To a business type, this sentiment should be obvious. Technical types often get led astray, however. They take for granted that an intricate piece of technology will be admired for what it can do, whether or not it actually delivers reliably. They assume that new technology can make its own rules, whether users like it or not. You can get away with that kind of thinking for awhile. (I should know, having committed both sins.) In the long haul, though, the competition will grind you down.

I've discussed some aspects of this topic in earlier essays. See **Essay 7: Awaiting Reply**, on the need to respond promptly to customer problems. **Essay 14: Shelfware** describes how programs become so annoying they end up on the shelf. And **Essay 16: Customer Service** talks about supporting software. Two recent experiences have encouraged me to revisit the topic. Both concern companies that sell good software products. But in each case, I found myself flabbergasted at the response I got to a service request.

Perhaps I am getting crustier with advancing age. I know I am less tolerant of poor service. Perhaps I resent having to buy so much software these days. I know I enjoyed writing my own for two decades. Or perhaps I am just sensitized to such issues by the ongoing trade debate between America and Japan. Certainly good service is essential to maintaining a good competitive position. Whatever the motivation, I feel the experiences are worth reciting here. Both make good cautionary tales for those of you who would program on purpose.

The first concerns Xerox Ventura Publisher. I have been using this type-setting software since its first release many years ago. With it I typeset letters, lecture materials, and all the books I publish these days. It has the heavy-duty capabilities I need and it mostly works fine.

At the end of 1990, I left home for a year in Australia. Just before leaving, I upgraded to the Windows version of Ventura. (See "Programming on Purpose: Font Follies, *Computer Language*, April 1991.) My plan was to finish writing a new book and revise another during my sojourn.

The new book was *The Standard C Library* (**Pla92**). As is so often the case for a large project, it took several months longer than I'd planned. A contributing factor was that Ventura under Windows (VPWin for short) began crashing as my chapters got larger. I assumed that I was hitting some capacity problem and began to dread each added word.

The problem eventually got so bad that I stopped trying to hide from it. I spent a whole day isolating the problem. Seems that the hyphenator couldn't digest cross references. Start editing a line and heaven help you if a cross reference jumped from one line to another. I finally got a two-line chapter to crash predictably. (The only reason that large chapters got more fragile was because they tended to accrete more cross references.) At least now I knew what to avoid.

Then I noticed that my borrowed Apple Laserwriter wasn't kerning properly. *Kerning* is the practice of squeezing together certain pairs of letters to improve appearances. A classic kerning pair in almost any font is "VA." My draft copy showed that certain pairs were squeezed too much. But a given pair would sometimes kern properly, then other times overdo it, even on the same page.

I could only hope that the problem was peculiar to the Laserwriter. The final page images were to come out of a 1200 dpi Monotype system. Well, they came out about as bad as ever. I was running late and on the wrong side of the planet for quick support. The book came out chock full of typos (my fault) and kerning gaffes (thanks to VPWin).

ow, I have paid for maintenance on Ventura Publisher for many years. That gives me the right to camp on hold, at my expense, until a telephone support person can talk to me. Perhaps it was a false economy, but I couldn't abide a week of half-hour trans-Pacific calls to chase down assistance. So I waited for the lull between book projects to pursue the matter.

I wrote a letter to Ventura Support outlining my problems. I asked for a fax number that I could use to chat with them. A couple of weeks later (normal Pacific delays) I got a reply. The first paragraph set the tone nicely:

Neither of the problems you briefly describe in your letter represent "bugs" in the software. They seem more likely to occur as a result of the configuration of your system. There is not enough information in your letter to enable us to do so at this point [sic]. Changing width tables as well as kerning work without problems if there aren't system conflicts.

The letter went on to observe that the serial number I gave in my letter was for a pre-Windows version of Ventura. Besides, my support agreement provided support only in the U.S.A.. What was I doing in Australia with such an agreement, anyway? It concluded with the address of the Australian sales office for Ventura. It did not include the fax number I requested.

The first sentence made me so angry that I had trouble reading the rest of the letter. You simply *do not* tell a customer that the bugs he is reporting aren't really bugs. As for the rest of it, I had to admit they were right. I'd sent them the wrong serial number from the wrong country. They didn't have to help me and they'd proved it. Congratulations.

I keep a small folder labeled, "Who's Always Right?" It's small because it seldom contains more than one letter from any given company. A typical letter is from my former insurance agent. She took a year and a half to stop charging me for a car I'd sold. Her letter demonstrated conclusively that it wasn't her fault. Prosecution so stipulates. Big deal.

Unfortunately, only Ventura sells support for VPWin. I had no competitor to go to. So I drafted a blistering reply and filed the letter. In fairness, I must report that I got back a fairly contrite letter. It allowed as how I might really have bugs and suggested a few things to try. It even included a fax number. Along the way, I learned that my bugs were hardly unique to me. Maybe Ventura hadn't heard of them, but quite a few other customers had. More than one had shelved VPWin in place of the GEM version because of the persistent kerning bugs. But it took me months to get such an admission out of Ventura support.

Meanwhile, my second book project was coming to a boil. Jim Brodie and I were reissuing our *Standard C* (**P&B89**) as *ANSI and ISO Standard C: Programmer's Reference* (**P&B92**). Time was getting tight and the kerning problems remained. In the end, I typeset the book by turning kerning off globally. I then hand-kerned the worst offenders. I have now upgraded to a newer version of VPWin with lots of neat new features. But it still can't kern reliably.

I should say that the Ventura support staff can be very helpful. When it comes to showing folks how to use Ventura Publisher, they are often quite good. But when it comes to finding and pushing through bug fixes, they can only wait on their betters. I am still waiting too.

My second experience concerns Checkfree. Their software lets you send out checks by electronic mail, just like the big guys. It's a fairly new service, and slightly scary. How do you trust that a few typed commands and a mysterious dataphone call will really pay your mortgage on time? How do you prove you tried if a few bytes go astray? Clearly, this is a business that must put a high priority on building consumer confidence. I waffled more than once before I finally sent in my application.

But eventually I did. Two weeks later (with no Pacific delays) I got my System Identification Number (SIN for short). I was ready to join the modern world of banking. There was only one small problem. My SIN was supposed to be my Social Security Number (SSN). But the folks at Checkfree had changed the first of two 7s in my SSN to a 9. What a nuisance.

So I called the Checkfree support number. They asked for my SSN. I told them they didn't want it. They asked again. I gave it to them. They told me I didn't exist. I explained the problem. At this point I got a set lecture about the difference between SINs and SSNs. Seems the two don't really have to match. That's just a convenient starting point. (Same tone of voice as those folks who announce unavoidable flight delays.)

I explained that I could understand that. (Programmer training can help you in real life, sometimes.) *But I really want my SIN and SSN to match, since that was my original intention.* Oh, that's easy (cheerfully). All you have to do is cancel this account and reapply. In another couple of weeks, you'll have your new SIN.

Isn't there some way you could just fix the problem, I asked in all innocence. Out of the question. *You mean, I have to go to all this trouble because you made a mistake?* Well, let me ask. After a delay, the cheerful voice again. No problem, if it's our mistake we'll just go ahead and fix it. You should be straightened out in just a day or two. *That's more like it.*

So I waited two days and sent a small batch of transactions under my corrected SIN (my SSN). They were accepted and acknowledged. Great. This service is not so bad. I got into the swing of things and began paying bills in earnest.

𝔄 week later I got a letter from Checkfree (dated a week earlier). It warned me that I had sent a batch of transactions under the *wrong* SIN. They were now in limbo awaiting clarification from me. No list of transactions. No mention of later batches. Yikes! My worst fear realized. Visions of angry creditors danced in my head.

I immediately called Checkfree. They asked for my SSN. I went through an abbreviated version of my earlier *pas de deux*. When I confessed to my "correct" SSN, the customer-support person was most helpful. He explained that they had re-examined my application and concluded that there was no need to change it. That 9 *could* be read as a 7, so the error was my fault. They were right and I was wrong.

I said I was led to believe they were going to fix the problem. My mistake again. I said I really didn't want to go through life with a SIN that was almost but not quite my SSN — particularly when they kept asking for the latter. He repeated the set lecture about why they don't have to be the same. I said I wanted them to match anyway. He repeated the drill about canceling my current account and reapplying. I asked for a list of transactions in limbo so I could unwind from the current mess. He allowed as how he couldn't tell me.

Somewhere around here, my voice went up half an octave and about ten decibels. My customer service person offered to hang up on me. I calmed down and asked to speak to his supervisor. He cheerfully passed me on to her like the proverbial buck. She was icy calm, but unbending. I got the same lectures from her as her minions. It was clear that I had unearthed a nugget of unalloyed Company Policy. I began to see how I would get treated if a $5,000 transaction ever went astray.

At that point, I was mad enough to drop Checkfree forever. But I was worried about those transactions. And I was curious. Was this treatment the aberration of a mismanaged customer-service staff? Or did it reflect policy passed down from on high? So I did what the letter told me to do. I sent e-mail under my "correct" SIN requesting reinstatement of the transactions sent under my "incorrect" SIN (my SSN). I also requested confirmation of all the transactions, so I could start to sort out my electronic checkbook. Then I sent my customary blistering letter, this time to the president of Checkfree.

Over the next week or two I got two replies. One was a letter from the icy supervisor. It documented in detail how Checkfree was right and I was wrong. It even included a photocopy of my offending application. (That'll treat me to cross my 7s for clarity.) I filed it under "Who's Always Right?" and forgot about it.

The second reply was a phone call, but not from the president. Instead, the woman explained that she wanted to understand why I was so upset. She then repeated all the lectures I had heard several times before. No doubt about it, I was wrong and they were right. I asked for a list of pending transactions. She could only tell me about those that had cleared the bank. Not much help.

I asked about my confirmation request. She assured me that all e-mail is logged and gets a response. *Couldn't prove it by me.* She hung up to investigate the matter. Called back to say that my e-mail had been logged, sure enough, but got no response. But please understand, that sort of thing Just Doesn't Happen.

Yup.

As of this writing, I have send out a couple dozen transactions via Checkfree. I have yet to receive a bank statement showing what has happened to any of them. Probably, they're all just fine. I worry from time to time, though, about what will happen if my proverbial $5,000 check goes astray. And I can't wait for someone to go into competition with Checkfree.

I repeat the moral of these two tales for emphasis. Even for a business built around computer software, the software is not central to the business. It is the service you provide to willing customers that counts most. Those customers don't have to be right. But then again, they don't have to be your customers either. □

fterword: These two encounters proved to be more than just isolated incidents. The Ventura kerning bug disappeared only when Microsoft upgraded Windows to version 3.1. Evidently the Windows PostScript driver was the culprit. Ventura has yet to fix any bugs I've sent their way. I do get occasional useful advice from them. And I find their maintenance fees cost effective if only for the discounts they earn me on upgrades.

As for Checkfree, I found that they had to write and mail conventional checks altogether too often. That led to a mishmash of check numbers and electronic transactions on my monthly bank statement, plus a few missed payment dates. I was spending more time balancing my monthly statement than I was saving over printing all checks with Quicken. It took me months to get my account under control after I canceled Checkfree. A few letter writers agreed with my conclusion that consumer electronic banking in the U.S.A. is not quite ready for prime time.

I believe these incidents also prove to be more than just cautionary tales. I find them altogether too typical of how customers get treated these days. If we're moving to a service economy, we'd better learn how to deliver service.

21 The Cycle of Complexity

When I started programming, almost thirty years ago, the in thing was FORTRAN II. By the standards of those days, it was a reasonably elegant language. You could write horrendous expressions using a notation that strongly resembled conventional mathematics. The FORTRAN compiler managed to translate those expressions to code that was usually correct and not all that inefficient. It sure beat writing assembly language most of the time.

Of course, dedicated assembly-language programmers sneered at FORTRAN programmers. The big machines in those days had a shade over 100 kilobytes of memory and a clock rate just over 200 KHz. (Yes!) It was clear to the old timers that you couldn't afford to waste space or time running suboptimal programs. FORTRAN was an amusing little sideline to the main stream of computing. Clearly, you had to wallow in the full complexity of assembly language if you wanted to write serious programs.

Nevertheless, FORTRAN flourished and assembly-language programming began its long, steady decline. True, FORTRAN left you little spare capacity. But it was *fast enough*. FORTRAN made computers available to a large group of new users — scientists and engineers who didn't have the time or the inclination to become assembly-language experts. As a result, computers got used more and the business of making those computers flourished.

That led the computer makers to design ever more ambitious FORTRAN compilers. (There was no separate software industry to speak of in those days. A hardware vendor provided an operating system and compilers at no extra cost.) FORTRAN II gave way to FORTRAN IV and its many variants. You could specify device-independent I/O, even asynchronous I/O. That led to richer job-control language (JCL) to tailor each execution of your FORTRAN program to a different set of I/O devices.

It wasn't long before all those scientists and engineers began to get a bit off balance. If you think assembly-language programming is bad, try coding JCL. Engineers walked around with little packets of JCL cards in their shirt pockets. These provided the incantations needed to run a FORTRAN program and print the results sensibly. Some shops even employed full-time JCL programmers (magicians) who made such talismans for the uninitiated.

Then IBM introduced System/360. It blended the technology, and culture, of both scientific and commercial programming into one heady stew. (Other companies did too — I cite OS/360 only as a leading example.) JCL got even more complex and the underlying OS ballooned. Running FORTRAN II on an IBM 7090, you gave up about 500 bytes of storage to the operating system. (Yes!) Under OS/360, you could kiss good-by hundreds of kilobytes of precious storage. (I use "precious" literally — memory cost tens of thousands of times more then than it does now.)

Still, the marketplace seemed to be demanding ever more complex operating systems and programming languages. How else to meet the needs of a growing and ever more diverse constituency? Each new software release offered still more complexity to provide still more ways to use these wondrous new computers.

Then along came the minicomputer. Scientists and engineers gave a shout of glee. Here, once again, were computers they could understand. No ornate operating systems or multiple languages. You got a toy OS, an assembler, and a FORTRAN compiler. An individual user could conceive, and even write, all the software for a nontrivial application.

Not only that, a single department or laboratory could afford its own computer. You could dedicate a machine to acquiring data or running an experiment. And it was all under the control of a handful of non experts. (Well, quite a few of us scientist types did get tainted with a love for writing complex computer programs.) No need to depend on the comp center staff — either the techies or the bureaucrats.

Of course, the comp center staff sneered at minicomputers. The big machines in those days were growing ever more powerful. Some even offered a megabyte or more of storage. (Yes!) It was clear to the main framers that you couldn't afford to waste your time playing with minicomputers. They were an amusing little sideline to the main stream of computing. Clearly, you had to wallow in the full complexity of a main-frame operating system if you wanted to write serious programs.

Nevertheless, the minicomputer flourished and the main frame began its long, steady decline. True, those smaller machines had little spare capacity. But they were *fast enough*. The minicomputer made computers available to a large group of new users — scientists and engineers who wanted to do hands-on computing, either interactive, embedded, or real time. As a result, computers got used more and the business of making computers flourished.

That led the computer makers to design ever more ambitious minicomputer systems. (There was still no separate software industry to speak of.) The simple operating systems gave way to clones of their main-frame predecessors, albeit somewhat scaled down. You could run COBOL programs, even specify multiple processes that cooperated or competed for the limited shared resources. That led to richer system interfaces to invoke all these wondrous new services.

It wasn't long before all those scientists and engineers began to get a bit off balance. If you think writing for a main-frame operating system is bad, try working with a cheap imitation. Engineers accumulated shelves full of manuals. These provided the incantations needed to run a FORTRAN program and print the result sensibly (if only you knew where to look). Some shops even employed full-time systems programmers (magicians) who made such talismans for the uninitiated.

Then Digital introduced VAX/VMS. It brought the technology, and culture, of both scientific and commercial programming into the world of minicomputers. (Other companies did too — I cite VMS only as a leading example.) The system interface got even more complex (if somewhat more orderly) and the underlying OS ballooned. Running a program under DEC's RT-11 operating system, you gave up about 2 kilobytes of storage. (Yes!) Under VMS, you could kiss good-by hundreds of kilobytes of precious storage. (Now "precious" means that memory cost only hundreds of times more then than it does currently.)

Still, the marketplace seemed to be demanding ever more complex minicomputer operating systems. How else to meet the needs of a growing and ever more diverse constituency? Each new software release offered still more complexity to provide still more ways to use these wondrous new computers.

Then along came the UNIX operating system. Scientists and engineers gave a shout of glee. Here, once again, was a system they could understand. You got a trim little operating system, a C compiler, and a set of killer little programs called software tools. An individual user could conceive, and even write, all the software for an extremely nontrivial application.

Not only that, a small group of people could concoct all its own software. You could write simple C programs, even shell scripts, to do things undreamed of with other systems. And it was all under the control of a handful of non experts. (Well, quite a few of us had to learn how to become UNIX system administrators.) No need to depend on the arcane knowledge of a bunch of minicomputer systems programmers — or the latest whims of the vendor.

Of course, the minicomputer vendors sneered at UNIX. The vendor-supplied operating systems in those days were growing ever more powerful. Some even began to rival main-frame systems in capabilities — not to mention storage requirements. It was clear to the minicomputer vendors that you couldn't afford to waste your time playing with UNIX. It was an amusing little sideline to the main stream of computing. Clearly, you had

to wallow in the full complexity of a minicomputer operating system if you
wanted to write serious programs.

Nevertheless, UNIX flourished and the minicomputer systems began
their long, steady decline. True, those early UNIX systems were primitive
in many important ways. But they were *sophisticated enough*. UNIX made
computers available to a large group of new users — scientists and engineers who wanted to develop powerful software applications without
becoming steeped in the arcana of any particular set of hardware. As a
result, computers got used more and the business of making computers
flourished.

That led the UNIX folks to add ever more elaborate capabilities to the
system. (There was now a software subindustry separate from the
hardware vendors.) The simple operating system gave way to clones of its
main-frame and minicomputer predecessors, albeit made somewhat more
elegant. UNIX accreted oodles of specialized utilities, in addition to its more
general software tools. Each system call, it seemed, needed an extra pa-
rameter or two to give it greater power. Some just couldn't be extended
enough. That led to even more system calls to invoke all sorts of wondrous
new services.

It wasn't long before all those scientists and engineers began to get a bit
off balance. Slowly, UNIX began to look like all those complex minicomputer operating systems that it had worked so hard to displace. The
three-ring binder no longer served as an adequate repository of all UNIX
documentation. Engineers accumulated shelves full of manuals. Worse,
UNIX shops started requiring experts. These provided the incantations
needed to run a simple C program and print the result to the proper printer
on the network. Some shops even employed full-time gurus (magicians)
who interpreted the entrails of system crashes and made talismans for the
uninitiated.

Then the UNIX community discovered "open systems." These were an
excuse to dump even more complexity into a once graceful little operating
system. Naturally, multiple groups are vying for the right to define what
constitutes openness. (The group in charge of an open system can thus
better close the UNIX market to its competitors.) These groups compete by
adding complex subsystems to UNIX at a prodigious rate. Presumably, the
open system with the greatest potential for doing something, and the least
likelihood of doing anything, will win. (But please don't think I'm biased
against this way of defining the platform we're all supposed to use for
writing future applications.)

While UNIX was evolving along these lines, along came the personal
computer. Everybody gave a shout of glee. Here is a system that
many people can understand. You get a tiny little operating system and a
handful of utilities. Your neighborhood software store will gladly sell you

lots more programs ready to run. If you want, you can even buy a C compiler and make your own without a lot of fuss.

Not only that, the computer is all yours. No need to compete with other time-sharing users for response time and disk space. Each individual or small group can tailor the hardware, software, and data storage to meet individual requirements. No need to depend on the whims and policies of a bureaucracy in charge of a shared resource.

Of course, those bureaucracies initially sneered at the personal computer. Serious computers require serious organizations to manage them. You can't expect individuals to make sensible decisions about what to buy or how to use computers properly. The personal computer was initially viewed as an amusing little sideline to the main stream of computing. Clearly, you had to wallow in the full complexity of computer arcana if you wanted to make adequate use of a computer.

Nevertheless, the personal computer has flourished and central control over computers has seen a long and steady decline. True, those early personal computers were primitive in many important ways. But they were *sophisticated enough.* The personal computer has made computing available to an enormous group of new users — ordinary civilians who have practically any kind of data to process from words to numbers to pictures. As a result, computers are getting used more and more every day and the business of making computers continues to flourish.

That has led the makers of personal computers, both hardware and software, to add ever more elaborate capabilities to their systems. The simple early operating systems have given way to graphical interfaces, multiprocessing, and networking. In some ways, that has made computers easier to use. But it has certainly made them much harder to program. It takes far more than a C compiler and a 200-page MS-DOS manual to turn out a state-of-the-art application these days.

I think it is fair to characterize many programmers of personal computers these days as being more than a bit off balance. The complexity you have to master to write for a windowing system is staggering. A typical graphical user interface has nearly a thousand services. These manipulate dozens of different data types. You can use an object-oriented language to structure this complexity to some extent, but it's still there. You have a lot of semantics to master to perform even the simplest of operations.

Still, the marketplace seems to be demanding even more complexity. Multimedia throws sound, animation, and tighter clocking into the stew. Pen-based systems and optical character recognition are growing in importance. Each such subsystem demands its own specialized interface. Where will it end?

I don't have a specific answer to that question, but I can make a rough guess. Look back over the cycles of complexity I just recited. They are but a few of a dozen or so I have witnessed in my adult career. You can probably sketch similar cycles in the development of computer chips, architecture, or programming languages. All follow a similar pattern.

Start with a simple design. If it's a good design, it will flourish. As it flourishes, it inevitably becomes embellished. That's the way most people think to improve on something they like. It seldom occurs to such people that the goodness of a design may stem from its elegance. Embellish it enough and the elegance gets lost somewhere along the way. Beyond that point, the original design can no longer be rescued. It takes a new departure, with a clean new design, to begin the cycle over again.

The trouble is, few of us can see that wonderful new design before it's ready to be born. (A lucky few of us can recognize it for something new and important when it finally does arrive.) We have to keep embellishing what we have to find out what works and what doesn't. Given enough experience, some insightful person will then give us that new departure. (And those heavily invested in the current complexity will assuredly pooh-pooh the new design as trivial and unimportant to the main stream of computing.)

Plus ça change, plus c'est la même chose. □

*A**fterword: I intended this essay as a ray of hope for today's programmers. It seems like the accretion of complexity will never end. Only a faith in historical cycles, and our limited tolerance for complexity, gives us hope that the accretion will become more tolerable. Note that past complexity never goes away. It just gets packaged better, so we can ignore most of it even as we profit from it.*

22 Pity the Typist

$\mathfrak{I}$ am a touch typist. My typing rate is a steady 50 words per minute on human-oriented text. For computer programs, data files, and other arcana, it is naturally much lower. Even for this sort of gibberish, however, my fingers still know mostly where to go. Or at least they want to think they do.

A pet peeve of mine for several decades is the whimsical attitude that hardware designers take toward keyboard layouts. (For my gripes about tactile feedback from keyboards, see "Programming on Purpose: Warm Fuzzies," *Computer Language*, October 1990.) They act as though there is something creative, perhaps even decorative, in a novel layout of keys. Sure, most of them (but not all) preserve the standard **QWERTY** layout of the letters. It's all those odd keys that computers delight in that keep us on a semipermanent scavenger hunt.

I suspect that your average keyboard designer is a bad typist. Most hardware types I've observed at the keyboard favor the Columbus method — discover a key and land on it. A few have their typing done by that most famous of typists, **mtf** — "my two fingers." Seldom do you see an engineer engage multiple fingers and thumbs.

How else do you explain all those new palmtops with keys that are:

- in alphabetical order
- in **QWERTY** order but with rows misaligned
- too cramped or unresponsive for any approach but Columbus or **mtf**

Much as I love my Compaq laptop, I'd also love to write essays like this one on a palmtop computer. But I won't not until the designers meet us trained typists halfway.

$\mathfrak{T}$he problem goes back a long way, of course. Christopher Sholes made the first practical typewriter back in 1867. It is now well known that the current **QWERTY** layout was adopted as a mechanical compromise. Seems those first typists were getting ahead of the hardware and repeatedly jamming the keys. The **QWERTY** layout is intentionally suboptimal to slow us all down. Over a century later, the form has long outlived its original function. In fact, it now interferes with the push to *improve* typing speed.

You probably also know that better layouts exist. The Dvorak keyboard has been shown repeatedly to be more sensible from a human standpoint. People can type noticeably faster with a Dvorak layout than with **QWERTY**, all other things being equal. Nevertheless, Dvorak remains a hobby horse ridden by only a dedicated and tiny minority.

I know of no better example of standards at work than typewriter keyboards. Here is living proof that a standard doesn't have to be technically superior to endure. It merely has to be *good enough*. That's always a hard lesson for us techies to swallow.

The Royal portable I hauled off to college differed only in insignificant ways from the mechanical clunkers of the nineteenth century. (Yes, they still made mechanical typewriters in the 1960s.) It had few punctuation keys that could be misplaced, at least compared to your typical computer keyboard of today. As I recall, the layout bore a remarkable resemblance to the typical IBM typewriter keyboard of the day.

We have IBM to thank for most of the stability, and sensibility, of typewriter keyboards. That company certainly understands the principle of *good enough* better than most enterprises. And every once in a while, IBM even unleashes some first-rate designers. They rightly dominated the office equipment marketplace for many decades. The influence of the IBM Selectric keyboard still persists well into the era of computerized word processing.

There have been a few setbacks, make no mistake. I remember when the first hobbyist keyboards appeared in the 1970s. They committed numerous barbarisms in the interest of controlling hardware costs. You could, for example, save a gate or two by shifting for the equals sign (=) instead of the plus (+). And so some folks did. (Who cares, anyway? Remember, Christopher Columbus was looking for India when he stumbled across America.)

The minicomputer vendors were hardly any better. They had bigger budgets, but no better sense of the practical. They found more places to hide the backslash (\) than you could possibly imagine. That probably was of more concern to us early UNIX types than to others. But everybody had to paw around for the more widely used control and alt shift keys.

Besides the extra shift keys, ASCII introduces over half a dozen characters not found on your Selectric golf-ball typing element. Each of these suffers the same fate as the wandering Jew who taunted Christ. They will probably not find a resting place until the Second Coming.

IBM struck again about a decade ago. The PC again showed that Big Blue could define a marketplace — and a slew of de facto standards in the bargain. Most keyboards started looking like the PC offering. My fingers began to feel at home once again. I even began to learn where to find all those new function keys and funny scrolling arrows. The PC keyboard wasn't a perfect standard, by any means, but it was *good enough*.

Then IBM introduced the "enhanced" AT keyboard. Some keys got rearranged just for the fun of it, I think. And Apple started pushing the

Macintosh. They had to prove they weren't slavishly imitating Big Blue. And Sun redefined the workstation market. Everyone knows that a workstation has different, and more serious needs, than a mere PC. Just when you thought it was safe to work on your touch-typing skills once again.

If you think I'm speaking just for the typing pool here, think again. Even people who believe that computers should talk and listen acknowledge that keyboards won't go away. We all use them to talk to a host of applications. (You can't point and click to say everything.) The more we can make our typing skills portable, and second nature, the more computers will fit smoothly into our daily activities. To the extent that computers are intimidating, their legitimate uses will remain stunted.

A particularly important application to us programmers is editing text. I have already harangued on that general topic in an earlier essay. (See "Programming on Purpose: Text Editors," *Computer Language*, May 1991.) We each form a mental model of what's happening to the text we edit. We rely on the screen display to reassure us that the text is changing the way we expect. If what we see is what we want to get, that's useful feedback. Any means is justified if we get the pattern of marks we want on screen (and later paper).

When we want to do more than generate marks, however, the job gets tougher. Not every keystroke can or should generate a printable character. We need a set of "meta keys" to give instructions instead of directly generating text. Sensible patterns of meta keystrokes constitute a language in their own right. It becomes yet another thing we need to learn as touch typists.

A typewriter has only a limited set of meta keys. You leave space between words with the space bar. You start a new line with the return key. You skip over to a tab stop with the tab key. Maybe you back up to overstrike a letter with the backspace key. You also switch between two interpretations of the keyboard by judicious use of the shift and shift-lock keys. (European typewriters also have "dead keys" to ease overstriking letters with accent marks.)

That's the document formatting language known to typists for over a century. Throw in a correcting key, or a bottle of White Out, and you've got the full set of editing commands. Not a lot to learn, but *good enough* to generate literally mountains of office correspondence over the years.

The computer has changed all that. From its earliest days, it has supported character and line deletion, usually with single-character commands. Those simple commands soon gave way to ever more complex meta-languages. At first, the editing commands consisted of printable characters. That necessitated a mode-sensitive editor. You had to make a point of switching between entering text and modifying what you'd entered. Start entering text in edit mode and the most fascinating things could happen — and often did.

So programmers began to favor modeless editors. Commandeer some keystrokes not likely to be entered by your average typist. Give each a useful meaning, and preferably one with some mnemonic value. You have three combinations of the control and alt shifts to apply to dozens of other keys, alone and shifted. The sky's the limit.

The sky, however, is no place for a touch typist. Your fingers can memorize only so many operations. If they differ between editors, you're in a bind. One response, a common one, is to stick with the editor you've learned to love, however old fashioned it becomes. Another is to learn little or nothing about the peculiarities of any one editor. However fast you type running text, you're sailing uncharted waters when you edit.

I'm pretty firmly in the second camp. I've seen too often what happens to people who master too much arcana. They become so invested in their knowledge that they resist learning anything new. I also move among various systems a lot. That keeps me from devoting much typing time to any one peculiar editor. I prefer being able to do a few simple edits rapidly to over specializing.

The WIMP interface is supposed to have fixed these problems. (*WIMP* stands for "windows, icons, menus, and pointing devices.") No funny keystrokes to memorize any more. Now you can perform natural, human-oriented operations to edit text. Everything is so intuitive that even beginners get it right. You can edit rapidly with few errors. Right?

If only that were true. What I find instead is just enough variation among text editing schemes to disrupt typing skills. Here, I use "typing" in the more general sense. It includes pointing and clicking with a mouse and navigating with cursor keys, not just striking keys on a keyboard. (Perhaps I should call it "touch mousing.")

What should the down-arrow key do, for instance? Move the cursor down to the next line, to be sure. But where on that line? If the cursor ends up within the line of text, the answer is fairly obvious. You want the cursor to stay in the same column. If it's beyond the current end of the line, however, you have to think harder. The answer you get depends on the model you assume for the displayed text.

One model is the "histogram of text." Each line has a length determined by its current contents. Position the cursor past the end of the line and it whangs back to the end. You can type trailing spaces if you want, but you can only feel them out by moving the cursor around. What goes into the file is what you type, period.

Another model is the "two-dimensional array of text." You can navigate anywhere around the array and drop new characters where you will.

Spaces presumably fill any untyped expanse of line. Similarly, trailing spaces presumably disappear when you write the file.

As you might guess, I favor the first model. The second involves too many presumptions for my deterministic tastes. Borland's Turbo C/C++ editor seems to follow the second model. It keeps dumping me in interstellar space when I navigate a source file. I find that to be odd behavior for a package that favors an economy of keystrokes.

But even within the histogram model you can find unfortunate variety. The Microsoft Windows Notepad utility whangs back to the end of the line. Then it decides that that's the column you want to be in. Windows Write has a different notion. It remembers the column you started out with, and clings to the ends of any shorter lines. I kinda prefer that behavior, but I'd rather have consistency.

I thought I'd like WinEdit. It has huge capacity, supports multiple file windows, and even searches with UNIX-like regular expressions. Then I discovered that it treats horizontal tabs as input-only characters. It writes the expanded spaces back to a file. I spent one afternoon repairing a dozen damaged files, then deleted WinEdit from my hard disk.

Of the half dozen editors I switch among, my favorite is a surprising one. Laplink Pro includes an MS-DOS-based, character-mode text editor almost as an afterthought. It has two file windows and an optional emacs-style split screen. It supports cut and paste to a clipboard as well as file merges. It is fast, has large capacity, and seldom crashes. It even counts words for me.

The author(s) of this handy editor took obvious pains to make it look like most GUI-based products. But they left out one operation. You can't specify a range of text by a mouse click, move, shift-click. You can only drag the mouse across the range. That has burned me any number of times. I now find myself avoiding the shift-click method even on editors that support it. Conditioned reflexes work both ways.

Yes, I know that some systems have style guides. They're supposed to eliminate unwanted variation among applications. Generally, they focus on the "user friendly" aspects of the WIMP interface. Less attention is paid to users who are more than naive. My experience is admittedly far broader than it is deep here. Still, I can't say I've discovered an island of sanity yet. At least not for us beleaguered touch typists. □

Afterword: There's a lot more I could say on this topic, but I've probably said enough here. If you aren't a touch typist, you encounter only a few of the problems I've harangued about. If you are, you're probably accustomed to such impediments. I just hope a few system designers (with some clout) are listening.

23 Criticism

Recently, I've been on the receiving end of a lot of criticism. That happens to all of us from time to time. Performance reviews are an inevitable part of any job. Even the president is answerable to the board of directors. And the board is answerable to the stockholders. Whatever your position in life, you can always find someone in a position to subject at least part of your behavior to critical review.

You may have seen the old cartoon of the university as a multi-story outhouse. Freshmen get the ground floor, sophs the next, and so on up the line. Professors aren't at the top, though. There are deans, trustees, then alumni. If there is a top, it is lost in the clouds. Different barnyard from the business world, but the same pecking order.

I happen to be "self employed." That doesn't make me immune to criticism, whatever you may think. It simply means that I have any number of bosses. My constituency is all the people for whom I write, edit, or give talks. Each has the opportunity, from time to time, to tell me where to get off. I may not always want to hear it, but I dare not tune it out. I ignore such information at my peril, just like everybody else.

It is unfortunate in many ways that my chosen constituency is highly technical. In principle, engineers and programmers are trained to be both analytical and rational. You'd think that techies would be just the sort of critics you need. They can provide a balanced perspective on your performance. They can focus on constructive criticism. They can distinguish objective measures from the purely subjective.

Think that and you would be wrong.

If there is a more critical group than a bunch of computer programmers, I've yet to find it. Programmers delight in finding bugs. A "bug" in the general sense can be any sort of behavior of which they disapprove. But it is not enough for a programmer to find a bug and point it out. Nosiree. That bug must be squashed once and for all.

As a consequence, programmers are not only hypercritical, they often overreact. Anything not amenable to objective measurement becomes a lightning rod for religious zealotry. Your opinion doesn't merely differ from mine, it is dangerously wrong. You are leading innocents astray with your ill-considered prattle. Shut up and go away.

I suspect there is also some truth in the nerd stereotype that the world imposes on all us techies. Many of us do indeed lack various social graces.

165

It never occurs to us to waste any air time broadcasting politeness or consideration. Our job is to deliver the unvarnished truth (as we see it). Leave it to the touchy-feely types to wallow in supportive blather.

It doesn't help that a technical education tends to be highly competitive. Few schools give brownie points for helping out fellow students (sadly enough). Even working in groups gets short shrift — until you get in the real world, that is. Little wonder that most of us are better at slicing up our fellow techies than helping them out.

I first became deeply aware of this aberration when I began attending standards meetings. I was appalled at the emotional frenzies stirred up by the most abstract and equivocal of issues. (I was chagrined when I got caught up in the emotional fray myself.) In the heat of the moment, the debate sometimes got personal. I once had to leave the room when someone accused me of deliberately lying to make my point. (I can indeed lie. Otherwise, being truthful is more a handicap than a virtue to me. But I save my lies for more important matters than mere programming language standards.)

It wasn't long before I formulated a basic law of technical debate — the strength of a techie's emotional attachment to a position varies inversely as the amount of objective evidence supporting that position. When emotions run high enough, the distinction between personalities and abstract ideas evaporates.

I saw a similar insensitivity while selling computer software. One man approached me at a trade show and smiled politely. He asked me why my company produced such mediocre software that was so full of bugs. He could have been asking after the health of a mutual acquaintance in the same tone of voice. I'm sure he was unaware of the gross unfairness of his characterization. He was certainly unaware of the personal hurt he caused.

If that were an isolated incident, it would be but a sad anecdote. Unfortunately, I had such encounters regularly. People who have never written a major piece of software, or brought it to market, are quick to make glib pronouncements. Tell me what you want as a consumer, by all means. That's your right and you honor me with your marketing data. But don't make offhand value judgments about a process you don't understand.

You can imagine how an olympic runner feels when a pudgy journalist asks her why she only came in second.

I have read reviews of my products that border on libel. To this day, I don't know what puts reviewers into an occasional feeding frenzy. I can tell you that the effect is personally painful. It can also hurt sales severely. I believe reviewers have a particular obligation to criticize wisely and fairly. That makes the pain of a bad review all the worse to me.

I notice that anonymity of any sort makes it easier for many to be critical. It offers an emotional distance that can be pernicious. Electronic mail seems to bring out the worst in some people, for example. The art of "flaming" is now widely practiced. It's bad enough to send a rude message to another via such an anonymous channel. To flame someone on an open forum is, to me, the height of insensitivity. Yet I see it all the time.

My son just recently joined The Sierra Network. It's a nationwide gaming arena loosely akin to, say, Prodigy. People can chat by sending comments to each other a line or two at a time. I note with interest that each message you receive comes with a "complain" button. (Social note — there is no "praise" button.) It seems to have at least some tempering effect on the dialog I have observed.

I edit a monthly magazine. The publisher and I recently sat down together for our first face-to-face since I'd gone off to Australia over a year ago. I fished for a compliment or two, got none. Instead, he told me that my responses to letters were too negative, too defensive. I wasn't providing enough positive feedback to readers.

I left our interview feeling depressed. Finally it hit me. The publisher had been too negative. He didn't provide me enough positive feedback. He at least had the decency to acknowledge what happened when I pointed it out. I got the reassurance I needed.

I am a product of competitive schools and work environments, like many of you. I can dish it out with the best of them. When I get zinged, I've learned long since to stuff the hurt fast. You won't catch me betraying any weakness. The net effect is that I have spent a good part of my life walking around numb. (If you're busy not feeling pain you're also busy not feeling much anything else.)

More recently, I have learned a simple trick. If I notice that I am numb or depressed, I seldom know why. So I think back to the last time I felt good. Then I look at what happened to change my mood. Invariably, it was some assault on my ego that shut me down. Often, the assault took the form of heavy-handed criticism. (Once you acknowledge the hurt and let yourself feel it, it passes.)

The stimulus for this essay was a batch of critiques that just came in the mail. They were for a series of talks I gave at Software Development '92. Many were positive and made me feel good. Some were constructive and made me feel grateful, if a bit chagrined. A few, however, were simply backhanded slurs. The one that hurt the most characterized one of my talks as "useless." Not "useless to me," mind you. Just "useless." Given the questions and comments of others in the room, the criticism was patently untrue. At the least, it was a gross overstatement.

Now I am more self confident than the average bear. I can convince myself intellectually that this person had his or her head wedged. I can even beat down any fears that I am rationalizing away the truth. But I can't stop the remark from hurting.

The big secret is that none of us ever really grows up. Inside every adult is a little kid who wants to have fun and, above all, wants to be loved. Pretend that kid isn't there and he just gets bratty. Treat him nice and he's the wellspring of much of your happiness and spontaneity.

One of the perversions of modern society is to deny the importance of our little kids. We pretend to rational debate when our little kids are throwing mudballs. We want to cry and get officious instead. We befuddle being right or being rich with being loved.

Back in the 1930s and 1940s there was an intellectual movement called general semantics. It argued that people were captive to fantasies about the world. That made them behave irrationally and, sometimes, self destructively. You should not, for example, punch somebody in the nose just for calling you names. While there is much truth to what the semanticists said, I believe they overstated the case. It is not true that "Sticks and stones may break my bones but names will never hurt me." An important part of our existence is in that "fantasy" world of images and beliefs. Names and other words are the very stuff of our reality.

There are people and principles that I would die for. From the standpoint of personal survivor, that is simply unsane. Nevertheless, I have no interest in curing myself of such aberrations.

I am not, by the way, opposed to all forms of criticism. Quite the contrary, I believe it is absolutely necessary. Rare is the person who can see all his or her shortcomings. We all profit from feedback from those with a cooler perspective.

The little kid in me revels in unstinting praise. He wants the same absolute approval that we all deserve from our parents, just for being who we are. The adult caretaker knows better, however. Yes-men are just as unhealthy as unlimited quantities of jelly beans.

The trick of criticism lies in how you express it. You need to deliver a message that can be heard by the adult without unduly arousing the child. Fail to do so and it matters not how right you are. You fail as a critic if you fail to make a difference.

Properly packaged, criticism can be seen for the gift that it truly is. I have colleagues who critique with a scalpel in each hand. Run their gantlet and you know you've got a thing worth publishing. Their remarks don't hurt because they're uniformly constructive. (Just be warned if any of these people politely decline to offer criticism. That means they don't think it's worth the effort.)

𝕴 hope that by this point I've convinced you to be more cautious with your critical words. Zinging your friends is a hard habit to break, but it can be done. And it should be. Withholding useful advice can be just as bad. You owe it to your friends and colleagues to learn when and how to criticize.

Here are a few guidelines:

Never confuse the person with the idea. Remember that little kid inside, who wants to be liked as much as you do. There's a world of difference between "You're wrong" and "I don't agree with what you just said."

State the positive first. Emphasize what's good about another person's ideas, or what you agree with. This may seem artificial at first, at least to people outside California. But it keeps the positives from getting lost in a shouting match. And it helps everyone find the common ground that much faster.

Try to state ways to improve an idea instead of tearing it down. One way to identify constructive criticism is to first list the three most important things to keep the same. Then list the three things you'd most like to change. (I didn't say "fix," I said "change.")

Try the Hegel approach — thesis, antithesis, synthesis. Is there a positive way you can combine viewpoints that apparently conflict? This is *not* the same as compromise the way most politicians practice the art. That is more a matter of relative capitulation, with the greater victory going to the stronger or smarter party.

Be humble. If you disagree with the majority, accept the possibility that your opinion might not be as compelling as you want to believe. Each of us is entitled to a private opinion. And in a democracy, the majority is entitled to rule in most matters.

Finally, go for consensus. This is *not* the same as unanimity. A minority can go unsatisfied in a consensus if the majority agrees that it has received a fair hearing. If you are that minority, save your tantrums for issues that are truly important to you. Don't sweat the small stuff.

Follow these guidelines and you will find that you're a more agreeable person. You may even be surprised to find that you get your way more often. In a cooperative work place, that can help everyone succeed. In an intertwined economy, it can help everyone prosper. I'm not saying that a sensible use of criticism is sufficient to bringing world peace. But it is necessary. □

𝕬fterword: This was one of my more successful essays. It stimulated an outpouring of letters from readers — uniformly supportive — that convinced me I touched a nerve. Interestingly enough, it was also easy to write. I just had to assemble a number of thoughts that had long begged for expression. Evidently, many others were waiting for similar thoughts to be expressed as well.

24 Piled Higher and Deeper

It's funny how the realization creeps up on you. Just a few short years ago, my software needs were much simpler. I used a C compiler, a home-grown operating system modeled on UNIX, and a host of software tools with similar roots. The most elaborate of these tools was a document formatter, and that was certainly no more complex than the C compiler. Printers and terminals were all character oriented, so I had no need for graphics software or pointing devices.

I wrote a large fraction of that software myself. What I didn't write was developed by other programmers in my company. True, one or two machines ran licensed copies of UNIX. Beyond that, however, we used next to no commercial software. And we managed to get quite a lot of work done, thank you.

One reason why we used so little outside software should be obvious. It simply wasn't available. UNIX is still a Balkanized marketplace, spread across multiple computer architectures. Only a few platforms are sufficiently numerous to support volume pricing of shrink-wrapped software. Before the advent of Sun workstations and the Intel 386, there were next to none. Even today, you often pay a premium for software that runs under UNIX.

I anguished about this situation when I struck off on my own. It didn't take me long to decide to switch to IBM PCs and compatibles. I hated to give up multi-tasking and UNIX-style command language. And MS-DOS is not a dream system by any standards, even for refugees from CP/M. But the economic payoff was unbeatable. I could actually buy software at reasonable prices instead of writing my own.

The first thing I learned was the importance of buying a PC with a "full" 640-kilobyte memory. Software had just escaped the shackles of the CP/M 64-kilobyte limit. (The PDP-11 was only slightly better in supporting separate 64-kilobyte code and data segments.) Pent up demand for larger address space sent programmers into a feeding frenzy. Overlaid programs spread out through memory. Pipelines got merged into monoliths. A mere factor of ten increase in memory size evaporated like morning dew.

Still, the kind of software I wanted to buy in those days fit comfortably in 640 kilobytes. Competing for that space was MS-DOS itself and any special device drivers, but that wasn't so bad. I soon learned to avoid "terminate and stay resident" (TSR) utilities. They ate memory like candy, fought civil wars with each other, and sooner or later did something surprising and not nice to my valuable data. In fact, the only problem software I had to live with was the PC-based games my son Geoffrey insisted on buying. They inevitably pushed to the limits memory capacity, CPU speed, and any notions of portability across PC clones.

It is now well known that the notorious 640-kilobyte boundary was set rather arbitrarily. The original PC engines, the Intel 8088 and 8086, could address 1,024 kilobytes with ease. IBM simply set aside a generous upper third of the address space for assorted ROMs and memory-mapped I/O controllers. Such spendthrift designs are hardly uncommon in our business, but they still cause grief. (See **Pla87**.) Incredible quantities of ingenuity go into work arounds for such limitations, rather than into the applications themselves.

In some ways this is simply a quibble, however. An extra 384 kilobytes would often be nice, but it's only a small percentage improvement. An application that needs more than a megabyte is still hurting. You're back in the world of overlays and pipelined execution. Or some other trickery. Burdened as it was with unexpected success, the PC marketplace grew with only a minimum of planning. People attacked the problem of limited memory on multiple fronts.

One approach was to offset the Intel 8088 limitations with a kind of bank-switching scheme. You can install additional *expanded* memory that is visible through a narrow window in the upper 384 kilobytes. Applications equipped to take advantage of expanded memory can manage this window to scribble throughout megabytes of additional storage. It ain't a flat address space, but it still beats swapping overlays on and off a disk.

Still another approach came for free with the Intel 80286 and later more powerful upgrades to the original 8088 and 8086. These newer CPUs could directly address 16 megabytes or more of *extended* memory. It is almost as easy to address as that first megabyte, except that you must also muck with a separate set of memory-management registers.

I won't go into all the intricacies. Many of you live with them more intimately than I ever want to. Suffice it to say here that the IBM PC architecture started out rococo. It has since grown more ornate. Trust me when I tell you that extended memory is generally better than expanded. But that doesn't stop software developers from using both with seeming whimsy, at least to this bystander.

I started caring about this stuff when I found I couldn't buy a C compiler that fit in 640 kilobytes anymore. Then I started typesetting with Ventura Publisher and kissed small computers good-by forever. Suddenly, I was spending days reading about memory boards and memory-management software. Next thing I knew, I was anguishing over how to partition memory between expanded and extended. (This was at a time when memory was selling at $600 per megabyte.) Enough was enough.

Programmers know well what to do when you have too much software. You add more software to manage the overload. Then you add still more software to monitor the manager and to optimize it. It's just like the old joke about college degrees. We all know what B.S. stands for (and it's not necessarily "Bachelor of Science.") M.S. is simply "More of the Same." And Ph.D. stands for "Piled Higher and Deeper." Willy nilly, I was starting to earn advanced degrees in PC-compatible software.

𝕸y first attempt at controlling the memory eaters was a neat little product called Quarterdeck DesqView. It has the gall to turn a PC into a multi-tasking system. Given all the dirty tricks that MS-DOS and various applications play, this is seemingly futile. Managing a birthday party for seven-year-olds is civilized by comparison. Nevertheless, DesqView can be amazingly robust. I used it for some time with good success. In fact, the only serious problems I had with it came when I tried to run some of Geoffrey's games. They pushed the state of the art much too hard to cohabit with any software as responsible as DesqView.

In the end, I abandoned most of DesqView. The part I kept is its memory manager, called QEMM. On a sufficiently powerful CPU, it can blur the distinction between expanded and extended memory. I still use QEMM386, Version 6.02, because it makes my life simpler. Quarterdeck can keep trying to outsmart all that nasty hardware and software. I gladly pay for the extra RAM that QEMM386 inhabits so long as it keeps winning those battles for me. (That's easier to say now that memory is selling for $50 per megabyte, of course.)

In fact, the only serious problem I've had lately with QEMM386 is caused by one of Geoffrey's newest video games. Seems ULTIMA VII insists on using its own memory manager. (It's called Voodoo, for what that's worth.) I spent an evening crafting a special boot diskette to eliminate all sorts of useful software I normally run. Even then, ULTIMA VII crashes on our old Compaq Deskpro (and many other machines, I'm told). Not a wise marketing choice.

𝕾o why did I abandon DesqView? Mostly because Microsoft finally got Windows more or less right. I needed Windows to run Corel Draw. And I began acquiring a taste for the bit-mapped graphics interface and pointing devices. When Ventura Publisher finally came out in a Windows edition, I figured what the hell. It was time to make Windows my principal base of operations.

In the end, it came down to power politics. Quarterdeck can fight the good fight for years to come. I'm sure they'll keep solving problems about as fast as hardware and software types keep making new ones for their product. Some vendors even make an effort to maintain compatibility with

DesqView. But herein lies the difference. You can be sure that *all* vendors will work hard to maintain compatibility with Windows. (I'm certainly not a fan of "might makes right." But I still carry an AT&T calling card.)

Next thing I knew, I was trucking around nearly 40 megabytes of software. That got me Windows running with QEMM386, and all the utilities that come with Windows for openers. Throw in Ventura Publisher, Corel Draw, and hundreds of assorted fonts, and you're talking serious disk real estate. (I don't even count the megabytes of games that magically accrete on any system that runs Windows.)

I should also point out that Windows applications make reasonable use of extended memory. That's yet another way to blur the 640-kilobyte boundary. Of course, that boundary is still there. Windows itself needs a reasonable amount of lower memory to work properly. You also want lots of lower memory so that MS-DOS sessions work decently under Windows. Still, you do make better use of extended memory. So much so that you have to keep buying more. My laptops have gone from 3.5 megabytes to 6, then to a current 10 megabytes because Windows enjoys using memory so much. At today's prices, I guess you can call that progress. In fact, the only problem I've found is with some of Geoffrey's video games. Either they don't cohabit well with Windows or they need the last ounce of memory when running in an MS-DOS session.

The past year has seen the growth of yet another pernicious trend, however. No longer do applications gobble a megabyte or two of disk space. Now each one sprawls over *ten to 40 megabytes*. The worst offenders in my little backwater are the latest C/C++ compiler packages. Each comes with oodles of libraries — for Windows and MS-DOS, for every conceivable memory model. They also have integrated environments, interactive debuggers, and special interfaces of all descriptions. (Seldom do the vendors provide clear guides to pruning this largess.) My latest book project requires that I exercise all the popular compiler packages. But I keep running out of room on my tiny little 120-megabyte disk!

My first response was, you guessed it, to buy more software. I installed Stacker on my laptop, but only after reading half a dozen reassuring reviews. Yes, it really does take good care of your data. Yes, it really does double your disk space (essentially) with no cost in performance. Trade off just a bit more RAM (and money) and you can pack ten pounds in a five pound sack. In fact, the only problem I've found with Stacker is with some of Geoffrey's video games. The latest ones come with ten or more megabytes of *precompressed* files. Often, Stacker can only compress them another five or ten per cent. (And ULTIMA VII, naturally, will have nothing to do with Stacker.)

Stacker bought me some breathing space, but at a price. I now carried around much too much software to back up easily. Diskettes were out of the question. I have tried cartridge tapes in the past, with mixed success. What I really wanted was a removable cartridge disk drive.

 took two laptops to Australia last year and a docking station that worked with both. While there, I bought a 44-megabyte Syquest cartridge drive that plugged into the docking station. That would have been ideal, except that the system never got to working reliably. In the end, I sent back the Syquest drive and sold the smaller laptop and docking station. Waiting at home was my old Compaq Deskpro 386. It looked like a better host for a cartridge drive. And Syquest was now offering an 88-megabyte version. So I crossed my fingers and bought the newer drive. After a few initial flakies, it has proved to be about as robust as I could hope for.

So I put up the latest versions of Windows, QEMM386, and Stacker on the Deskpro to make it a decent backup machine. The only problem was, my wife Tana decided that the Deskpro was now a usable machine. She took it over to do our accounting with Quicken and her own work with Microsoft Word. Now my problem was one of logistics. Periodically, I had to schlep the laptop from my office to Tana's. Once there, Laplink Pro makes it a breeze to copy files from laptop to cartridge disk. But I still found myself slopping compilers and book images all over hell. And Tana found herself competing for disk space with Geoffrey, who keeps buying ever larger video games.

I anguished for a spell, then capitulated. It was past time that we installed a network in the house. It was also past time that we bought the latest and greatest in PCs. These days, that translates to a 50 MHz 80486 with an EISA bus, a 320-megabyte drive, a super high-speed modem, etc, etc. I figured I could store my compilers on the 486 and ship data around the house on the network. Tana figured that Geoffrey would naturally gravitate to the most powerful computer in the house and leave her alone. Geoffrey figured that a 486 would make an adequate starting point for a serious computer. (He's been eyeing games that need a CD-ROM and a heavy-duty sound card.)

Only trouble is, the network software also eats RAM. You try to cram all the pieces into the upper 384 kilobytes, but they don't always fit. (Remember all those ROMs and device registers.) What doesn't fit steals space from the lower 640 kilobytes. And that's where we came in, if you recall.

 nstalling that network makes a story unto itself. (See "Programming on Purpose: Through the Grapevine," *Computer Language,* October 1992.) For now, I'll end this saga with a few simple observations:

Complexity breeds complexity. Much of the software I now load every day is there to do battle with overly complex hardware. Still more does battle with the complex software that has gone before. Rarely does any improvement lead to less software.

The more flavors of storage you have, the more opportunities you have to run out of something. My computers all have lower memory, upper memory, extended memory, and disks. (They could also have expanded memory, but I don't let them.) Each causes a different set of problems. Most solutions steal from one resource to feed another.

Finally, **there is no such thing as enough computer for an ambitious and resourceful twelve-year-old who loves video games.** □

Afterword: You might look on this essay as a continuation of an earlier one on growing complexity. (See **Essay 21: The Cycle of Complexity**.*) Like all good tongue-in-cheek humor, it is more than half serious.*

I can report that all this hardware and software has been working fine. Tana insisted on her own 486 laptop, so the Deskpro has reverted to being a general utility machine. On the other hand, Geoffrey has tightened his grip on the most powerful machine. And his games keep getting bigger.

25 Lawyers

Don't get your hopes up. This essay is *not* going to be a pastiche of lawyer jokes. (I do have some humdingers, though.) It's not even a diatribe on the evils of unbridled litigation. (But feed me two martinis and you'll hear all you ever need on that topic as well.) Think of it more as a user's guide to legal services in the computing profession.

When I started this series of essays almost six and a half years ago, I planned to talk about program design methods. I did so primarily for the first year or so. Then I succumbed to an overwhelming urge and wrote an essay on ethics. (See **Essay 1: Honestly Now**.) I have since wandered farther and farther afield. I still cover technical issues of interest to programmers. But I am just as likely to discuss matters of business, culture, or personal growth.

Believe it or not, all these essays have a common theme. Developing software for computers is a nontrivial enterprise. It differs from other professions in important ways. It endeavors to control more complexity than any other undertaking I know. And, despite legitimate criticism, it has been remarkably successful at building on its earlier accomplishments.

The software business has also become a generator of considerable wealth. You can try to capture some of that wealth, just watch it go by, or get screwed out of it. I find no particular virtue or vice in any of those postures. But I favor those who would be captains of their souls. Whatever you do, do it with malice aforethought. In particular, if you write computer programs, then program on purpose.

Complexity and cash make a heady brew. It attracts sharks. Even the nicest people get a little strange when the sums get serious. And software is so hard to protect from thievery. That's why it's important for you to delimit clear boundaries. Employees and contractors need to know who owns the fruits of their labors. Customers need to know what they bought and what they can do with it. Competitors need to know what is proprietary and what is public domain.

That's where the lawyers come in. It's their job to give advice and to make paper. The advice should warn you when you start to swim outside the shark nets. Or when you're leaving blood in the water. (Sorry for the raw images — that's what a year of living on a beach in Australia does to your imagination.) The paper should protect you from your own stupidity.

Or from predators who walk on two legs. (More than one three-piece suit hides a dorsal fin.)

Lawyers should take a more aggressive role only when you screw up. Annoy someone else enough and you've got a lawsuit on your hands. Then you need *lots* of advice and paper, not to mention lots of hours of your precious time briefing lawyers and reviewing those stacks of paper. You may as well hand your Day Timer over to the legal department. Even if you don't end up in court, you can kiss good-by enough time, money, and psychic energy to renovate downtown Newark.

Americans spend altogether too much time and money on lawyers. We all know that. But you shouldn't blame the lawyers completely. Sure, some of them instigate unnecessary litigation. And they all have a vested interest in playing Let's You and Him Fight. But they wouldn't get away with it if the demand wasn't there.

To me, it's much like blaming drug dealers for the vast demand that exists for drugs. Bleach is bad for you too, but you don't see too many jerks flogging quart bottles outside school yards. Nobody wants the stuff, except to make sweat socks whiter. Sadly, *lots* of people, in and out of school, feel the need to curdle their brains on a regular basis. Decrease that need and your friendly neighborhood pusher will soon switch to another nefarious trade.

The American love affair with litigation predates its drug habit by well over a century. I learned this fascinating tidbit on one of my visits to Sturbridge Village in southern Massachusetts. Sturbridge is a working recreation of a generic New England town from the early 1800s. Seems the early United States set great store by lawyers and judges. After all, this was a nation of laws, and the law was supposed to be the impartial arbiter of social conflicts. So people took their squabbles to the town lawyer, and the local judge, at the least excuse.

Sound familiar? Well, it isn't. The practice of law differs fundamentally between then and now. In those simpler times, you made your case, got a judgment, and lived with it. Delays were less likely and appeals were much rarer. Neglecting the inevitable pockets of corruption among judges, you can say that the system basically worked as intended.

Today, the system has been largely perverted. Delays, injunctions, and other pretrial maneuvers let people with money intimidate those without. It is the long pending *threat* of a trial that wears down many a party with a legitimate case. The trial itself becomes an exercise in trickery and obfuscation. Seldom is the race to the swift or the battle to the strong. Instead, time and chance happeneth to them all. And both time and chance are bad business investments in this arena.

If it were done when 'tis done, then 'twere well it were done quickly —
to steal from Shakespeare as well as the Bible. But nothing happens quickly
in the legal process. And nothing is ever done when 'tis done. There are
appeals, counter claims, and no end of motions. Once again, the party who
can afford legions of lawyers has the intrinsic advantage.

If enough money is at stake, most managers dare not stop the legal
process until all avenues have been exhausted. Better to win a Pyrrhic
victory and keep your job, or go down fighting with the stockholders'
money. In either case, you can always move on to the next company if you
don't like what's left of the one you're nominally defending.

That's why I feel that an excess of lawyers is a symptom, not a cause. It's
the managers who start fights and who keep them going. Too often, they
defer to legal advice to the detriment of the enterprise because that is safer
for their short-term goals. Or worse, they get caught up in being right and
lose all business perspective. (I won't even discuss the endemic lack of
ethics or sense of social responsibility. That's a topic for another diatribe.)

So let's pretend that you don't want to get eaten alive by legal fees and
follies. We will also pretend that you are fairly honest and plan to run a
legitimate business within the letter and spirit of the law. (That's actually a
necessary attribute of any long-term business, but you'll never convince
the weasels of the world.) How then do you keep a high-tech business such
as computer software well clear of the shoals of litigation?

It's not as hard as you might think. (Of course, I speak as one who has
pissed away a large fraction of a million dollars over the past decade on
legal fees that I should have avoided. Who are you going to believe, me or
the guy who's never had to kick himself?) Just remember a few simple
principles when you deal with lawyers.

Principle: **Lawyers do law, you do the business.** If you get nothing else
out of this essay, hang onto this principle. It is the one I find least
understood among techies. Even business types lose track of it altogether
too often.

The problem begins when you ask a lawyer for advice. It may concern
a single business deal. Or you may be devising licensing terms to offer all
comers. What you want is terms that are attractive enough to meet customer needs. They must also be safe enough to ensure that you stay in
business. In either event, you must steer a narrow course.

On the one side, you can fail to protect your own interest. That may cost
you ownership of your intellectual property. Or it may leave you open to
large and growing liabilities. Whether revenues go down or expenses go
up, you go out of business when the profits disappear.

On the other side, you can fail to be competitive. Your customers may
find your licensing terms too arbitrary or restrictive. Or a competitor may

be willing to settle for fewer protections. Whether you're an ambitious tortoise or a reluctant hare, you can lose the race.

Lawyers are most comfortable helping tortoises thicken their shells. Partly that is their training. They are taught to write ironclad language, then dig a moat and throw in a couple of guard dogs for good measure. It is a rare lawyer who meditates long upon the ways of the rabbit. There are too many risks involved when your only defense is staying light and moving fast. But that is the essence of good business. You have limited windows of opportunity and limited resources to pursue them. You must move fast and get a good return on your investment. Otherwise, you'll lose out sooner or later to someone who can do more with less.

The worst lawyer I ever met, at least for giving business advice, believed in the bogey man. Ask him whether a course was prudent and he would dredge up the most outlandish dangers you could imagine. He delighted in fashioning protections against the least likely of occurrences. Of course, he did so on his client's nickel. And he always left you feeling like you were on the verge of being sued by IBM and the Justice Department, in tandem.

The best lawyer I ever met, at least in the same sense, understood the distinction between law and business. He would tell you the most probable risks and the worst-case exposure you had to plan for. He would point out the place where extra legal protection began to cost substantially more than the likely savings. And he tried to leave you with the kind of protections developed by IBM for their own enterprises.

Most lawyers, naturally, fall in the vast middle ground. Just know that typical legal advice errs on the conservative side. The next principle explains why.

principle: **Lawyers can't win.** Let's say that a corporate lawyer encourages a bit of risk taking. If all goes well, the business types will pat themselves on the back for being daring enough to take that advice. If the company loses in any way, however, guess who gets the blame.

A conservative stance is much easier for a lawyer to defend. That's the prudent course, and a lawyer's job is to preach prudence. You can't blame Legal if the customer balks at the terms. Everyone knows that customers demand the sky. Someone has to look out for the best interests of the company.

Of course, Marketing doesn't see it that way. They are convinced that they can sell anything, if only the engineers stop nattering about irrelevant performance limitations and the lawyers stop insulting the customers. And guess who's better represented at the next meeting of the board of directors. You can bet that the case for the lawyers won't be as persuasive as for those who make the *real* profits.

Combining these two principles puts you back in the driver's seat. Stop trying to get good business advice from the lawyers you consult. They don't often think that way. More to the point, they don't dare give advice based on sound business principles. Accept the fact that lawyers can only give you legal advice. You must take the responsibility for interpreting it and acting on it as you see fit.

You can gripe if a lawyer fails to apprise you of a legal risk. You have no gripe if you fail to act on it. You also have no gripe if you act so conservatively that you queer the business. Use the lawyers where they're useful. Otherwise, run the business yourself.

Principle: **Lawyers talk to lawyers, you talk to people.** I cringe whenever I get a call or a visit from a lawyer acting on behalf of another client. That's because I know that much will get lost between me and the client. It doesn't matter whether I'm buying or selling. In either case, I can expect to waste time and money better spent otherwise.

Lawyers have their own ways of proceeding — and their own goals. For the reasons I cited above, these often interfere with the business at hand. However many legalisms must be hammered out for a given deal to go down, you don't want to let them set the initial agenda. When and if you have a good business deal, you can then generate the paper to match.

Good lawyers know this and stay out of the way. They enter the negotiations only when the other side gets their lawyers involved. Then lawyers talk to lawyers, to make paper that both sides can agree on. But the business terms are the province of the business decision makers. They must talk to each other. If they hide behind lawyers, it's probably because some of them are cowardly or insecure. Possibly, one or more participants don't want the deal to happen at all. So they egg the lawyers on until somebody (inevitably) queers things.

Principle: **Lawyers should keep you out of court, not in it.** A popular myth is that a good contract lays the groundwork for a successful court case. Your lawyers are supposed to rig things so that you will win, at least on all the important points. At least so the theory goes. But that is about as far from the truth as you can get.

First of all, no deal of any significance can survive without a fair measure of good will. (I might exclude certain drug deals, but just barely.) Both sides need some assurance that the other party is acting mostly in good faith, if only out of "enlightened self interest." (That's "selfishness" translated into 1990s double speak.) A contract full of gotchas is not a good foundation on which to build such faith.

Second and more important, a contract should not be written for the eyes of a judge or jury. Consider, if it's clear to both parties who will win and who will lose a court case, the case will never end up in court. The stuff of litigation is ambiguity. Only when both sides can delude themselves into thinking that each can win do they end up squaring off in court. Then the air fills with conflicting interpretations and counter charges of bad faith.

A lawyer's job is to make paper that is as clear as possible to all concerned. Legalisms should be used only to improve precision, never to obfuscate. Nothing should be left to the imagination, or to some future "friendly" resolution. Friendship goes out the window when serious sums start to fire the imagination of one or more participants in a business deal.

Your lawyer should be able to tell you what an agreement says about every possible future eventuality. You as a technical type should be able to develop an exhaustive list and check it through. If you don't understand something, don't write off your confusion as legal ignorance. Hang in there until you understand (and approve) the business terms. If necessary, find another lawyer who can see you through to a clear understanding.

Principle: **Once you go to court, you've lost.** I think I made this point clearly enough in my introductory remarks. I simply close with two supporting observations.

First and most important, there are no Perry Masons in the legal profession. Your lawyer will *not* stay up nights trying to figure out who really copied the code (or whatever). Expect no dazzling cross examinations or dramatic confessions on the witness stand. You'll be lucky if your lawyer remembers the names of the principal protagonists. Don't even *hope* that anybody besides you (and your opponent) understand any technical issues.

Second, even if you win big, you might not collect anything. Lawyers are remarkably powerless to enforce court judgments. The best ones bluster and intimidate. The worst ones just walk away. All of them collect their fees whether you get paid or not. And why shouldn't they? A lawyer's job is to help you with the law. Straightening out your business, or your life, is up to you. □

Afterword: Believe it or not, this column garnered good feedback from lawyers. More than one said that it cast their profession in an unusually fair light. I just wanted to break the traditional dependency/despondency cycle between client and lawyer. No profession should be saddled with so much responsibility, or so much acrimony.

26 Bankers

Many years ago, two of my friends were ardent feminists. Wherever possible, they sought out other women when they needed various professional services. In the 1970s, however, they couldn't always succeed. They grudgingly admitted that two men were important in their lives. A woman in her twenties in suburban New Jersey couldn't survive without an auto mechanic and a gynecologist.

More recently, I have heard echoes of that complaint from some of my technical friends who would be entrepreneurs. Male or female, techies share a disdain for "suits" — those people who insist on wearing neckties even to picnics. In this modern era of growing informality, you can go a long time between suits. But some are still unavoidable, at least outside California. Rarely can you start and run a business without dealing with two quintessential suits, lawyers and bankers.

I discussed lawyers in the previous essay. (See **Essay 25: Lawyers**.) I even managed to do so without telling a single lawyer joke. In this essay, I discuss those people who have the money you need. Some are called bankers, some investors, some venture capitalists. (Some are called other names as well by people who don't share their values. Of these, "vulture capitalists" is the most printable.)

The worst problem with people who wear suits is that they expect you to do the same. You can get away without if you're paying the bills, but not if you need to make a good impression. And when you put on a suit, you have to adopt an attitude to match. You have to convey just the right combination of maverick self confidence and groveling humility. Otherwise, the money people won't believe that you'll earn enough to pay them back what you borrow.

We technical types tend to be single minded when it comes to money matters. We see a chance to make a wonderful new kind of product or service and we're gone. Just give us some money and stand out of the way. A year or three of hard work will make us all millionaires.

The money types have heard all this before. They're happy to see you get rich, provided they also get a bit richer in the bargain. But they want some assurances that you can pull off your ambitious dreams. That's why they demand annoying details such as market studies and business plans. They need to believe that you can *run* a business as well as start one. Otherwise, they'll put their money somewhere safer.

𝔜ou may be shocked to learn who your biggest competitor is for the money you need. It's the U.S. Government. Last time I looked, Uncle Sam was paying out $50 billion *per month* in interest on treasury bills. That's over a million dollars a minute. Plenty of that to go around. And T-bills are widely regarded as a safe investment. (Put another way, when the U.S. Government starts reneging on its debts, the world will have *lots* of financial problems.)

Anybody with a few hundred thousand to spare can park it in T-bills, collect the interest, and pay the taxes. Your job is to convince one or more of those bodies that you can yield a better return after taxes than Uncle Sam. If you can't, why should they let you play with their money?

It's worse than that, of course. You are bound to be a bigger risk than your basic T-bill. A startup in search of seed money is a bigger risk still than a small company looking to finance growth. The greater the perceived risk, the greater the expected return.

You should be grateful that you have access to money at all. Once upon a time, people had no incentive to loan money. (Usury was originally the crime of charging *any* interest on a loan, not excessive interest.) The only way to accumulate a large sum was by hard work and hoarding. You couldn't even earn interest on the money that you were saving. In fact, your biggest hope was that nobody would find it and steal it.

Over the past few centuries, money has become steadily easier to borrow. The real explosion in borrowing began just a few decades ago, however. Where our grandparents saved to buy cars and houses, we sign our names, pay large quantities of interest, and pray for inflation. Bankers have grown ever more creative in finding ways to create liquidity (and earn interest, of course). The good news is that the world economy now offers us all many more opportunities for success. The bad news is that the failures have become all the more spectacular.

But you don't care about that, except when discussing politics. What you want is a chance to pursue your own personal dreams. That's why you're willing to talk to the suits. They have money and you need it.

What follows is a brief guide to dealing with money people. It is aimed at the technical entrepreneur, and his or her henchpeople. Like the guide to using lawyers that I presented in the last essay, I cast it in the form of a handful of guiding principles. As before, I start with the most important.

𝔓rinciple: **Never raise money to start a business just to make money.** It saddens me whenever I see a friend take out a second mortgage to set up an office. Desks, postage meters, and secretaries are important trappings of a business, to be sure. But they are not the most important. Anyone who focuses on appearances first usually does so because the basics aren't in place.

The most basic of basics is customers. Somebody out there must want to buy what you want to sell. The next most basic is a drive to excel in your chosen business. Remember what I said about return on investment above. You'd better have something going for you if you expect high profit and/or growth.

Real entrepreneurs succeed because they really want to build something new and special. Getting rich is a nice side effect. It vindicates their efforts and provides a neat way to keep score. But it is not the driving force. If you can get rich by the mechanical application of money, so can the people who have lots of money. They don't have to share the wealth with you.

I started my company in the living room of our two-bedroom apartment in Manhattan. We had a healthy positive cash flow before we hired any support staff. Perhaps we wasted coding talent stuffing software in shipping bags. On the other hand, we didn't fret that our limited cash was going to pay interest on borrowed money.

Principle: **Venture capitalists are only interested in high-risk ventures that are safe.** If you need cash to start a company, or grow it rapidly, chances are that your local bank won't lend you the money. (You can use your house as equity, perhaps, but not your newborn business.) The canonical way to fund a high-tech startup is to sell part of the stock to venture capitalists. These are people who specialize in high-risk ventures. As I explained before, they expect a high return for their troubles.

Dozens of books will tell you how to start a company. Nearly all take for granted that you will begin by raising hundreds of thousands, even millions of dollars of venture capital. Thus, they talk at length about how to package your business plan, resumes, and so forth for maximum appeal. They describe the venture-capital community, its putative psychology and current fads. In doing so, they are almost as bad as my friends who hock their homes to buy rosewood desks. The longer you can wait before you have to raise capital, the less that capital is going to cost you in terms of ownership.

My company was almost four years old before I talked to my first venture capitalist. I was fortunate in many ways, but I was also careful with cash flow. The software business doesn't require high overheads, at least until maintenance becomes a serious burden. If you can live without all the trappings, you can really start many such enterprises on a shoestring.

But if you have to raise venture capital, don't despair. The money is still out there, waiting to be placed. It will do you more good than you can possibly imagine to prepare all the documents that serious investors demand. And, despite horror tales to the contrary, venture capitalists are not all ogres.

Again, I was fortunate in this area. I got to do business with several of the best venture capitalists in the Boston area. And Boston is second only to Silicon Valley in its selection of investors. I never felt pressured to make the quick buck — these people were willing to grow a business over many years. And I felt the investors respected my efforts, despite all the mistakes I made.

One thing I noted with amusement was the lemming-like nature of venture capitalists. They all know each other and they all gossip. As a result, they all chase fads with teen-age abandon. If you have the enterprise of the month and a good tale to tell, you can be overrun with suitors. Hit the wrong month and you'll clock a lot of time in reception areas.

That's why I state this principle as I do. Venture capitalists want high risk opportunities because they want high return on investment. But they also want some assurance that the risk is not foolhardy. Thus, they look for safety in numbers.

Principle: **Venture capitalists know how to run a business, but they don't know how to run *your* business.** What disappointed me most about venture capitalists was their limitations. I confess that I have a tendency to look for white knights. I keep hoping that someone will come along, take one look at my problems, and say confidently, "Step aside, kid, I'll handle this." By now, I have learned that the people who will fill that role usually want your soul as collateral.

The good thing about venture capitalists is that they tend to be active investors. That means they want to attend board meetings several times a year, even if they have little or no voting power. Since they see the insides of many companies with problems similar to yours, they bring a lot of experience to the party. And since they have a stake in your success, they are seldom shy about sharing that experience.

The problem is, nearly all that experience is generic. They don't know squat about writing software, or overhauling laptops, or whatever it is you do. They just bought into your dream enough to take a chance on you. Remember, if they really knew how to make a tidy profit doing what you're doing, they wouldn't have bothered with you in the first place.

Generic experience is still useful. A lot of the business of running a business is strictly business. It has nothing to do with whether you're producing document formatters or plumbing fixtures. In such matters, you should listen to professional advice whenever possible. You must then make the tough decision about whether your enterprise is an exception.

My investors were very gentle in such matters. Often they would respond to my plans by saying, "Well, that's an interesting approach. We've seen it tried a dozen times before and it's always failed. It will be interesting to see if you succeed." Want to guess what usually happened? But even when I ignored the warnings, I still appreciated the advice.

Principle: **Bankers don't want to lend money to people who need it.** You don't always have to trade equity to get money. Once you have a running cash-flow engine, you should qualify for more conventional business loans. Rarely will your banker volunteer this information, however. You have to ask. Sometimes you have to threaten to take your business to another bank to get decent terms.

Bankers tend to be *much* more conservative with loans than are venture capitalists with investments. (Third-world countries and patently crooked real-estate developers are obviously exempt from this conservatism, for reasons that escape me.) You will be asked for personal guarantees, which you should resist as much as possible. You will be zinged with fees and hamstrung with constraints more ways than you can count. Your only defense is to shop around, then take the best deal offered.

What you have to realize is that bankers don't want to lend you money for the same reason you want to borrow it. They're happy to bleed interest from a well-oiled cash generator. They're sometimes willing to smooth the growth of a company that is already successful. What they do *not* want to do is provide you with venture funds to pursue new opportunities. And they do *not* want to give you a cushion of credit against bad times. But those are exactly the reasons why you want to borrow someone else's money whenever possible.

Principle: **The time to arrange a line of credit is when you need it least.** This principle follows directly from the previous one. Once you get in a cash-flow pinch, your options get severely limited. Bankers don't want to loan you money then, because the risk is higher that you might fold before you pay it all back. Even if they're willing to take your loan application, you have a speed mismatch. You want the loan to clear fast so you can make the next payroll. They want to take extra time to be extra safe. (It's called "due diligence" in the financial trade, and heaven help the loan officer who can't demonstrate due diligence in investigating a loan that later goes sour.)

So what you do is cultivate your banker when times are good. Get a line of credit in place while you both have the leisure time and warm fuzzy feelings to pull it off. Secure it with a lien on your receivables, or your equipment if you have enough. Pay a maintenance fee to keep it alive if you must. *Don't* put up your house, your kids' college fund, or control of the company.

Even then, you should know that banks are great at reneging when times get bad. Credit lines evaporate like fairy gold when bank vice presidents get scared. Which leads in turn to the next principle.

Principle: **Bankers hate surprises more than they hate missed payments.** About a decade ago, I ran into a spate of trouble with my company. The first call I made was to my lawyer, who battened down the hatches. The second was to my contact at the Bank of Boston. Over breakfast the next morning, I told him all the sordid details. Those were the sanest two acts I committed that month. (As you might guess, it was largely my stupidity that caused the spate to begin with.)

As it turned out, we missed no loan payments in the ensuing months of turmoil. But our financial figures performed gyrations that would have scared a Mafia loan shark. Having the bankers involved in the solution saved them from being a major part of the problem. The bank was even instrumental in helping clean up the mess once the troubles eventually got resolved.

Principle: **The money people are looking out for your best interests, believe it or not.** I end with this principle because it's the thought you should take with you. Venture capitalists and bankers stand to profit only if you succeed. Even more important, they stand to lose if you go under. (Seizing your collateral offers some comfort, but it still costs loan officers major brownie points within the bank.)

Still more important, the pros can make a harsher assessment of your financial prospects than you can when times get tough. They have the experience. They are not blinded by your optimism. And they are not muddled by your fears. Keep them properly informed and they will even respect your right to hang on as long as possible.

My investors didn't get near the return they were looking for when I sold the company. The days of rapid growth were ending even as they bought in. Nevertheless, I felt that they gave me good advice — advice good for me, personally, that is — right up to the end. And I believe we parted friends.

I value that friendship, even with people who wear suits to picnics. □

*Afterword: With this essay, I come full circle from the first member of this collection. (See **Essay 1: Honestly, Now**.) I began with several hard-earned lessons in ethics. Along the way, I visited an assortment of people issues in this interesting trade. I end with some useful lore about the people I've met in the computer software business.*

When I started my own company, I didn't know where I was going. I had no vision of how large I wanted the company to be, or what it would be doing in ten years, or what my role should be then. I knew enough to be scared by that lack of vision. You can't complain if things don't go as you'd hoped — not if you didn't know what you were hoping for early enough to make a difference.

ne thing I did get right from the start. I knew that a company was a thing of people. Not money, not technology. They are mere ingredients. So I was careful to enjoy the people I've met along the way — be they employees, customers, or competitors. And I still enjoy the people I work with at least as much as the technology that fascinates me.

Making money is nice. Making good software and good words is better. Making friends is the best reward of all.

Appendix A List of Columns

The following list gives the publication date, destination, and title of each installment of "Programming on Purpose" published in *Computer Language* through December 1992. For example, the entry

Jul 1986   Design   1 Which Tool is Best?

tells you that the essay "Programming on Purpose: Which Tool is Best?" was first published in the July 1986 edition of *Computer Language*. You can also find it as Essay 1 in the collection *Programming on Purpose: Essays on Software Design*, Prentice-Hall, 1993. The other two collections are *Essays on Software People* and *Essays on Software Technology*.

Date	Collection	#	Title
Jul 1986	Design	1	Which Tool is Best?
Aug 1986	Design	2	Writing Predicates
Sep 1986	Design	3	Generating Data
Oct 1986	Design	4	Finite-State Machines
Nov 1986	Design	5	Recognizing Input
Dec 1986	Design	5	Recognizing Input, Part 2
Jan 1987	Design	6	Handling Exceptions
Feb 1987	Design	7	Which Tool is Next?
Mar 1987	Design	8	Order Out of Chaos
Apr 1987	Technology	1	You Must Be Joking
May 1987	Design	9	Marrying Data Structures
Jun 1987	Design	10	Divorcing Data Structures
Jul 1987	Design	11	Who's the Boss?
Aug 1987	Design	12	By Any Other Name
Sep 1987	People	1	Honestly, Now
Oct 1987	Design	13	Searching
Nov 1987	Design	14	Synchronization
Dec 1987	Design	14	Synchronization, Part 2

Date	Collection	#	Title
Jan 1988	Design	15	Which Tool is Last?
Feb 1988	Technology	2	Computer Arithmetic
Mar 1988	Technology	3	Floating-Point Arithmetic
Apr 1988	Technology	4	The Central Folly
May 1988	Technology	5	Safe Math
Jun 1988	Technology	6	Do-It-Yourself Math Functions
Jul 1988	Design	16	A Designer's Bibliography
Aug 1988	Design	17	A Designer's Reference Shelf
Sep 1988	People	2	You Can't Do That
Oct 1988	Technology	7	Locking the Barn Door
Nov 1988	Technology	8	Half a Secret
Dec 1988	People	3	Protecting Intellectual Property
Jan 1989	People	4	What and How
Feb 1989	People	5	Skin and Bones
Mar 1989	Technology	9	It's (Almost) Alive
Apr 1989	Technology	10	The (Almost) Right Stuff
May 1989	People	6	Product Reviews
Jun 1989	People	7	Awaiting Reply
Jul 1989	Design	18	A Preoccupation with Time
Aug 1989	Design	19	Structuring Time
Sep 1989	People	8	Soup or Art?
Oct 1989	People	9	The Seven Warning Signs
Nov 1989	Design	20	Abstract It
Dec 1989	Design	21	Encapsulate It
Jan 1990	Design	22	Inherit It
Feb 1990	People	10	The Politics of Standards
Mar 1990	People	11	Setting the Standard
Apr 1990	Technology	11	Instant Lies
May 1990	People	12	All the Standard Reasons
Jun 1990	People	13	The Physicist as Programmer
Jul 1990	Technology	12	What Meets the Eye
Aug 1990	Technology	13	Technicolor and Cinemascope
Sep 1990	Technology	14	What Meets the Ear
Oct 1990	Technology	15	Warm Fuzzies
Nov 1990	People	14	Shelfware
Dec 1990	People	15	It's Not My Fault

Date	Collection	#	Title
Jan 1991	People	16	Customer Service
Feb 1991	Design	23	Heresies of Software Design
Mar 1991	People	17	Heresies of Software Management
Apr 1991	Technology	16	Font Follies
May 1991	Technology	17	Text Editors
Jun 1991	Technology	18	Approximating Functions
Jul 1991	Technology	19	Economizing Polynomials
Aug 1991	People	18	Watching the Watchers
Sep 1991	People	19	Washing the Watchers
Oct 1991	Technology	20	Technical Documentation
Nov 1991	Technology	21	All I Want to Do Is
Dec 1991	Technology	22	Programming for the Billions
Jan 1992	Technology	23	All Sorts of Sorts
Feb 1992	Technology	24	Transforming Strings
Mar 1992	Design	24	Remedial Software Engineering
Apr 1992	Technology	25	Books for Our Times
May 1992	People	20	Who's Always Right?
Jun 1992	People	21	The Cycle of Complexity
Jul 1992	People	22	Pity the Typist
Aug 1992	People	23	Criticism
Sep 1992	People	24	Plled Higher and Deeper
Oct 1992	Technology	26	Through the Grapevine
Nov 1992	People	25	Lawyers
Dec 1992	People	26	Bankers

Appendix B   Bibliography

The references that follow are all cited in the essays in this collection. I do not include references to "Programming on Purpose" — Appendix A summarizes all of those essays.

Als88 — R. Alsop, "It's Slim Pickings in Product Name Game," *Wall Street Journal*, p. B1, 29 November 1988.

C&W80 — W. Cody and W. Waite, *Software Manual for the Elementary Functions*, Prentice-Hall, 1980.

Cha89a — D. Chandler, "A paradox of the body: Order may be unhealthy," *Boston Globe*, p. 4, 16 January 1989.

Cha89b — D. Chandler, "Fractals: Out of the studio, into the lab," *Boston Globe*, p. 45, 16 January 1989.

Cli90 — W. Clinger, "How to Read Floating-Point Numbers Accurately," *Proceedings of the ACM SGPLAN '90 Conference on Programming Design and Implementation*, p. 92, *ACM*, 1990.

G&M74 — W. Gentleman and S. Marovich, "More on Algorithms that Reveal Properties of Floating-Point Arithmetic Units," *Communications of the ACM*, 17:5, p. 276, May 1974.

Gar90 — S. Garfinkel, "Get Ready for GNU Software," *Computerworld*, p. 102, 6 August 1990.

Gro88 — G. Groenewold, "Rules of the Game: As Simple as ABC," *Unix Review*, p. 42, October 1988.

Hum89 — W. Humphrey, *Managing the Software Process*, Addison-Wesley, 1989.

Ian88 — J. Iandiorio, "Pennwalt Corp. v. Durand-Wayland, Inc.," *The Reflector*, p. 4, Boston Section IEEE, August 1988.

J&W74 — K. Jensen and N. Wirth, *PASCAL User Manual and Report*, Springer Verlag, 1974.

K&P76 — B. Kernighan and P. Plauger, *Software Tools*, Addison-Wesley, 1976.

K&R78 — B. Kernighan and D. Ritchie, *The C Programming Language*, Prentice-Hall, 1978.

Ker88 — A. Kernan, "Art and Law," *Princeton Alumni Weekly*, p. 34, 12 October, 1988.

Knu68 — D. Knuth, *The Art of Computer Programming, Volume 1: Fundamental Algorithms* Addison-Wesley, 1968.

Lan89 — C. Langdon, Editor, *Artificial Life: The Proceedings of an Interdisciplinary Workshop on the Synthesis and Simulation of Living Systems Held September, 1987 in Los Alamos, New Mexico,* Addison-Wesley, 1989.

LGU88 — Lucash, Gesmer & Updegrove, "Vault Corp. v. Quaid Software," *Technology Law Bulletin,* p. 2, October 1988.

P&B89 — P. Plauger and J. Brodie, *Standard C,* Microsoft Press, 1989.

P&B92 — P. Plauger and J. Brodie, *ANSI and ISO Standard C,* Microsoft Press, 1992.

Pla87 — P. Plauger, "Son of PC Meets the C Monster," *Computer Language,* p. 41, February 1987.

Pla90 — P. Plauger, "Standard C: Wha Gang Agley," *The C Users Journal,* April and May 1990.

Pla92 — P. Plauger, *The Standard C Library,* Prentice-Hall, 1992.

Plu91 — T. Plum, "Building a Standard is Hard; Testing it is Just as Difficult," *Computer Language,* p. 38, May 1991.

S&W90 — G. Steele, Jr. and J. White, "How to Print Floating-Point Numbers Accurately," *Proceedings of the ACM SGPLAN '90 Conference on Programming Design and Implementation,* p. 112, *ACM,* 1990.

Sal89 — R. Saltus, "Scientists link attitude to course of AIDS," *Boston Globe,* p. 3, 16 January 1989.

Sam89 — P. Samuelson, "Why the Look and Feel of Software User Interfaces Should Not Be Protected by Copyright Law," *Communications of the ACM* 32:5, p. 563, May 1989.

Val89 — T. Valeo, "A glimpse of how mind produces art," *Boston Globe,* p. 45, 16 January 1989.

Wag86 — J. Wagner, *The Search for Signs of Intelligent Life in the Universe,* Harper and Row, 1986.

Wal88 — P. Waldman, "Software-Copyright Laws are in State of Confusion," *The Wall Street Journal,* p. 21, 21 March 1988.

Y&C79 — E. Yourdon and L. Constantine, *Structured Design,* Prentice-Hall, 1979.

Index

𝕬

ACM 55, 94, 142, 195-196
Ada
   See language
   See Lovelace
AFNOR 135-136
Air Force
   See U.S.
Alexander the Great 9
Algol 68
   See language
Alsop, Ronald 31, 195
American Physical Society 94
amnesiac 103
ANSI 69-75, 85- 88, 131-137, 149, 196
Apple Computer Corporation 17, 26-28, 53-58, 148, 160
Apple II
   See computer
Apple Laserwriter 148
Apple Macintosh
   See computer
as-if rule 79-80
ASCII
   See character set
assembly
   See language
AT&T Corporation 20, 22-23, 33-34, 87, 91, 134, 143, 174
Axe
   See software

𝕭

Babbage, Charles 34
BAL
   See language
bankers 1, 183-188
Barnum, P.T. 61

BASIC
   See language
Baum, L. Frank 67
bear with me 62-63
behavior
   implementation-defined 81-82
   locale-specific 81
   undefined 81, 83, 92
   unspecified 81
Bell Laboratories 13, 20, 23, 33-34, 66, 91, 99, 143
Bible 179
Binney and Smith 32
Borland 28, 118, 163
Boston Globe 4, 195-196
Bradley, Bill 46
Brodie, Jim 85, 149, 196
BSI 135-136

𝕮

C
   See language
C Standard 69-71, 75-92, 134, 136, 139
C Users Journal 86, 196
C++
   See language
Campbell's Soup 53
Capone, Al 37
Carbon Copy
   See software
Chandler, D. 195
character set
   ASCII 46, 70, 160
   ISO 646 70
chatterbox 103
Checkfree
   See software
Christ, Jesus 159-160
Clarke, Arthur C. 21-22